T3-BPX-040

INTERNATIONAL BANK REGULATION

James C. Baker

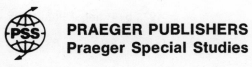

PRAEGER PUBLISHERS
Praeger Special Studies

New York • London • Sydney • Toronto

Library of Congress Cataloging in Publication Data

Baker, James Calvin, 1935–
  International bank regulation.

  Includes bibliographical references and index.
  1. Banks and banking, International. I. Title.
K1088.B34   341.7'51   76-19545

ISBN 0-03-028936-X

PRAEGER PUBLISHERS
PRAEGER SPECIAL STUDIES
383 Madison Avenue, New York, N.Y. 10017, U.S.A.

Published in the United States of America in 1978
by Praeger Publishers,
A Division of Holt, Rinehart and Winston, CBS, Inc.

89   038   987654321

© 1978 by Praeger Publishers

All rights reserved

Printed in the United States of America

341.751
B167i

To
Douglas Meikle,
A Professor Who Motivated
Many to Strive
for a Graduate Education

The financial foundation of worldwide business is comprised of the mortar of the international banking system. Commercial banks, credit banks, merchant banks, banques d'affaires, universal banks—whatever they are called around the world—are the catalysts for the growth of the industrial sector in the developed as well as the developing world. They are the principal actors among the various financial intermediaries that facilitate the savings/investment equation by channeling surplus funds to the demand side of the equation.

Banks, because of their fiduciary nature, have always been considered a little more sacred than the usual nonfinancial corporation. They use the money of others to fuel the economy and can, by their money-creating ability, affect the monetary policy of their own nations, as well as that of other nations. Thus, it is quite important that this phase of their operations be carefully monitored and regulated.

Many company and financial laws have been enacted because of this exalted, but feared, position of banks. During the 1920s and early 1930s, literally thousands of banks failed and were declared insolvent. With these failures, the life savings of millions of individuals disappeared, and many business failures occurred. Thus, legislatures in many nations, most notably the United States, placed restrictions on banking operations or established systems to assist problem banks or reimburse depositors of failed banks.

During the 1955-75 period, banking and business grew at a phenomenal rate on a multinational basis. The two complemented each other and grew concomitantly. Banks, however, like business firms, resorted to many so-called go-go operations on a worldwide basis, and by the early 1970s, several large and notorious banking failures had occurred.

As a result of the bank failures and losses of the last decade, the relevant audience of bank performance—business journalists, government regulators, legislators, academicians, businessmen, and depositors—began to demand new controls with which banks could be regulated and supervised.

The primary subject of this book is the regulation and supervision of banks on a worldwide basis. In addition, the reasons for current patterns of regulation and supervision, as well as proposals for future adoption, will be discussed and analyzed in this book.

The author's interest in this subject was nurtured by a year spent at Federal Deposit Insurance Corporation (FDIC) as a Federal

Faculty Fellow, under the sponsorship of the American Assembly of Collegiate Schools of Business and the Sears Roebuck Foundation in 1975-76, and the following year as a part-time consultant with FDIC. This agency lagged behind the Federal Reserve System and the U.S. comptroller of the currency by light-years in its mastery of the world of international finance and international banking. I assisted the agency in closing the gap by a few centimeters. As a result, while at FDIC, I participated in several major studies of various aspects of international bank regulation and supervision; these were valuable in the formulation of this overall study.

As with any research in the area of international finance, two major limitations are found in this treatment of international bank regulation. First, the statistical data contained in such a study may be dated by time of publication. However, it is meant to serve primarily as illustrative material. Second, the nations whose systems of bank regulation and supervision are covered in this book are limited to the major banking countries of the world, as well as to selected developing areas that are rapidly becoming significant factors of the worldwide economy. Thus, only bank regulation in the United States, Japan, Canada, West Europe, and the Middle Eastern nations is discussed, and with regard primarily to international banking.

Several periodicals, as well as other miscellaneous sources of information, should be highlighted to assist students of international banking and its regulation and supervision. The monthly publications from England, Euromoney, the Banker, and the Bankers Magazine, are valuable sources of data on worldwide banking. The first two mentioned publish supplemental sections on banking in selected countries, as does the Economist. Some periodicals publish annual reports on international banking. These include the Economist, Far Eastern Economic Review, and Institutional Investor. Banking journals in the United States occasionally publish international banking articles. These include Journal of Commercial Bank Lending, the Bankers Magazine, Journal of Bank Research, Issues in Bank Regulation, Bankers Monthly Magazine, Magazine of Bank Administration, and Journal of Money, Credit, and Banking.

Several publications contain useful statistical series on international banking. These include World Financial Markets, published weekly by Morgan Guaranty Bank; the Federal Reserve Bulletin; Bank of England Quarterly; Lloyds Bank Review; Barclays Review; and the Journal of the Banca Nazionale del Lavoro. In addition, public data on international banking are available from the central banks and bank regulatory agencies of the leading nations. In the United States, for example, the G.11 and FR 886 series offer excellent data on foreign banking in the United States and are obtainable from the Federal Reserve System.

Acknowledgment is due several people for their assistance with this study. Among them must be mentioned Mary T. Mitchell, deputy director of the Division of Bank Supervision at FDIC, for whom I worked; Gerald Lamberti, project and planning branch specialist at FDIC, whose ascerbic wit and meticulous editing improved many manuscripts that have been made a part of this work; Janice Bradburn, research assistant at FDIC, who gathered much of the data and material; Jack Severeins of Cleveland State University, who collaborated on a study of foreign bank securities affiliates in the United States; Glenda Jackson of the Federal Reserve Board staff, who furnished statistics of foreign bank operations in the United States; Jane d'Arista, staff member of the Committee on Banking, Finance and Urban Affairs, U.S. House of Representatives, who expressed ideas developed in studies of foreign bank regulation; and Thomas Stuhldreher, doctoral candidate in international banking at Kent State University, who assisted in conceptualizing the framework for the analysis of U.S. regulation of foreign banking discussed in this book. Others, too numerous to mention, have contributed to this study in many ways. These include those government agency and U.S. and foreign bank officials who testified at several congressional hearings I attended; graduate students in several financial institutions courses at Kent State University; staff members in the Research Division at FDIC; and bankers whom I have interviewed during the past decade in various studies of international banking. Finally, the final drafts were typed and made more coherent by my wife, who made a yeoman effort to iron out the many inconsistencies of the manuscript while running the household and surviving the Great Blizzard of 1978. Her final editing of the manuscript improved it significantly.

The author is responsible for any errors in fact or judgment concerning this manuscript. Aside from any that might be present, it is hoped this brief discussion of an important problem will serve as a catalyst for others to do further research in this area of international finance.

Note: After this manuscript was written, H.R. 10899, the International Banking Act of 1978 (with some amendments of material found in H.R. 13876), was passed by the U.S. House of Representatives and was sent to the Senate for deliberation.

CONTENTS

APPENDIXES

LIST OF TABLES AND FIGURE

Table		Page

Figure

1
INTERNATIONAL BANKING:
GROWTH AND CAUSAL FACTORS

INTRODUCTION

During the past two decades, both multinational corporate and banking activities have grown at a phenomenal rate. American companies have made more than $135 billion of direct investments in foreign countries, and foreign investment in the United States has risen dramatically during this period. Japanese and German firms are establishing new plants almost monthly in foreign countries, the most recent in the United States being a Volkswagen plant under construction in Pennsylvania and a Honda plant planned for Ohio. The Arabs, with surplus oil revenues, are beginning to make significant portfolio investments in foreign companies.

Concomitant with this expansion in multinational corporate investment has been the significant growth of international banking operations, specifically by banks headquartered in the industrial countries, but not limited to banks from such nations. Banks in several less developed countries (LDCs) have been moving abroad slowly. The Arab banks represent one major example.

For many decades, of course, the British banks were the most internationalized of any banking system in the world. The British Commonwealth necessitated such a banking system, and even today, British banks probably have more branches located abroad than any other country.

U.S. INTERNATIONAL BANKING

The United States is a Johnny-come-lately to the arena of international banking. U.S. banks moved aborad significantly when U.S. multinational corporations (MNCs) began to increase their overseas investments during the last two or three decades. To finance U.S.

1

corporate activity overseas, U.S. banks have established hundreds of new foreign branches.

The period since 1960 has been one of phenomenal growth for U.S. banks' international operations. In 1960, only eight U.S. banks had branches abroad, and these branches had total assets of $3.5 billion. By year-end 1972, 108 U.S. banks had 627 branches, with $90 billion in assets. By 1977, more than 140 U.S. banks had more than 750 branches operating overseas, with total assets of more than $225 billion.[1] See Table 1.1 for comparative data concerning foreign branch and domestic office assets of U.S. banks. These data demonstrate that, since 1970, U.S. banks' foreign operations as a percentage of their total operations have increased dramatically.

In addition to these branch operations, U.S. banks also own and operate a variety of subsidiaries and affiliates, both domestically and abroad, which carry on international activities. These affiliates and subsidiaries are owned wholly or partially by Edge Act companies (EACs) of U.S. banks, allowed by Section 25A of the Federal Reserve Act to carry on international activities of U.S. banks,[2] and by bank holding company affiliates, a practice permitted by the 1970 amendment to the Bank Holding Company Act. The banking assets of these subsidiaries combined with the assets of U.S. banks' overseas branches at year-end 1975 amounted to $194 billion, versus $7.5 billion at mid-

TABLE 1.1

Comparison of Assets of Foreign Branches and Domestic Offices
of All Insured Commercial Banks in the United States, 1970–77
(billions of dollars)

Date	Foreign Branches	Domestic Offices	Total Domestic and Foreign	Foreign as Percent of Total
December 1970	47.4	576.2	623.6	7.6
December 1971	61.3	640.3	701.6	8.7
December 1972	78.2	739.0	817.2	9.6
December 1973	121.9	835.2	957.1	12.7
December 1974	151.9	919.6	1,071.5	14.2
December 1975	176.5	938.4	1,134.9	15.6
December 1976	219.5	1,010.8	1,230.3	17.8
December 1977	257.5	1,145.4	1,402.9	18.4

Sources: Federal Reserve Bulletin 60 (March 1974): A86; 62 (March 1976): A14 and A70; 63 (March 1977): A16 and A62; 63 (March 1978): A16 and A62.

1965^3 and, as mentioned, to more than \$225 billion unofficially by 1977.

EACs are located domestically in the United States and are allowed to invest in foreign banks and other financial institutions, as well as take deposits, make loans, and carry on international trade financing, foreign exchange operations, and Eurocurrency market activities. They are regulated by the Federal Reserve System and are permitted to locate in a state other than that in which the parent is located (but for international banking operations only). For example, Bank of America (BankAmerica) has EACs in San Francisco, Chicago, New York, Houston, and Miami. A total of 116 EACs had been established and were operating at year-end 1975, with total assets of \$10.6 billion and total capital of \$1.3 billion.[4] However, since most countries in which U.S. banks are operating grant full-banking status to branch operations, U.S. banks, as can be seen by the data, prefer to operate abroad by establishing branches.

In addition to these branch and EAC operations, the 30 largest U.S. commercial banks had, at year-end 1974, more than 300 subsidiaries overseas in which their ownership interest was 50 percent or more. The equity holdings in these subsidiaries amounted to \$750 million. These banks also owned more than \$850 million equity in more than 600 other foreign joint ventures and affiliates.[5]

As implied by the above-mentioned fact that approximately 140 U.S. banks are engaged in international operations, international banking by U.S. banks is highly concentrated when one considers the 14,500 or so U.S. banks operating at present. To demonstrate further the concentration of U.S. international banking, consider that of 125 U.S. banks with overseas branches at year-end 1974, 80 had only a single "shell" branch in either the Cayman Islands or Nassau, with total assets of only \$4.1 billion. A further 25 U.S. banks had 49 branches that were not shells, whose total assets were \$8.6 billion.

Thus, overseas operations were concentrated in only 20 U.S. banks, which owned more than 80 percent of the total overseas branches and more than 90 percent of these branches' assets.

These 20 multinational banks are dominant in U.S. banking. They own 30 percent of all domestic assets of U.S. banks, and their combined domestic and foreign branch assets amount to 37 percent of the combined domestic and foreign branch assets of all U.S. banks. The average amount of assets held overseas by these 20 banks is approximately 35 percent of their total assets.[6]

The overseas branches of U.S. banks are located on all continents, but aside from the more than 120 branches—shell operations—in the Caribbean, nearly 30 percent of the total U.S. bank branches are located in Latin America, more than 20 percent in Western Europe, and nearly 20 percent in Asia. A location breakdown by region

TABLE 1.2

Overseas Branches of U.S. Member Banks, 1965–75[a]

Country of Location	1965	1966	1967	1968	1969	1970	1971	1972	1973	1974	1975
Belgium–Luxembourg	2	4	6	8	9	11	11	8	8	15	15
France	4	4	4	6	7	11	12	15	17	15	17
Germany	3	6	8	9	14	17	21	22	27	30	30
Greece	1	1	1	2	5	8	9	13	14	16	18
Italy	1	1	1	2	2	3	4	6	7	8	10
The Netherlands	3	3	3	3	5	7	7	7	6	6	6
Switzerland	1	1	2	3	3	6	7	8	8	9	9
United Kingdom	17	21	21	24	32	37	41	45	49	52	55
Total Europe[b]	32	43	48	59	80	103	116	128	142	157	167
Bahamas	2	3	3	3	8	32	60	73	94	91	80
Cayman Islands	—	—	—	—	—	—	—	—	2	32	44
Total Caribbean[c]	5	9	9	10	22	53	89	107	131	164	164
Argentina	16	17	17	25	33	38	38	38	38	38	37
Brazil	15	15	15	15	15	15	16	19	21	21	19
Colombia	5	6	6	8	15	23	26	28	28	32	36
Panama	10	12	15	19	21	26	29	29	32	33	33
Total Latin America[d]	72	79	93	123	155	182	191	195	190	195	198
Taiwan	—	2	2	2	2	2	2	2	3	5	7
Hong Kong	6	6	8	10	12	13	13	15	19	23	24
India	5	6	8	8	11	11	11	11	11	11	11

Indonesia	—	—	—	—	4	6	6	6	6	6	6
Japan	13	14	14	14	14	15	15	17	21	25	31
Lebanon	3	3	3	3	3	3	3	3	3	3	3
Persian Gulf[e]	2	3	3	3	3	3	8	11	10	10	11
Singapore	—	8	8	8	8	9	11	11	11	14	18
Total Asia[f]	45	55	63	69	78	83	91	98	112	126	143
Total Africa[g]	3	2	2	3	3	1	2	2	2	2	5
Overseas areas of the United States	23	23	29	31	35	38	43	47	50	55	55
Grand total	180	211	244	295	373	460	532	577	627	699	732
U.S. member banks with overseas branches	11	13	13	15	26	53	79	91	107	125	125

[a] As of January 1.

[b] Also includes Austria, Ireland, Monaco, and Romania.

[c] Also includes Barbados, Haiti, Jamaica, Netherlands Antilles, Trinidad-Tobago, British Virgin Islands, and other West Indian Islands.

[d] Also includes Bolivia, Chile (no resident U.S. branches as of January 1, 1975), Dominican Republic, Ecuador, El Salvador, Guatemala, Guyana, Honduras, Mexico, Nicaragua, Paraguay, Peru, Uruguay, and Venezuela.

[e] Includes Bahrain, Qatar, Saudi Arabia, and United Arab Emirates.

[f] Also includes Brunei, Fiji Islands, Israel, Jordan, Korea, Malaysia, Pakistan, the Philippines, Thailand, and Vietnam.

[g] Includes Liberia, Kenya, Mauritius, and Nigeria (no resident U.S. branches as of January 1, 1975).

Source: Allen B. Frankel, "International Banking: Part I," Business Conditions (economic review of the Federal Reserve Bank of Chicago) (September 1975), p. 5.

and country is presented in Table 1.2. The largest growth during the 1965-75 period in the number of U.S. bank branches overseas has been in Western Europe, with a fivefold increase in branches during that decade.

In terms of profitability, the largest U.S. banks derive nearly 50 percent of total earnings from international activities. Since 1970, the 13 U.S. banks with the largest international operations had a compound annual growth rate of 36.4 percent in international earnings. Their total earnings from abroad during this period rose from $177 million in 1970 to $836 million in 1975. The compound annual growth rate for domestic operations of these banks during this period was 0.7 percent, and their growth in foreign earnings represented 95 percent of total earnings made by these banks since 1970.[7]

REASONS FOR GROWTH OF U.S.
INTERNATIONAL BANKING

One principal reason already given for the growth of U.S. banking operations during the past two decades has been the growth of U.S. multinational corporate activities. However, perhaps an even more overriding reason for the growth in recent years can be attributed to the capital controls placed on financial flows by the U.S. government during the 1964-74 period. These controls were the Interest Equalization Tax, first proposed by the Kennedy administration and passed into law in 1964, a tax levied on portfolio purchases of foreign securities by American residents from foreign residents; the Voluntary Foreign Credit Restraints Program, administered by the Federal Reserve Board, which limited U.S. banks' loans to overseas borrowers; and the Foreign Direct Investment Program, administered by the U.S. Commerce Department, which limited financial outflows by U.S. MNCs to overseas subsidiaries. This latter program began as a voluntary plan in 1964 but was made mandatory in 1968. These controls were all lifted by presidential decree in 1974. Their imposition encouraged the growth of the Eurocurrency market, which became a principal source of working capital and long-term funds needed by international companies.

The objective of these controls was to limit outflows of funds from the United States, thus alleviating balance-of-payments deficits. A direct effect of such controls was the motivation of U.S. banks to expand overseas operations from only a handful of banks with foreign branches to more than 140 banks operating abroad by the beginning of 1976. Thus, the growth of MNCs, international banking, and Eurocurrency market activities occurred concurrently and phenomenally during this period.[8]

FOREIGN BANKS IN THE UNITED STATES

A second wave of growth in international banking that should be recognized is that of foreign banks operating in the United States. Foreign banks' assets in the United States in 1965, which amounted to only $7 billion, increased to $24.3 billion in 1972 and to about $72 billion in late 1977.[9] As of June 30, 1977, 222 foreign institutions were operating more than 400 offices in the United States, were comprised of nearly all the 50 largest foreign banks, and had made $17.5 billion worth of domestic commercial and industrial loans. This latter figure represented about 15 percent of such loans made by large U.S. banks, which file weekly reports with the Federal Reserve Board.[10] The foreign institutions are not all banks in the American sense of the word. Some are banks, some are foreign investment companies, some are joint ventures, some are consortia, and some are merely representative offices of parent financial institutions. In various surveys published in the United States, these institutions all seem to be classified as banks. Selected data about principal assets and liabilities of foreign banks operating in the United States are shown in Table 1.3. These foreign banks had total U.S. assets of $77.1 billion as of June 30, 1977. However, this represents only one-third of total assets held by U.S. banks abroad and less than 7 percent of all domestic assets of U.S. banks.

Foreign banks have developed rapidly during the 1965-75 period for a number of reasons. Among the most important of these are the following:[11]

1. to provide financial services to the U.S. subsidiaries of non-U.S.-based companies that are clients of the foreign parent bank
2. to serve as a dollar source for the foreign parent bank
3. to establish contacts with the U.S. securities markets
4. to have better access to U.S. money markets;
5. to escape banking restrictions in their parent banks' countries
6. to tap the retail banking market in the United States, especially of certain ethnic groups
7. to facilitate international payments settlements.

Specifically, the 222 foreign financial institutions are represented in the United States by 34 subsidiaries and 188 branches, agencies, New York Investment Companies (NYICs), and other affiliates. More than 100 representative offices have also been opened in the United States. Most of these operations are located in California, New York City, and Chicago, although foreign banks are increasingly locating in Houston, by means of representative offices, and in Atlanta, since Georgia recently enacted legislation permitting foreign

TABLE 1.3

Principal Assets and Liabilities of Foreign Banks in the United States, End-Quarter, 1977
(millions of dollars)

Item	March 31	June 30	September 30
Assets			
Cash	12,492	14,382	12,413
Investments	4,371	4,231	4,675
Loans	37,846	39,795	45,220
Customers' liabilities on acceptances and letters of credit	3,350	3,584	3,244
Due from directly related institutions	12,843	13,612	14,870
Other assets	1,597	1,504	1,784
Total assets	72,499	77,106	82,206
Liabilities			
Demand deposits and credit balances	11,617	13,105	15,661
Time and savings deposits	16,080	16,795	17,176
Other borrowing	15,023	16,021	16,353
Liabilities on acceptances and letters of credit	3,429	3,718	3,394
Other liabilities	1,072	1,108	1,300
Due to directly related institutions	23,131	24,155	26,013
Reserves and capital accounts	2,148	2,205	2,308
Total liabilities, reserves, and capital accounts	72,499	77,106	82,206

Source: Federal Reserve Statistical Release, "Monthly Report of Condition for U.S. Agencies, Branches and Domestic Banking Subsidiaries of Foreign Banks as of Report Date in October 1977," mimeographed (Washington, D.C.: Federal Reserve Board of Governors, December 12, 1977) (G.11 series).

banks to form agencies in that state. To give some idea of the recent expansion of foreign banking in the United States, unofficial data compiled by the Federal Reserve Board shows that during the period July 1 to September 30, 1977, foreign bank institutions increased from the 222 mentioned earlier to 240, and their total assets increased from $77.1 billion to $82.2 billion.

As mentioned above, foreign banks have organized by means of six different structures in the United States: as subsidiaries, branches, agencies, securities affiliates, New York Investment Companies, or representative offices. Whereas nearly all U.S. overseas offices are initiated as branches, foreign bank operations in this country are organized in this manner because of the statutory requirements of the states in which they operate.

Foreign Bank Branches

Foreign bank branches can perform full-line banking in New York but are ineligible under current federal banking laws for Federal Deposit Insurance Corporation (FDIC) insurance of deposits because they are not covered by the Federal Deposit Insurance Act. As of year-end 1976, 70 such branches were in operation in the United States, having total assets of $28 billion, or 37 percent of total foreign bank assets in the United States.

Foreign Bank Subsidiaries

Foreign banks wishing to participate in any large way in retail banking are required (by competition) to obtain FDIC insurance of deposits in their U.S. operations. Thus, in California, where foreign banks have had strong retail banking interests, they must form a subsidiary in order to obtain FDIC deposit insurance. As of year-end 1976, 36 such subsidiaries had total assets in the United States, amounting to $16.339 billion, or 21 percent of total foreign bank assets in the United States.

Foreign Bank Agencies

More than 90 foreign bank agencies hold more than 40 percent of all foreign banking assets in this country (or $30 billion). About half of their funds are obtained from sister or parent banks, and the remainder comes from interbank markets or from corporate customers. They cannot accept deposits but are permitted to maintain

credit balances. Agencies finance international trade, deal in bills
of exchange, manage dollar balances for their parents, act as agents
of the home central bank, deal in the Eurocurrency markets, and may
operate trust departments if local state law permits.[12]

NYICs

The New York State Banking Law has permitted formation of so-
called New York Investment Companies, banking groups that are required to report to the Federal Reserve Board and which operate much
as foreign bank agencies do. Only five such banking institutions have
been established. The most notable example of an NYIC is the European-American Banking Corporation, the group that acquired most of
the operations of the failed Franklin National Bank. These five banking establishments have combined assets amounting to less than $4
billion.

Foreign Bank Securities Affiliates

Some foreign banks own and operate securities affiliates. Although the Federal Reserve Board publishes statistics concerning
foreign bank subsidiaries, branches, agencies, and New York Investment Companies, for some reason, it does not do so for foreign bank-
owned securities affiliates. This may be a result of the nonbanking,
investment operations only aspect of the business of foreign securities
affiliates, activities of interest to the Securities and Exchange Commission.
Thus, no agency seems to publish adequate, if any, information
on foreign bank securities affiliates. Federal Reserve Board Vice-
Chairman Stephen S. Gardner attached some data on these affiliates
to his testimony before the Senate Subcommittee on Financial Institutions hearings in 1976.[13] This was merely an updated version of
similar information submitted by then Vice-Chairman George W.
Mitchell in testimony given earlier that year and which listed some
17 securities affiliates owned or controlled by foreign banks. Other
sources, in the form of annual surveys by such publications as Finance
Magazine, the American Banker, and Institutional Investor, report
the existence of as many as 37 such U.S.-located securities affiliates.
However, a detailed analysis of these 37 show most to be owned
by foreign investment companies and not by banks. Only eight seem
to be foreign bank securities affiliates.[14] These eight affiliates perform investment-brokerage-type activities, underwrite securities,
serve as specialist firms on regional securities exchanges, do no com-

mercial banking business, and have managements separate from any branch, agency, or subsidiary affiliation the foreign parent bank may operate in the United States.

Of these eight, six are ranked in the top 300 U.S. investment companies, according to the annual directory published by Finance Magazine; the largest ranks only 52nd. The combined capital of these six is less than 10 percent that of Merrill Lynch and under 2 percent of the capital of the top 25 securities firms in the United States. They are all located in New York City. The best estimate of their total capital is $55 to $65 million.

Representative Offices

The representative, or "rep," office is quite prevalent in this country. By mid-1977, at least 102 representative offices were being operated by foreign banks in the United States.[15] The rep office does not perform banking functions but acts as a public relations office of the parent bank and provides the customer with at least some presence of the parent foreign bank. Rep offices are low-cost operations, easy to form, require little or no regulatory supervision, and perform services that are of a primarily informational or public relations character.

Conclusions

Banks probably prefer branches to subsidiaries, when such is possible, for a number of reasons. The loan limits of branches are based on the parents' capital positions, whereas for subsidiaries, such limits are based on the subsidiaries' own limited capital. The branch carries the parent's name, whereas the subsidiary usually has to operate on its own name. The branch has more flexibility in moving funds, because state authorities can more clearly separate a subsidiary's operations from those of the parent, at least in a legal sense. The subsidiary has a more complex organizational structure and must have U.S. resident directors. Under present statutory requirements, these foreign operations cannot operate EACs, allowed U.S. banks, since all directors of an Edge subsidiary are required to be U.S. citizens.[16] In addition, branches and agencies of foreign banks are not subject to the Bank Holding Company Act.[17]

Foreign banks have some form of presence in 13 states, the District of Columbia, Puerto Rico, and the U.S. Virgin Islands. Except for those subsidiaries in California whose deposits are insured by FDIC, these foreign banking operations are regulated by the states in which they operate. A number of states actually prohibit foreign banking operations; others have no statutes concerning such operations. In fact, the president of the San Francisco Federal Reserve Bank, John J. Balles, has referred to the present framework of foreign bank regulation in the United States as "state patchwork."[18]

BANKING IN EUROPE

Banking in Western Europe has also shown a large amount of growth. During the past two decades, continental European as well as British banks have grown at home, as well as in their foreign operations. Much of this is a result of the influx of U.S. MNC operations into Europe and the concomitant growth of the Eurocurrency market, centered primarily in London, Luxembourg, and West Germany.

The burgeoning Eurocurrency market—estimated to be approximately $525 billion[19]—has attracted many foreign banks to Europe, but it has also furnished much of the growth of Europe's banks. For example, 125 of the top 300 worldwide banks ranked at year-end 1975 are headquartered in Western Europe,[20] and most of these banks are prime market-makers in the Eurocurrency market. The development of international banking in Europe has also been attributed to the growth of foreign trade markets during the "boom" years, the challenge of U.S. banks in foreign markets, and the trend toward global interdependence.[21]

These banks, which circle the Western European nations, have expanded not only domestically but also in international markets. Barclays and Lloyds Banks in the United Kingdom, for example, have expanded abroad rapidly in recent years. Barclays has 1,715 offices outside the United Kingdom, and Lloyds has opened 501 offices in foreign countries.[22] In France, the big French banks have created trading company subsidiaries as a means of overcoming restrictions in France and as a way to utilize their extremely liquid position to expand internationally, especially in key target areas, such as the United States.[23] The French banking market has become overbanked; thus, Société Générale, Crédit Lyonnais, Banque Nationale de Paris, and Banque de Paris et des Pays-Bas have established trading companies and are leasing equipment, placing bonds, and establishing branches on a worldwide basis.

In Germany, the concept of universal banking is practiced (all commercial and investment banking operations are carried out by one institution). More than 3,500 German financial institutions, with business volume of $700 billion, are expanding rapidly domestically and internationally. The credit banks contributed nearly 25 percent of this volume. These include Deutsche Bank, Dresdner Bank, and Commerzbank. Deutsche Bank, in 1977, derived 30 percent of its profits from foreign banking. As the local markets for these banks have shrunk, they have followed their clients overseas. The "big three" have been a force in international financial markets since 1970, but now, all German banks, including the state savings banks and cooperatives, are going international. It has been estimated that German banks have increased overseas branch offices from 23 in 1973 to 48 in 1977.[24]

Finally, in Switzerland, the scandal involving the Chiasso branch of Credit Suisse, several bank failures, and managerial weaknesses in the banking system all have caused concern and chagrin on the part of bank regulatory officials. The three big Swiss banks—Union Bank of Switzerland, Swiss Bank Corporation, and Swiss Credit Bank—have all more than doubled in size of gross assets since 1968.[25] A large amount of this growth was centered in international expansion, especially in an effort to wrest control of the Eurobond market from U.S. and British banks. The problems of recent years may suppress the Swiss banking expansion.

ARAB AND JAPANESE BANKING

Arab Banking

The Arab banking world deserves to be mentioned in this sketch of worldwide banking. The excess oil revenues that have accrued in recent years to Arab members of the Organization of Petroleum Exporting Countries (OPEC) have created a need for banking expansion in these countries. Middle Eastern members of OPEC had surpluses of $36 billion in 1975 and an estimated $28 billion in 1976.[26] In addition, the Lebanese Civil War has nearly eliminated Beirut as a banking center in the Middle East, setting the scene for Kuwait, Abu Dhabi, or Bahrain to become the Arab financial center.

Banks in this area are highly concentrated and, in most nations, many are nationalized. Egypt has four nationalized commercial banks. Jordan's system is comprised of four Jordanian and five foreign banks. Kuwait, with a very high per capita income, has a banking system comprised of a central bank and five commercial banks, wholly owned by Kuwaitis; international activity of these banks is a prime factor of banking growth there.[27] Foreign banks are not allowed to open branches in Kuwait but can participate there in the form of investment companies.

Bahrain has been suggested as a center for Middle Eastern banking operations. The nation has good communications facilities,

Concorde Jet Liner service, a small population, favorable ties with
other Arab countries, is in a favorable time zone, has a history of
political stability, and has large oil revenue reserves.[28] Its banking
system includes Arab, U.S., Pakistani, Iranian, and British banks,
and 32 offshore banking units have been licensed to operate in Bahrain.
The Bahrain Monetary Agency was formed in 1973 and became a full-
fledged central bank in 1975. Major worldwide banks are being encouraged to establish offices there.

Finally, the United Arab Emirates (UAE), a federation of seven
constituent emirates located in the coastal areas of the Saudi peninsula, have experienced large oil receipts of more than $5 billion an-
nually. The banking system has grown from 20 commercial banks—
14 of these foreign, in 1973, when the UAE Currency Board, the
monetary authority, was established—to 45 banks licensed in 1976,
with 39 operating 200 branches and another 97 approved. This represents a very large and competitive banking system for a region with a
population of less than 500,000.[29] Total banking assets in the UAE
more than quadrupled from 1973 to 1976, and more than half is invested
in foreign assets.[30]

Japanese Banking

Japan has a banking system that has undergone significant
changes since the end of World War II. It can be classified into three
areas: (1) the Bank of Japan—the central bank of Japan; (2) private
financial institutions, consisting of commercial banks, specialized
financial institutions, and miscellaneous institutions, such as securities and insurance firms; and (3) government financial institutions,
such as the Japan Development Bank and the Export-Import Bank of
Japan.

The Bank of Japan is the central bank and, as such, controls
the banking sector and the money supply by acting as note-issuing
bank, the banker's bank, and banker for the central government.
The Bank of Japan executes monetary policy through its discount policy, open market operations, and reserve requirements on deposits
in much the same way as the Federal Reserve System operates.

Japanese banks are classified as ordinary banks, long-term
credit banks, and foreign exchange banks. Ordinary banks were authorized by the Banking Law of 1927 and consist of city banks and local banks. These two types have 35 percent of all deposits in Japanese
financial institutions. All ordinary banks control nearly 42 percent
of all deposits. Foreign exchange banks were established by the Foreign Exchange Bank Law of 1954, and long-term credit banks were
authorized by the Long-Term Credit Bank Law of 1952.[31]

City and local banks engage mostly in short-term financing, conduct commercial banking operations, and occasionally extend medium- and long-term loans. Most of their deposit resources are from time deposits. They must obtain permission from the Minister of Finance to do foreign exchange trading.

As of year-end 1975, there were 87 ordinary banks; of these, 13 were city banks, and 74 were local banks. City banks have branches throughout the nation and are very large organizations, whereas most local banks are medium and small sized. The Bank of Tokyo, a city bank, is also a specialized foreign exchange bank. By year-end 1975, deposits had increased to $666 million, with a record increase in 1975.[32]

City banks' lending is 60 percent to enterprises with more than 100 million yen capital, whereas 60 percent of local banks' lending is to companies smaller than 100 million yen in capital. Long-term credit banks engage in long-term financing by raising funds from debenture issues. Their deposit business is limited to wholesale operations. Three such banks are operating: the Industrial Bank of Japan, the Long-Term Credit Bank of Japan, and the Nippon Fudosan Bank. In addition to these banks, Japan has trust banks, small business financial institutions, mutual loan and savings banks, credit associations, credit cooperatives, and special agricultural-, forestry-, and fisheries-financing institutions.

Japanese banks have begun, in recent years, to expand abroad. The largest banks have established subsidiaries in the rich retail markets in California. Among these are the Sumitomo Bank and Bank of Tokyo. Sumitomo has just opened an office in Houston, a center of great interest to foreign bankers.[33] In conclusion, Japanese banks have begun to resemble American banks in many aspects of their operations.[34]

IMPLICATIONS AND PROBLEMS OF INTERNATIONAL BANKING GROWTH

During the last two decades of international banking growth, several failures and losses have been incurred by large banks, especially in industrialized countries. In 1967, Intra Bank of Lebanon failed. This was one of the largest banks in the Middle East and had significant correspondent relationships with multinational banks in other countries. In Germany, I. D. Herstatt, the largest private bank, failed in 1974, primarily because of large foreign exchange losses, and two large state banks, Hessische Landesbank Girozentrale and Westdeutsche Landesbank Girozentrale, suffered severe losses from foreign exchange dealing and bad real estate loans. Banca Privata of

Italy and several secondary banks in the United Kingdom failed. In Switzerland, where banking has been considered conservative and almost a sacred business, the Lugano office of Lloyds Bank International suffered large foreign exchange losses; a United Bank of California branch in Basel failed because of losses resulting from illegal commodities trading by bank management; and, in 1977, a Chiasso branch of Credit Suisse reported large losses resulting from the granting of illegal guarantees to investors.[35] In France, Banque Baud failed, and even the large state bank of the USSR has been reported to be having problems.

Finally, in the United States, the eight largest bank failures of all time occurred. The three largest were U.S. National Bank of San Diego in 1973 (a result of corrupt management), Franklin National Bank in 1974 (a result of poor management and overextension of foreign exchange trading), and Hamilton National Bank in 1976 (from bad real estate loans). A relatively large number of bank failures occurred in recent years: 13 in 1975 and 12 in 1976. In addition, in recent years, the U.S. federal bank regulatory officials have reported large numbers of banks classified as problem banks by their agencies.

Most of these worldwide banking problems have stemmed from the recession and inflation prevalent during this period, as well as from the "go-go" banking carried on by international banks on a widespread basis. The world business cycle has been a contributing factor, as well as foreign exchange and real estate losses in Europe and the United States; losses by Eurocurrency banks incurred on loans to a declining world oil tanker market; and the resultant decline in bank assets on a worldwide basis. Some effect also may have been felt from losses on loans to LDCs and, in the United States, on shaky municipal loans, especially New York City paper.[36]

The major thrust of these worldwide banking failures and losses has been the ever-increasing discussion by legislative and executive agencies in major nations calling for revamped regulatory powers. In the United Kingdom, a white paper was published in 1976 asking for more stringent measures for bank entry, reporting operations, increased bank capital and liquidity standards, and possible insurance of bank deposits.

In other European countries, these and other bank regulatory measures have been introduced. In France, a small bank failed; its deposits were covered by the central government and the banking system. In Germany, a very comprehensive deposit insurance scheme was established in 1976. The European Economic Community (EEC) has been discussing the harmonization of banking laws among member countries.

In the United States, several proposals have been introduced in Congress to regulate and supervise at the federal level foreign banks operating in the United States.[37] One such bill, passed by the House of Representatives in 1976, was considered again in 1977 and was re-introduced in 1978. New reporting standards for foreign operations of U.S. banks were put into effect in 1978.

Finally, the Federal Reserve Board has been instrumental in pursuing a tighter international banking regulatory system. In 1973, it established a Steering Committee on International Bank Regulation, with a primary objective of studying legislation to control overseas activities of U.S. banks and domestic activities of foreign-based banks. The Board also has been a participant in the activities of the Blunden committee, a committee of representatives from central banks of various countries. Its activities and hearings have been held at the Bank for International Settlements in Basel, Switzerland.[38]

The Blunden committee, named after George Blunden, who is chairman of the Bank of England, was formed in 1975 by the governors of the central banks of the Group of Ten and ten leading industrialized nations, and is formally entitled the Committee on Banking Regulations and Supervisory Practices. Its purpose is to encourage and facilitate liaison and cooperation among these central banks on matters dealing with procedures and problems of bank supervision and regulation in each respective Group Ten country.[39]

These proposals and discussions will be the subject of detailed analysis in subsequent chapters of this book. The regulation of international activities of U.S. banks and of foreign banks operating in the United States will be analyzed in the next two chapters. Proposals made by U.S. bank regulatory agencies and congressional committees will be included in this discussion.

In addition, bank regulation in selected Western European and Arab countries, as well as Japan, will be described and analyzed in the following chapters. The growth and structure of banking in these countries will not be a primary subject, except where necessary to make a point concerning bank regulation and supervision. Other studies have accomplished this purpose.[40]

NOTES

1. U.S. Federal Reserve System data.

2. See James C. Baker and M. Gerald Bradford, American Banks Abroad: Edge Act Companies and Multinational Banking (New York: Praeger Publishers, 1974); Douglas H. Lemmonds, "Edge Corporations: A Microcosm of International Banking Trends," Federal Reserve Bank of Richmond Monthly Review 59 (September 1973): 15-16; John E. Leimone, "Edge Act Corporations: An Added Dimension to Southeastern International Banking," Federal Reserve Bank of At-

lanta Monthly Review 59 (September 1974): 130–38; James C. Baker, "Nationwide Branch Banking: The Edge Act Corporation and Other Methods," Issues in Bank Regulation 1 (Summer 1977): 31–36; Donald E. Baer, "Expansion of Miami Edge Act Corporations," Federal Reserve Bank of Atlanta Economic Review 62 (September/October 1977): 112–17.

3. C. Frederic Wiegold, "Brimmer Asks Fed Revamp to Allow U.S. Banks More Activities Overseas," The American Banker 141 (May 3, 1976): 1.

4. Federal Reserve Board data.

5. Paul A. Volcker, "Growth of International Banking Brings Problems in Regulation," The American Banker 141 (October 6, 1976): 4.

6. For an analysis of U.S. bank branch operations overseas, see Compendium of Papers Prepared for the FINE Study, prepared by the staff of the U.S. House of Representatives Committee on Banking, Currency and Housing, 94th Cong., 2d sess., June 1976, pp. 803–38.

7. Thomas H. Hanley, United States Multinational Banking: Current and Prospective Strategies (New York: Salomon Brothers, 1976), p. 3.

8. For excellent coverage and descriptive analysis of the Eurocurrency market, see Paul Einzig, The Euro-Dollar System: Practice and Theory of International Interest Rates (New York: St. Martin's Press, 1973), and Jane Sneddon Little, Euro-Dollars: The Money-Market Gypsies (New York: Harper & Row, 1975).

9. Chris Welles, "Bankers, Bankers Everywhere—But How Much Business Are They Getting?" Institutional Investor 11 (September 1977): 116; and Federal Reserve System data.

10. Ibid.

11. Jeffrey S. Arpan and David A. Ricks, "Foreign Banking in the U.S.," unpublished working paper. Arpan is with Georgia State University and Ricks is with Ohio State University.

12. Franklin R. Edwards and Jack Zwick, "Foreign Banks in the United States: Activities and Regulatory Issues" (Research Paper no. 80), mimeographed (New York: Graduate School of Business, Columbia University, 1974), pp. 11–12.

13. Statistical Appendix to Statement on H.R. 13876 by Stephen S. Gardner, vice-chairman, Federal Reserve Board, to the Subcommittee on Financial Institutions of the Senate Committee on Banking, 94th Cong., 2d sess., August 31, 1976.

14. James C. Baker and Jacobus T. Severeins, "Federal Regulation of Foreign Banking in the United States: Implications for Foreign Securities Affiliates' (paper presented at the Annual Meeting of the Southern Finance Association, New Orleans, November 1977).

15. "The Foreign Bank Roster," Institutional Investor 11 (September 1977): 143–75.

16. Baker and Bradford, American Banks Abroad.

17. Henry Harfield, "Legal Considerations in International Banking," The Banking Law Journal 91 (August 1974): 636.

18. "Required Reading: Federal Rule over Foreign Banks Would End State Patchwork," The American Banker 140 (August 13, 1975): 4.

19. "Dollar's Woes Worry Many Foreigners, Too," The Wall Street Journal, November 28, 1977, p. 1.

20. "The Top 300 Banks in the World," The Banker 126 (June 1976): 645–702.

21. Klaas Peter Jacobs, "The Development of International and Multinational Banking in Europe," Columbia Journal of World Business 10 (Winter 1975): 33.

22. Robin Pringle, "The British Big Four Stake Their Claim," The Banker 127 (August 1977): 115.

23. "French Banks Turn Traders," Business Week, November 21, 1977, p. 148.

24. "Germany's Drive to Be the No. 2 Banker," Business Week, December 5, 1977, pp. 53, 56.

25. "Why Swiss Banks Need a Housecleaning," Business Week, June 6, 1977, p. 102.

26. E. R. Shaw, "Arab Funds in Euro-Markets," The Bankers Magazine (United Kingdom) 220 (June 1976): 23; and "Arab Banks and International Lending Markets," The Banker 126 (August 1976): 957, 959.

27. Barry Moule, "Banking and Financial Developments in Kuwait," The Banker 122 (November 1972): 1399.

28. K. R. Day, "Bahrain's Development as a Financial Centre," The Banker 126 (June 1976): 585.

29. N. A. Sarma, "The Financial System of the United Arab Emirates," Euromoney, March 1976, pp. 46–47.

30. Ibid., p. 47.

31. Philip Thorn, ed., Banking Structures and Sources of Finance in the Far East (London: Financial Times, 1974), p. 10.

32. John G. Roberts, "Prospects Brighter for Japanese Banking," Burroughs Clearing House 60 (June 1976): 18.

33. "Why Foreign Banks Like Houston So Much," Business Week, December 5, 1977, p. 39.

34. Paul Gleason, "Japanese Banks Edge Closer to U.S. Style," Banking 48 (July 1976): 86.

35. Eric Morgenthaler, "Chiasso Connection: Scandal at Border Bank Jolts Swiss Financiers and Italian Investors," The Wall Street Journal, May 16, 1977, pp. 1, 27.

36. "Banking on the Boom," The Economist Survey on World Finance 258 (February 14, 1976): 9.

37. Robert Johnston, "Proposals for Federal Control of Foreign Banks," Federal Reserve Bank of San Francisco Economic Review, Spring 1976, pp. 32-39.

38. See George W. Mitchell, "How the Fed Sees Multinational Bank Regulation," The Banker 124 (July 1974): 757, 759-60; and "Foreign Bank Regulation in the USA: I—The Federal Reserve Proposals," The Banker 125 (January 1975): 47, 49, 51.

39. Paul A. Volcker, "Growth of International Banking Brings Problems in Regulation," The American Banker 141 (October 6, 1976): 2.

40. See, for example, Francis A. Lees and Maximo Eng, International Financial Markets (New York: Praeger Publishers, 1975).

2

REGULATION OF
INTERNATIONAL OPERATIONS
OF AMERICAN BANKS

INTRODUCTION

Regulation of international operations of American banks is the subject of this chapter. Much of this regulation is related to that performed by federal and state agencies over the overall operations of all 14,500 or so U.S. banks. However, an attempt will be made to recognize the dichotomy between domestic and international banking, to discuss the latter, and to leave the reader to peruse the rich literature on the subject of general bank regulation and supervision.[1]

It was mentioned previously that only about 140 of the approximately 14,500 U.S. banks are engaged in international operations of some kind. In fact, international banking is highly concentrated when considering these 140 banks. Only 20 banks own 80 to 90 percent of the overseas branch operations, and although 50 U.S. banks have foreign exchange trading facilities that are at least moderately active, half of all U.S. foreign exchange trading is concentrated in 25 banks.[2]

At this point, the dual banking system in the United States should be mentioned. This unique character of American banking is quite relevant because it affects several aspects of international bank regulation and is intertwined with the subject of international reciprocity in banking laws here and abroad.

The dual banking system grew out of the establishment in 1863-64 of a national banking system by the National Bank Act, which permitted banks to be chartered by the federal government. Thus, national banks are supervised by the U.S. comptroller of the currency, state-chartered banks by the Federal Reserve System if they are member banks, and state-chartered nonmember banks by state bank commissions and, if their deposits are insured by FDIC, by this latter agency. No other major country has such a system, that is, where banks may be supervised dually at either the federal level or at the state level, depending on whether they are chartered at the national or state levels.

In this chapter, several aspects of international banking operations will be analyzed in terms of regulation and supervision of these activities. Since all U.S. banks engaged in international business have deposit insurance and are predominantly Federal Reserve member banks with national charters, the regulatory and supervisory thrust will be from the federal level. Thus, little or no discussion will be made of state regulatory functions in this chapter. The involvement of states will be a significant factor in Chapter 3 with regard to regulation of foreign banks operating in the United States.

The board of governors of the Federal Reserve System has primary regulatory authority over international operations of U.S. banks.[3] The statutory authority for this responsibility is garnered from the following: (1) Section 25 of the Federal Reserve Act, as amended in 1916, 1962, and 1966; (2) Section 25(A) of the Federal Reserve Act (the Edge Act of 1919); and (3) the Bank Holding Company Act of 1956, as amended in 1966 and 1970. From this authority, the board regulates the following aspects of U.S. banks' international operations:

1. Branches (statutory authority over member banks from Section 25 of the Federal Reserve Act, implemented by the Board's Regulation M)

2. Direct equity participations in foreign banks (statutory authority also from Section 25 and Regulation M)

3. Equity participations in foreign banking and nonbanking firms by U.S. bank-holding companies (statutory authority from the Bank Holding Company Act of 1956, as amended in 1970, implemented by Regulation Y)

4. Branches and agencies of EAC or agreement corporation subsidiaries of a bank, and equity participations by such subsidiaries in foreign banking or nonbanking firms (statutory authority from Sections 25 and 25(A) of Federal Reserve Act, implemented by Regulation K).

As will be discussed later, the U.S. comptroller of the currency has responsibility for examination of overseas branches of national banks. State bank commissioners have complete authority to examine overseas branches of state-chartered nonmember banks but share this authority with FDIC. They also share jurisdiction over such activities of state-chartered member banks with the Federal Reserve System. The Fed, however, does have complete responsibility in supervising Edge Act operations of state-chartered banks, as well as foreign business of domestic bank holding companies that own state banks.[4]

The structure of international operations of U.S. banks that is subject to federal supervision and regulation is presented in Figure 2.1. Since a bank holding company operation is depicted, federal authorities have complete jurisdiction over these activities. Other aspects of supervision—specifically, examination—will be discussed in subsequent sections of this chapter.

OVERSEAS BRANCH OPERATIONS

General Operations

U.S. banks' branches in London represent the most important part of U.S. international banking operations, because they have the largest share of overseas assets and supply a large portion of funds to other foreign branches. As shown in Table 1.2, the number of U.S. branches in the United Kingdom—most of these in London—increased more than threefold from 1965 to 1975. London has been the center of the Eurocurrency interbank market, and it is the London Interbank Offer Rate (LIBOR) that is the key rate set in this market. With the strengthening of the pound on the foreign exchange markets during 1977, there is little question that London will remain the Eurocurrency market center.

The business of foreign branches of U.S. banks is difficult to fully identify because of the generalized or aggregated data (or complete lack thereof). Their activities may include trade financing, financing overseas offices of MNCs headquartered in the United States, making development loans to LDCs, foreign exchange trading, and so forth. However, a real information gap exists in the area of economic and financial analysis of their operations.

The locations of these branches, be they London or the Caribbean, are advantageous for a number of reasons. London, for example, is a financial center, where funds in the Eurocurrency market are available from a variety of sources. The Cayman Islands have tax advantages because of their tax haven nature.

However, interbank loans do have a relatively low return. A Federal Reserve Board survey of London branches of 15 U.S. banks in 1972 found the average return on these loans was 0.12 percent, compared with a much higher 0.79 percent return on such loans in the domestic U.S. market.

In spite of the tremendous growth in U.S. bank branching overseas, the return on assets of foreign branches and subsidiaries seems to be relatively low, and a significant difference does exist between the returns for the two organizational types. For all overseas branches, the return on assets in 1974 was 0.50 percent; for overseas subsidiaries, it was 0.30 percent.

FIGURE 2.1

Organizational Structure of U.S. Banks
and Their Affiliates Overseas

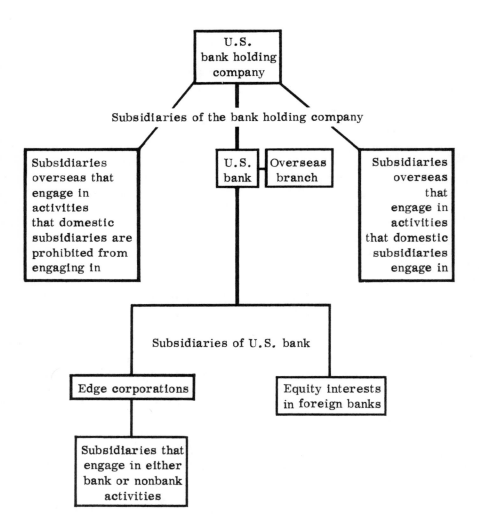

Source: Allen Frankel, "International Banking—Structural Aspects of Regulation," Business Conditions (economic review by Federal Reserve Bank of Chicago), October 1974, p. 5.

Riskiness of U.S. Overseas Branches

Although data for the past few years show that the loan loss experience has been much better for U.S. banks' international loans than for domestic loans, in general, the riskiness of U.S. overseas branch operations is higher than for domestic branches for several reasons. First, approximately 30 percent of assets and liabilities of overseas branches is payable in currencies other than dollars. Exchange market crises make such activities prone to the same problems as incurred by Franklin National Bank and Bankhaus Herstatt.[5]

Second, the trend in recent years to term lending by U.S. overseas branches has increased their riskiness. At year-end 1971, only 8 percent of the total assets of these branches were term loans. In 1975, term loans amounted to 20 percent of total assets of the foreign branches of the 21 largest U.S. banks.[6] The competition in the term-lending market is very intense, as demonstrated by the narrow spread on such loans of 0.75 to 1.5 percent, a spread inadequate for all but the very largest banks.

Third, the sources of funds for U.S. banks' overseas branches is a factor that increases their riskiness. Only about 13 percent of their liabilities can be considered stable, since they represent deposits of private individuals and corporations (which are relatively good customers). Prior to 1974, about 60 percent of these funds were supplied by other non-U.S.-based banks. After the Herstatt and Franklin failures, interbank liabilities of U.S. foreign branches dropped by $8 billion, or to about 11 percent of liabilities. Some of this decline was offset by OPEC deposits, but only about half the necessary funds were furnished and then only to the bigger banks. Thus, the price of funds rose during the process.[7]

Fourth, the rising cost of overseas branch operations and other facilities has increased their riskiness. A London branch costs more than $1 million per year to operate. A representative office in Tokyo may cost only $200,000 or more annually. The London branch would need $80 to $100 million in loans to reach the break-even point, whereas the Tokyo rep office would need only $15 to $20 million in loan volume.[8] These rising costs are the result of competition for funds in the international financial markets. Thus, many foreign branch operations are only marginally profitable, eliminating small banks from adequately servicing MNCs.

If the international department needs in the domestic office of a full-service bank are considered, one can easily see how going abroad can increase both the complexity and the amount of financing necessary. For example, such a department in a bank with merely $1.5 billion in deposits would need a manager, international lending and business development officers, an operations manager and staff, foreign correspondent bank relationships, agency-type accounts, credit files on all banks and companies with which the bank did business, country risk analysis capabilities, an international credit officer, access to an outside international attorney, a note teller for all international loans, foreign exchange and Eurocurrency expertise, and so on.[9]

These risk factors and the declining profitability have resulted in some branch closings in London and Continental Europe by a few U.S. banks. Other closings are being considered. However, the Federal Reserve Board and the U.S. comptroller of the currency have made it difficult to close overseas branches because of the belief that the overall image of U.S. bank operations will be weakened by such actions.

It has been previously mentioned that U.S. banks have experienced less loan losses from overseas operations than they have from domestic operations, even though foreign and domestic loan losses have increased absolutely and in proportion to loans outstanding during the 1972-74 period. The riskiness of these operations has been lessened by international diversification of the loan portfolios, as practiced by large U.S. banks.[10]

U.S. Regulation of U.S. Bank Operations Overseas

Nearly all overseas branches of U.S. banks are owned by nationally chartered banks. Thus, the U.S. comptroller of the currency has primary jurisdiction over the supervision of these branches. In fact, for the past few years, the comptroller's office, in conjunction with the Federal Reserve Board and FDIC, has held seminars and classes in international banking at the Rosslyn, Virginia, FDIC Training Center for their bank examiners. As a result of this training, according to the office of the comptroller data, there are 150 national bank examiners trained in international examining. The comptroller's office has examined the branches of U.S. national banks in more than 20 countries annually since 1967 and has sent an average of 116 examiners abroad annually for these examinations since 1972.

The overseas branches of U.S. banks are examined in much the same way as are domestic offices. The comptroller has an overseas office in London to facilitate this process. Six national bank examiners are assigned to this office to examine the 23 U.S. branches in London. Of course, these examinations must be made with the consent of the host government, and diplomatic protocol is observed. Some nations, such as Switzerland, preclude bank examination by foreign government agencies. In these cases, U.S. officials must rely on the host government examinations, reports, and analyses of

U.S. banking operations in those countries. Although this arrangement has been questioned by congressional committees, thus far, other governments imposing such a regulatory process have cooperated to the extent that no problems have occurred.

The Federal Reserve Board maintains an International Banking Section and participates with the comptroller's office in some supervisory functions but, primarily, leaves examination of foreign operations to the comptroller, while performing data-gathering and analytical functions. The Fed does practice a regulatory philosophy when dealing with the international operations of U.S. banks by restricting U.S. bank activities overseas to banking and financially related activities. The Fed does directly examine and supervise those international operations of state-chartered member banks.

The Fed does become involved in monetary policy, balance-of-payments, and branch application considerations. [11] Reserve requirements under Regulation M have been established against borrowings by member banks from their foreign branches and lending by these branches to U.S. residents. (Regulation M was formulated for balance-of-payments reasons, as well as to implement monetary policy objectives, because these reserve requirements affect the costs and the volume of such transactions.)

The Fed did promulgate guidelines under the Voluntary Foreign Credits Restraints (VFCR) Program for balance-of-payments reasons. The VFCR Program, terminated in 1974, limited the volume of foreign lending and investing of U.S. banks and nonbank financial institutions.

The Federal Reserve Board also acts on applications by member banks to establish or acquire foreign branches or affiliates under the Federal Reserve Act. Overseas U.S. branches may apply for permission from the Fed to engage in some financially related activities not permitted U.S. domestic banks but permitted local foreign banks. Such applications are reviewed to ensure that both the foreign branch and parent bank have the financial and managerial resources to carry out the foreign expansion. [12]

Finally, an area of the Fed's jurisdiction has had a pronounced indirect effect on the growth of U.S. banks' overseas operations. Regulation Q, implemented by the Federal Reserve System, limits the rate of interest U.S. banks are permitted to pay on deposits received in domestic offices. During tight monetary policy periods in the United States, such as in 1966 and 1969-70, when interest rates were quite high, U.S. banks could not compete for funds with other alternatives, such as U.S. government Treasury bills; thus, they experienced a runoff of deposits in domestic offices.

U.S. banks, therefore, turned to foreign branches, which were not subject to Regulation Q and which could pay higher interest rates for funds. These deposits were then transferred back to domestic offices for use in lending. U.S. banks used their foreign operations to get around tight monetary policies practiced by the Fed. This activity encouraged much of the growth in U.S. banks' overseas branch operations and necessitated the promulgation of Regulation M, mentioned earlier, with which the Fed could impose reserve requirements against new funds acquired abroad by U.S. banks' foreign branches.[13]

FDIC has very little examination activity to perform. This agency has supervisory jurisdiction over only state-chartered nonmember banks. At present, only one of these has an overseas branch that necessitates examination. FDIC examiners have made three total examinations of the branches of two U.S. banks. Approximately 39 shell branches have been opened in the Caribbean by state-chartered nonmember banks during the past decade. Shell branches are merely offices where a separate set of books are kept to record offshore banking transactions. In fact, former Federal Reserve Board Governor Andrew Brimmer classified shells as "really nothing more than a paper projection in foreign terms of business actually conducted from the banks' own head offices in the United States."[14] Since a similar set of books is kept in the parent office, FDIC examiners are able to examine the international data transacted by the shell branch by examining the parent bank main office.[15]

Thus, from a greater to a lesser extent, all three federal bank regulatory agencies become involved in the supervision and/or regulation of U.S. foreign bank operations. U.S. branch deposits overseas are not insured by FDIC; thus, except insofar as FDIC is involved in examining the small amount of overseas operations of state-chartered nonmember banks, most U.S. regulation and supervision of these operations is carried out by the Federal Reserve System or the U.S. comptroller of the currency.

FOREIGN EXCHANGE OPERATIONS

Foreign exchange operations of U.S. banks have grown greatly during the past few years. Two reasons for this growth can be identified. First, the floating exchange rate system adopted by major industrial nations has been a contributing factor. Second, a large portion of the loans and deposits of U.S. banks have been denominated in currencies other than the dollar. Thus, foreign exchange is necessary to settle regular international commercial transactions and to balance international payment positions. Firms and individuals also operate in the forward exchange market in order to hedge the risk that foreign exchange rates may move adversely before the final settlement date. In addition, speculators and arbitrageurs also operate in this market for purposes of making profits on currency rate movements.

Since the 1974 failures of Herstatt and Franklin and the $100 million foreign exchange loss by Westdeutsche Landesbank, there has been a general concern by bank regulators (worldwide) that the floating exchange rate system has increased the risks attendant to banks' foreign exchange operations. The risk problem involved in banks' foreign exchange operations is that they necessarily have to take positions in foreign currencies in order to maintain the market sufficient to accommodate the needs of their customers to buy and sell foreign currency balances for ordinary commercial transactions. Banks, thus, incur a foreign exchange risk but may also make profits in these operations. In fact, bankers have testified in congressional hearings that foreign exchange trading volume must be about seven times their foreign exchange needs for settling ordinary international trade transactions. This seven to one trading ratio is needed to maintain the market and the liquidity required to render the best prices available in the amounts needed for their customers.

In order for a bank to avoid overexposure to losses in its foreign exchange position, its management must set prudent limits on the various market and credit risks, as well as implement audit and other internal control procedures to police the trading limits set. Specifically, net position limits, maturity gap limits, and customer limits should be formulated.

Net position limits are those on a bank's overall net long or short position with respect to a currency. They restrict the bank's exposure to changes in spot and forward exchange rates and, at the same time, allow traders flexibility to be temporarily long or short in a currency, while acting as dealers.

Maturity gap limits moderate the mismatching of maturities between outstanding commitments to receive and deliver balances in a given foreign currency. This mismatching is inevitable if a bank is adequately serving customers' needs to buy or sell currencies for future delivery.

Finally, customer limits are designed to control the credit risk involved in foreign exchange trading incurred when a customer is unable to fulfill a foreign exchange contract into which he or she has entered with the bank. The customer might cancel the contract or be unable at settlement date to deliver funds after the bank has delivered the foreign exchange.

A key problem facing regulators is the characteristic absence of information. Little or no public information on foreign exchange markets is available. Since Herstatt and Franklin, regulatory agencies have designed forms to compile data on banks' operations in foreign exchange, and much new data were made available in 1978 (see Appendix A). The best available data show the top 12 U.S. multinational banks to have year-end 1974 gross volume of $40 billion buys and $40 billion sells, although these figures are probably greatly understated, because they include only contracts of foreign branches. Many U.S. regional banks deal in foreign exchange through an EAC located in New York. Several New York banks execute many contracts in the home office.

A further problem complicating the lack of adequate information about foreign exchange trading is that these transactions are generally interbank in nature and commonly exceed legal lending limits. Such transactions are free of the restraints of loan limits; thus, the risk is higher. In early 1974, Franklin National Bank's foreign exchange contracts with banks owned by Michele Sindona or affiliates were both in excess of Franklin's legal limits on loans to one borrower and in excess of capital.

Because of this concern and the speculation in trading out of weak currencies into strong currencies, the Federal Reserve Board implemented a survey in 1974 of foreign exchange operations of 32 member banks to obtain a "cross-sectional view of the policies and controls that U.S. banks employed in their foreign exchange operations."[16] About 50 U.S. banks have at least moderately active foreign exchange trading operations, although only about half of these conduct the vast majority of such operations in the United States. It was these latter that were included in the sample.

Thus, the most serious problem facing bank regulators in the area of foreign exchange trading is the lack of adequate information. An attempt to remedy this situation is being made by all three federal bank regulatory agencies. FDIC has been formulating new bank examination pages and questionnaires for examiner use, involving queries concerning foreign exchange, international loans, international letters of credit and acceptance, and Eurocurrency transactions. The foreign exchange questionnaire includes (1) a position analysis, in which the bank's foreign currency open position exposure will be compared with the bank's total capital and reserves; (2) a maturity distribution (gap) analysis, to determine the extent long and short maturities in foreign currency assets, liabilities, and forward contracts are matched; and (3) a revaluation and income/loss analysis, to determine the bank's net unrealized profit or loss in foreign currencies on examination date and to reflect the bank's historical income or loss derived from foreign exchange activities. This material has been supplemented with an international examiner aids package, which assists the examiner in dealing with international operations data.

Finally, beginning with the quarterly call report for March 1978, a detailed comprehensive report was required by the Federal Reserve Board for international operations of U.S. banks. A proposal for an attachment to the Consolidated/Foreign/Domestic Call and Income Report was circulated among the federal bank regulatory agencies in early 1977. It affects only about 150 U.S. banks—those having foreign offices or Edge Act subsidiaries. Some foreign exchange trading information will be solicited in the new call report.

INTERBANK/EUROCURRENCY OPERATIONS

The Eurocurrency market has grown concomitantly with multi-national corporate and banking operations during the past 20 years. The market is comprised of currencies held in deposits that are available for reinvestment outside the country in which they are denominated. Thus, a Eurodollar is a dollar deposited anywhere outside the United States; a Euromark is a mark deposited outside West Germany. The market also is comprised of Eurosterling, Euroyen, Eurofrancs—both French and Swiss, and so forth. The magnitude of the market is highly immeasurable. Reliable sources have estimated it to be about $525 billion, with over half denominated in Eurodollars.

The market is generally short term in nature, although Eurocurrency credit and Eurobond markets exist for long-term and medium-term financing. It is a wholesale market, with a high degree of interbank activity, centered primarily around London; thus, the so-called London Interbank Rate, or LIBOR, as the interest rate governing Eurocurrency transactions is known. A typical transaction is from call to one year to maturity for $1 to $5 million in amount. Transfers are by telephone or teletype, with a letter of confirmation as the only customary documentation. No withholding tax is levied on interest; the market is highly impersonal; and no government controls of any consequence are present to hamper market trading. Banks dealing in Eurocurrencies hold reserves but are generally exempt from mandatory reserves. This factor is highly advantageous from the standpoint of both profitability and flexibility.

It seems that five major problems can be delineated, all of which have serious implications for international banking in general and for U.S. banks' international operations specifically. These include: (1) tiering of the market; (2) a market whose operations are based on mutual trust; (3) lack of adequate information on Eurocurrency operations; (4) the issue of credit creation in the Eurocurrency markets, which contributes to worldwide inflation; and (5) the lack of international or national government controls on the market.

The problem of tiering of the market arose after the 1974 collapse of Bankhaus Herstatt in West Germany. Deposit markets were frozen, and bankers began to make more detailed investigations of banks with which they had dealt. The structure of the interbank market then changed from one comprised of four major bank groups layered around the money brokers to one that was, and still is, six-tiered, each a clearly definable group paying a different rate for Euromoney. After Herstatt, most business went to only a few very large banks. The others were squeezed out of the market. The top tier might pay up to 2 percent under the market rate for large amounts of, say, Arab money. The spread is normally about 0.75 percent. The cost of Eurocurrency increased to the borrower, since only a few banks were making a market. Another more subtle result of the tiered markets is that national tax authorities had difficulty determining the cost of funds to international bank branches in their jurisdictions.

A second problem concerns the mutual trust with which international banking must depend. After Bankhaus Herstatt, this mutual trust, characterized by verbal communications made by telephone or face to face and later confirmed by telex or letter, began to dissipate. Foreign exchange and currency operations, even spot transactions, were undertaken only with the largest banking institutions.

Interbank operations also operate on generally accepted assumptions. For example, a dollar interbank deposit made for five years will have interest payable at the end of each year unless stipulated otherwise. A depositor or banker need not specify the interest payment provisions when quoting a deposit rate. The terms are generally known to both sides.

A series of incidents in recent years have resulted in lawsuits challenging this mutual trust. One transaction concerned a $100 million loan to the Colocotronis shipping group to finance ultralarge crude oil carriers. These tankers did not produce revenues, and the shipowner could not service the Eurocurrency loan. A second case involved three irrevocable letters of credit opened by Creditanstalt-Bankverein in favor of a Dutch company. The third case involved several banks that made Eurocurrency loans to the government of Zaire. The terms of a loan agreement between the U.S. Export-Import Bank and Zaire gave the former first rights to exchange earnings from Zaire's mineral operations. This restriction imposed by the U.S. Export-Import Bank has since been lifted.

Because of these incidents and the possible legal ramifications, as well as economic implications, to the banks involved, the verbal agreements that characterize international interbank operations may be replaced with very comprehensive, costly, and complex documentation, which can only result in hindering international commercial operations and reducing overall banking profits in these areas.

A third problem in Eurocurrency operations and one that has serious implications for bank regulation is the lack of information available about the business of nonbank borrowers in Eurocurrency markets. Most of the data are generalized and aggregated. For example, foreign branches of U.S. banks report the location of branches where loans are made but do not report the country origin of the borrower, unless the borrower is a U.S. national. This does not make supervision of these markets very easy. In fact, such inadequacy probably precludes proper supervision and regulation.

Fourth, the issue of credit creation in the Eurocurrency markets contributes to worldwide inflation and has been singled out as a major problem of international finance. No one is quite sure just how much is added to the world money supply by a $1 deposit in the Euromarkets. Because of the lack of variety of reserve requirements, the multiplier effect seems indeterminate. The multiplier may be about 2.5 to 3 because of leakages throughout the monetary system.

However, these problems all lead to a fifth problem, and that is the lack of international or national control over the Eurocurrency markets. The stability of the international monetary system may be progressively jeopardized by this lack of control. Monetary policy may be thwarted by Euromarket operations, as it was in 1969 in the United States.

A recent example of Eurocurrency operations in small nations that have lax monetary controls occurred when a loan to a Teheran bank was made by the Cayman Islands branch of the Crocker National Bank of San Francisco, along with three Dutch subsidiaries of Japanese companies and 16 other institutions. A further such example concerns a note issue by Ljublianska Banka of Slovenia, Yugoslavia, managed partly by a New York investment firm and denominated in Kuwaiti dinars deposited in the Eurocurrency market. Some regulators see worldwide crises emanating from these markets if the following occur: country defaults, large bank failures, 1974-type tiering of the market, and loss of mutual trust among dealers.

Thus, in the past, federal regulation of U.S. banks' operations in the Eurocurrency market has concentrated on balance-of-payments considerations with the VFCR program (terminated in 1974). At present, reserve requirements under Regulation M are imposed by the Fed for both balance-of-payments and monetary policy considerations. These requirements have seemingly been only moderately effective. New reporting requirements included in the 1978 call reports is a first step toward gaining more adequate information about U.S. banks' Eurocurrency market operations. (See Appendix A for the new requirements.)

Little or no controls are imposed by foreign governments on Eurocurrency transactions. The monetary policy of these countries may be made less effective by massive Eurocurrency operations. Thus, some of these nations have suggested the imposition of new controls on this burgeoning market.

LOANS TO DEVELOPING NATIONS

During 1976-77, one of the most serious problems discussed about U.S. banks' international operations concerned loans to other governments, specifically, LDCs. Congressional leaders, bank regulators, and journalists became increasingly concerned about the magnitude of U.S. banks' lending to LDCs and about the level of debt service that these nations had incurred in recent years.[17]

The crux of the problem is that lending by U.S. banks to LDCs has increased in the past few years and drastically in the last two years. At year-end 1973, LDCs had a total long-term and short-term official and private debt of $86 billion. The International Monetary Fund (IMF) estimated that LDCs, by year-end 1975, owed overseas banks $250 billion (this probably included short- and long-term loans, whereas the above figure was long-term loans only) and that $97 billion of that was owed U.S. banks and their overseas branches. Even the experts cannot agree on the amount, but at any rate, LDCs do owe large amounts to U.S. banks.

The best American estimate for year-end 1976 was published by the Federal Reserve Board (based on data from the IMF, the World Bank and the Bank for International Settlements).[18] This source estimated total long- and short-term debt of the non-oil-producing LDCs to have been about $180 billion. About half of this was owed to commercial banks in the industrial countries. Most of this, about $140 billion, was long term. The remaining short-term obligations were mainly liabilities owed to commercial banks. More than half the commercial bank lending could be attributed to U.S. banks, the remainder was loaned by Canadian, European, and Japanese banks.[19]

The major concern, to be brief, is that the oil price increases severely aggravated LDCs' balance-of-payments deficits, which generally, in toto, are large. Normal debt servicing by LDCs, thus, became quite difficult in 1974-75, and the fear of default or, at the least, rescheduling of debt payments became a common threat.

Analysis of the non-oil-producing LDCs shows their government long-term debts to be about $140 billion, with half this owed to the private sector, mostly to banks. This, coupled with borrowing by the private sector in these LDCs, means amortization charges in 1976 of $12 billion, with $7 to $10 billion in interest charges. Add to this $30 billion needed for current balance-of-payments deficit financing in 1976. Thus, 1976 foreign exchange needs of these LDCs was nearly $52 billion.[20]

Much of the debt financing of LDCs has come from the Eurocurrency markets. In fact, two-thirds of such credit has gone to only six nations: Argentina, Brazil, Mexico, Peru, the Philippines, and South Korea. According to Business Week, with regard to 1975 long-term bank debt, Brazil owed $3 billion; Mexico, $2.9 billion; Greece, $1.4 billion; Argentina, $815 million; Zaire, $775 million; Peru, $703 million; and Chile, $573 million. [21]

The nations owing these amounts must be analyzed in terms of their economic environments. Brazil is developing rapidly. Chile has instituted a severe austerity program. Greece has some of the benefits of EEC membership. OPEC oil charges declined drastically in 1976, and LDCs, in general, had improved balance-of-payments positions. Thus, foreign exchange earnings for them were much better in 1976 and improved further in 1977. Still, the austerity programs they have implemented will hinder their growth.

Rescheduling has already occurred with Zaire, Chile, and other countries. There will be more rescheduling of debt, but defaults should not occur. Defaults are too drastic in their consequences, so that the IMF, Bank for International Settlements, Federal Reserve System, and World Bank will work to avoid any defaults. Banks have lost and may continue to lose money on some of these loans. However, it is possible for loan losses on overseas operations to remain relatively low and below domestic levels, as they have in the recent past.

U.S. banks already are analyzing LDC loans much more carefully (the press coverage in 1976 was primarily based on 1974 and 1975 results). It is interesting to note that charge-offs cited in a recent survey predicted Argentina, Mexico, and Zaire to be among the most probable to require rescheduling of their loans. Among the leaders in that survey, however, were charge-offs in the United Kingdom and the United States. First National City Bank of New York (Citibank) remained very optimistic about LDC lending and debt problems in 1976 and 1977. Citibank has more than 2,000 offices in more than 100 countries. Thus, their forecasts are highly respected. [22]

It should be added that the U.S. Treasury Department estimated on August 2, 1976, that lending to foreign countries by U.S. banks would increase by $11 billion in 1976, compared with $14.9 billion in 1975 and $26.6 billion in 1974. The estimate for 1977 remained about the same as that for 1976. Demand for credit in developed countries has declined, but in LDCs, especially non-oil-producing nations, it has increased. However, banks are reluctant to boost higher risk loans to LDCs.

One can add to this analysis the fact that much of the U.S. bank lending to LDCs is by the top 20 multinational banks, which have well-diversified portfolios. In fact, five of these account for nearly half of overseas lending. The widening profit margins of these banks during the 1976–77 period relieved pressure on their capital positions, their overseas loan write-offs were fractional, and loan demand declined. Thus, these banks ought to be able to cope with an occasional rescheduling of debt.

One final note to this section should be included. A further implication of LDC lending has not so much to do with the safety and soundness of banks as it has to do with foreign economic policy formulation by the U.S. government. Policy can be implemented by U.S. agencies. For example, the Export-Import Bank may decide not to guarantee credits or make loans to a certain country, for example, Chile, and U.S. banks may then follow suit. An economic squeeze may be placed on the nation, the government may fall, and then the U.S. government may decide to support the new government, with U.S. banks falling into line.

Private investors, including banks, may forecast better returns from South Korea than from India or from a particular government in Chile. Thus, from an economic standpoint, such policies, with or without official sanction, are rational. New institutional mechanisms will have to be established to solve these other problems, and the banker will have to use better economic judgment when making a portfolio decision to lend to an LDC. [23]

Conclusions

The area of lending to LDCs by U.S. banks has caused federal bank regulatory officials grave concern during the past few years, as the foregoing analysis certainly infers. The public, through the press, has become agitated by the possible worldwide disruption in the safety and soundness of the banking and monetary system that widespread defaults and renegotiations on debt by LDCs could bring. [24]

U.S. regulatory agencies, in cooperation with international financial institutions, such as IMF, have recently begun to analyze various methods for assessing the riskiness of countries. The U.S. Export-Import Bank has developed a model for measuring country risk. [25] The Federal Reserve Bank of San Francisco has devoted research to the problem of country risk. [26] The U.S. comptroller of the currency has developed elaborate procedures for evaluation of foreign public sector loans to be used in conjunction with the regular examination of national banks' overall international operations. [27] The author was involved in assisting FDIC in developing country risk assessment models during the 1976-78 period. Several large U.S. banks have developed in-house analytical models for evaluating foreign loans. [28] (See Appendix B for coverage of selected country risk assessment models.)

In addition to these activities, other research has been devoted in recent years to compiling data on LDCs' economic status or on the role of private banks in the development process. Euromoney has begun to publish a comprehensive analysis on the state of country credit, covering both developed and developing nations.[29] Citicorp, the bank holding company for Citibank of New York, has furnished a detailed analysis of bank lending to LDCs.[30] Finally, the most detailed statistics, although usually dated by nearly two years, on LDC borrowing are the World Debt Tables and Borrowing in International Capital Markets, both published by the World Bank.

The increasing comprehensiveness of data gathering and model building by U.S. federal bank regulatory agencies and by large U.S. multinational banks is resulting in better regulation and supervision in the area of lending to LDCs. This activity and the vigilance of congressional committees and the press will result in filling the regulatory gaps in an area of banking that could cause a collapse in the safety and soundness of the worldwide financial system.

REGULATION OF CAPITAL ADEQUACY
FOR OVERSEAS OPERATIONS

When overseas operations are considered, capital adequacy is a major problem area. The loan limits imposed on U.S. banks are generally based on the parent's capital. Since overseas branches do not have capital, their loan limits are based on the parent's capital; this gives branches of major banks a competitive edge vis-a-vis local host country banks. It also permits branches to operate at a higher level of loan activity than might be safe. The higher risk inherent in some operations permitted overseas branches (but disallowed the parent) also points toward imposition of some type of capital adequacy regulation on overseas branch operations.

Foreign U.S. branches, for example, are permitted to do ordinary banking business and financially related business. Thus, they are permitted to do some business overseas not permitted domestic banks in the United States but cannot enter into equity situations or underwriting activities allowed banks in the foreign host country. The financial operations permitted foreign branches but not allowed domestic banks may increase the risk of both the overseas operation as well as the parent bank. Without the capital base in the branch operations, more strain is placed on the parent's capital cushion, thus jeopardizing the safety and soundness of the bank as a whole.

In order to alleviate this, Federal Reserve System and national bank examiners from the comptroller's office generally analyze such overseas operations in great detail. The loans connected to these activities will be meticulously watched and the capital level of the parent bank will be taken into consideration in order to ensure that capital is adequate to support such operations. The Franklin National Bank/Sindona connection and lending by that bank in excess of loan limits taught several lessons to federal bank regulators.

EAC REGULATION

EACs are wholly owned subsidiaries of U.S. banks, are located in the United States, and are established to handle only international banking transactions. They are permitted under the Edge Act of 1919 (named after Senator Walter Edge of New Jersey), an amendment to the Federal Reserve Act.[31]

The Edge Act amendment is actually Section 25(A) of the Federal Reserve Act. The Federal Reserve Board has jurisdiction over EACs and regulates them under Regulation K. Charters for EACs are granted by application to the Fed, and each EAC must be capitalized with a minimum $2 million.

As of June 30, 1977, 116 EACs were operating, with total assets of nearly $11 billion. Of these, 58 were organized to carry out international banking operations: taking deposits, making loans, financing foreign trade, trading in foreign exchange, operating in the Eurocurrency markets, as opposed to financial operations, such as making direct investments in foreign financial institutions and nonfinancial companies and underwriting securities flotations. Thus, generally speaking, EACs have been organized as either banking or finance institutions, even though they are permitted by amendments to the Edge Act to perform both type activities in the same EAC.

EACs are restricted in lending to any single borrower no more than 10 percent of the EAC's capital and surplus.[32] They must furnish semiannual reports on operations to the Federal Reserve Board and are examined annually by it.

The primary advantage of EACs is their ability to locate outside their headquarters state, giving them freedom to branch across state lines without state permission, a practice prohibited national banks by the McFadden Act. By June 1977, 62 EACs had been formed outside their parent banks' home states. For example, BankAmerica has located EACs in San Francisco, Chicago, New York, Houston, and Miami.

The ability of EACs to engage in both commercial and investment banking activities and to branch nationwide makes them a significant factor in their parent banks' international operations. They will continue to grow by competing regionally for international business.

CONCLUSIONS

Several other minor areas of regulation and supervision of international operations of U.S. banks can be analyzed. One such area is U.S. banks' participation in joint ventures and international consortia. The latter, however, have not grown in recent years, and large international banks may have become disenchanted with them; thus, their regulation (by the Federal Reserve System) may be an inconsequential factor.

One growing aspect of international financing that is closely regulated by the Federal Reserve System should be mentioned in this section. This is the bankers' acceptance. Its creation is similar to that of demand deposits and, thus, is within the monetary regulation function of the Fed.

A bankers' acceptance is a draft, authorized by a letter of credit, which is accepted by the drawee bank by the stamping of the word accepted across the face of the draft. The bankers' acceptance can then be discounted in the market by the holder. It is a way of facilitating the financing of international trade.[33]

A bank can create a total amount of bankers' acceptances that does not exceed 50 percent of the bank's capital and surplus unless prior Fed approval has been given. In addition, the total amount of bankers' acceptances drawn by a single drawer is limited to 10 percent of the bank's capital and surplus. The use of bankers' acceptances is limited to foreign trade and to domestic shipment of goods and storage of readily marketable commodities, provided a bank obtains a warehouse receipt or other evidence of the transaction.[34]

This chapter has presented a brief survey of the major areas of federal regulation and supervision of U.S. banks' international operations. Several proposals have been advanced for strengthening this regulation. These proposals will be discussed in the concluding chapter.

NOTES

1. See, for example, The Federal Reserve System: Purposes and Functions (Washington, D.C.: The Federal Reserve Board, 1974); and the annual reports of the Federal Reserve Board, U.S. Comptroller of the Currency, and Federal Deposit Insurance Corporation.

2. From a Federal Reserve Board foreign exchange operations survey of 32 member banks in 1974 obtained from the Division of Banking Supervision and Regulation, Federal Reserve Board, Washington, D.C., 1975.

3. Allen Frankel, "International Banking—Structural Aspects of Regulation," Business Conditions (economic review by the Federal Reserve Bank of Chicago), October 1974, pp. 3-4.

4. Ibid., p. 4.

5. Fernand St Germain, "Banks' Foreign Activities Raise Questions of Risk and Diversion of Credit," The Money Manager 5 (May 3, 1976): 10.

6. Ibid.

7. Ibid.

8. Peter S. Rose, "International Banking: Problems and Prospects," The Southern Banker 145 (May 1976): 33.

9. T. E. Hitselberger, "Regional Banks: What Price International?" The Southern Banker 145 (May 1976): 25.

10. Fred B. Ruckdeschel, "Risk in Foreign and Domestic Lending Activities of U.S. Banks," Columbia Journal of World Business 10 (Winter 1975): 50-54.

11. The Federal Reserve System: Purposes and Functions, pp. 104-6.

12. "Required Reading: Growth of International Banking Brings Problems in Regulation," The American Banker 141 (April 29, 1976): 8.

13. Allen B. Frankel, "International Banking: Part I," Business Conditions (economic review by the Federal Reserve Bank of Chicago), September 1975, p. 4.

14. C. Frederic Wiegold, "Brimmer Asks Fed Revamp to Allow US Banks More Activities Overseas," The American Banker 141 (May 3, 1976): 1.

15. FDIC furnished this information from a 1976 Survey of State-Chartered Nonmember Banks with International Operations.

16. A report on this survey was published by the Federal Reserve Board, November 21, 1975, and can be obtained from the Division of Banking Supervision and Regulation, Federal Reserve Board, Washington, D.C. The section cited is from p. 1.

17. See Antoine W. van Agtmael, "How Business Has Dealt with Political Risk," Financial Executive 44 (January 1976): 26-30; "The LDCs Battle the Danger of Default," Business Week, March 1, 1976, pp. 54-55; Charles S. Ganoe, "U.S. Banks International Loans under Scrutiny," Euromoney, March 1976, pp. 13-14; S. M. Yassukovich, "The Growing Political Threat to International Lending," Euromoney, April 1976, pp. 10, 12, 14-15; Antoine W. van Agtmael, "Evaluating the Risks of Lending to Developing Countries," Euromoney, April 1976, pp. 16, 18, 20, 22, 25, 27-28; Richard D. Hill, "Growing Role of Bank Analysis of Less Developed Countries," Finance 94 (June 1976): 2-3.

18. David C. Beek, "Commercial Bank Lending to the Developing Countries," Federal Reserve Bank of New York Quarterly Review, Summer 1977, p. 5.

19. See also the "Supplement on International Lending," IMF Survey 6 (June 6, 1977): 177-88.

20. See also Stephen H. Goodman, "Debt Service Ratios Look Healthy but There May Be a Bumpy Rollover," Euromoney, June 1977, pp. 93-94, 97, 99.

21. "The LDCs Battle the Danger of Default," Business Week, March 1, 1976, pp. 54-55.

22. "A First Look at the Developing Countries' Debt," Monthly Economic Letter (Citibank) (June 1976), pp. 4-15.

23. For sources that are optimistic about the plight of LDCs and international banks lending to them, see Charles N. Stabler, "Bankers and Their Foreign Loans," The Wall Street Journal, January 29, 1976, p. 10; Kevin Pakenham, "The Debts of Less Developed Countries—The Challenge for Commercial Banks," Journal of Commercial Bank Lending 58 (May 1976): 19-28; series of articles on the subject in the June 1976 Monthly Economic Letter published by Citibank; G. A. Costanzo, "Lending to Developing Countries—Why the Gloom Is Overdone," The Banker 126 (June 1976): 581-83; "Worry, but Not Panic, over Bank Loans to the Poor," The Economist 258 (June 26, 1976): 66. Finally, for references that paint a very pessimistic picture, including the possibility of a severe international monetary crisis as a result of defaults by LDCs, see Ann Crittenden, "Loans Abroad Stir Worry," The New York Times, January 15, 1976, pp. 1, 56; Janet Porter, "Zaire Eurocurrency Loan Is Suspended," The Journal of Commerce, January 27, 1976, pp. 1, 8; Emma Rothschild, "Banks: The Coming Crisis," The New York Review of Books 23 (May 27, 1976): 16-22; a U.S. House of Representatives Committee on Banking, Currency and Housing News Release, "Reuss Warns Commercial Banks on Loans to Politics of Debt," The New York Review of Books 23 (June 24, 1976): 25-32; "Reuss Has His Doubts about LDC Borrowing," Business Week, June 28, 1976, pp. 32, 34; "Heavy, Heavy," Forbes, July 1, 1976, p. 76; Gordon Platt, "Banks, Analysts See Ill Wind from Press as Biggest Danger to LDC House of Cards," The Money Manager 5 (July 12, 1976), p. 35.

24. See Charles S. Ganoe, "US Banks' International Loans under Scrutiny," Euromoney, March 1976, pp. 11-13; S. M. Yassukovich, "The Growing Political Threat to International Lending," Euromoney, April 1976, pp. 10, 12, 14-15; "Reuss Has His Doubts about LDC Borrowing," Business Week, June 28, 1976, pp. 32, 34; Josef C. Brada, "Foreign Debt Defaults and International Banking," Bulletin of Business Research (The Ohio State University) 52 (June 1977): 4-6.

25. Stephen Goodman, "How the Big U.S. Banks Really Evaluate Sovereign Risks," Euromoney, February 1977, pp. 105, 107-8, 110.

26. Nicholas Sargen, "Country Risk," Business and Financial Letter, March 18, 1977, pp. 1-3.

27. Robert R. Bench, "How the US Comptroller of the Currency Analyzes Country Risk," Euromoney, August 1977, pp. 47-48, 50-51.

28. See, for example, Bruce Brackenridge, "Country Exposure, Country Limits, and Lending to LDC's," Journal of Commercial Bank Lending 59 (July 1977): 3-13; and Charles F. Mansfield, Jr., "An Ap-

proach to Evaluating Foreign Bank Credit Risk," Journal of Commercial Bank Lending 59 (August 1977): 44-55.

29. "The State of Country Credit," Euromoney, October 1977, pp. 63-111.

30. Irving S. Friedman, The Emerging Role of Private Banks in the Developing World (New York: Citicorp, 1977).

31. See James C. Baker and M. Gerald Bradford, American Banks Abroad: Edge Act Companies and Multinational Banking (New York: Praeger Publishers, 1974); Ronald E. Couvault, "Foreign Branches and Edge Act Corporations," National Banking Review 1 (December 1963): 247-54; Douglas H. Lemmonds, "Edge Corporations: A Microcosm of International Banking Trends," Federal Reserve Bank of Richmond Monthly Review 59 (September 1973): 15-16; John E. Leimone, "Edge Act Corporations: An Added Dimension to Southeastern International Banking," Federal Reserve Bank of Atlanta Monthly Review 59 (September 1974): 130-38; James C. Baker, "Nationwide Branch Banking: The Edge Act Corporation and Other Methods," Issues in Bank Regulation 1 (Summer 1977): 31-36; Donald E. Baer, "Expansion of Miami Edge Act Corporations," Federal Reserve Bank of Atlanta Economic Review 62 (September/October 1977): 112-17.

32. Regulation K, Section 211.9(b), Federal Reserve System.

33. Rita Rodriguez and E. Eugene Carter, International Financial Management (Englewood Cliffs, N.J.: Prentice-Hall, 1976), pp. 168-69.

34. Edward W. Reed et al., Commercial Banking (Englewood Cliffs, N.J.: Prentice-Hall, 1976), p. 380.

3

U.S. REGULATION OF
FOREIGN BANKING

INTRODUCTION

During 1973, a Steering Committee on International Bank Regulation was formed by the Federal Reserve Board, with George W. Mitchell, former vice-chairman of the board, as chairman of the committee. The steering committee's assignment was two-pronged in nature: to assess the operations of foreign banks in the United States and to examine board regulatory policies and supervisory practices concerned with the international activities of U.S. banks.[1] A bill was proposed by the Fed in 1974 and introduced in the House of Representatives as H.R. 5617 (the Foreign Bank Act of 1975), as a beginning toward accomplishing the first of the steering committee's two assignments.

Foreign-owned banks operating in the United States generally function outside the jurisdiction of federal regulation, although the Federal Reserve Board has statutory authority in the regulation of international operations of U.S. banks. Because of the growth of operations by foreign banks in recent years and the hodgepodge of state regulation of foreign banks by those states in which they are located, some banking authorities, including Congressmen, have advocated that they be regulated or supervised at the federal level. Some of these authorities have favored the Federal Reserve Board as the logical agency to fulfill this role.

Furthermore, in recent years, Congress has been concerned about the growth of foreign banking in this country; for a number of reasons, certain Congressmen believe that the issues of monetary policy and the safety and soundness of U.S. banking will be served by legislation that will insure federal supervision and regulation of foreign banks in the United States. For example, some Congressmen believe that because banks can exert much influence over their communities' economic life, the growth of foreign investment in the

United States, and in U.S. banking in particular, is cause for some apprehension. Furthermore, some Congressmen are concerned that the petrodollars being generated by the oil-exporting nations may be used to acquire controlling interests in the U.S. banking sector. A few examples exist where U.S. banks have been acquired by individuals from the oil-producing nations.[2]

Concern has also been expressed by some Congressmen that foreign banks are allowed to operate in areas that are prohibited to domestic banks and that domestic banks are allowed activities prohibited to foreign banks. Whether or not these are significant concerns, they may have prompted some Congressmen to support Federal Reserve Board authorization to regulate foreign banks in the United States.

Finally, Congress has been concerned increasingly with the safety and soundness of the U.S. banking system. Since the bankruptcy of Intra Bank in 1967—Lebanon's largest bank, with extensive worldwide holdings—coupled with the Franklin National and Herstatt bank failures, in which foreign exchange operations represented a large part of the problem, some Congressmen have expressed concern that international banking is in need of tighter supervision and regulation, especially at the federal level. Some of these same Congressmen believe that the large growth of foreign banking in the United States also has resulted in a large amount of volatile international banking assets being outside the jurisdiction of U.S. monetary policy.

The purpose of this chapter is to discuss the current status of regulation and supervision of foreign banking operations in the United States. Some general comments are set forth in the next section, and these are followed by detailed analyses of state and federal regulation of these activities. Various legislative proposals made since 1966 to establish federal regulation of foreign banking in the United States will be analyzed in Chapter 4.

Foreign banking operations in the United States primarily are supervised by the banking authorities of the 12 states in which they have operations.[3] Foreign bank subsidiaries are subject to the U.S. Bank Holding Company Act, whereas foreign branches and agencies are not. If the subsidiaries have deposits insured by FDIC, such operations are subject to FDIC review and supervision.

Foreign bank operations, in addition to what has already been discussed, may be allowed to operate or be prohibited from operating in areas where opposite regulations are imposed on domestic banks. For example, foreign banks may initiate operations in more than one state, if the laws of such states allow this, whereas U.S. banks are prohibited from interstate bank branching by the McFadden Act. On the other hand, some eight or so securities affiliates are owned by foreign banks and allowed full-scale investment banking operations.

Domestic banks are precluded by the Glass-Steagall Act from certain investment banking activities, such as underwriting and brokerage operations.[4] The foreign affiliates were grandfathered under the 1970 amendment to the Bank Holding Company Act, and foreign banks were allowed to retain these firms. Also under present statutory requirements, foreign banks in the United States cannot operate or own EACs. All directors of an EAC must be U.S. citizens, and a majority of the ownership of an EAC must be held by the parent U.S. bank.[5]

Furthermore, foreign banking units in this country are not required to be members of the Federal Reserve System and, thus, are not subject to monetary policy considerations imposed by the Fed, for example, reserve requirements. On the other hand, these institutions cannot borrow from the Fed at the rediscount window.

As this brief overview implies, John Balles's description of the regulation of foreign banks in the United States as a "state patchwork" is quite appropriate.[6] The growth of foreign banking in the United States and the type structure these institutions utilize to operate are determinants of the international banking development strategy formulated by the foreign parent bank and are also among the reasons for the several proposals (in addition to congressional concern) to regulate foreign banking in the United States.

Before discussing in detail the regulation and supervision of foreign bank operations in the United States, a more complete demographic picture than that offered in Chapter 1 should be presented. Although the data presented in this section may not be absolutely up-to-date, the information, nevertheless, depicts the trend in foreign banking operations located in the United States.

Although more than 200 foreign bank institutions reported asset and liability data for year-end 1976, official data are not available at the time of writing. Year-end 1975 data are presented in Table 3.1 for 184 reporting institutions.

Most of the foreign bank operations, regardless of organizational format, are located in New York City, Chicago, or California (primarily in San Francisco or Los Angeles). Foreign bank operations in these locations are presented in Tables 3.2, 3.3, and 3.4. Table 3.2 includes a list of foreign banks by country of representation that are located in California. In Table 3.3, foreign banks operating in New York are listed by country of origin and organizational status. Finally, assets of foreign banks located in Chicago are presented in Table 3.4.

State Regulation of Foreign Banks

It was mentioned previously that almost all regulation and supervision of foreign bank operations in the United States are imple-

TABLE 3.1

Assets and Liabilities of Offices of Foreign Banks in the United States, December 1975
(millions of dollars)

Assets and Liabilities	Agencies	Branches	Commercial Banks	Investment Companies	Total United States	Total Chicago
Assets						
Total assets	27,875	20,285	13,386	2,753	64,300	1,555
Loans and credits	13,040	5,702	6,400	1,253	26,394	732
U.S.	10,390	3,392	3,464	901	18,147	596
Foreign	2,618	2,147	657	326	5,748	127
Miscellaneous U.S. loans, including retail	32	163	2,279	26	2,500	10
Money market assets	3,584	6,258	3,474	557	13,873	518
Interbank assets	2,940	5,677	1,179	317	10,113	484
U.S. banks	2,175	4,153	1,049	161	7,538	387
Foreign banks	764	1,524	131	156	2,575	97
Loans to security dealers	286	145	62	0	492	5
U.S. government and agency securities	359	436	2,233	240	3,268	30
Miscellaneous assets	844	624	1,545	310	3,323	54
Assets from parent and affiliates	10,407	7,702	1,967	633	20,709	251
Clearing balances due from others	1,390	3,673	1,632	464	7,159	115

Due from U.S. banking affiliates	4,445	721	102	22	5,290	33
Due from foreign parent and affiliates	4,571	3,307	234	147	8,260	103

Liabilities and Equity

Total liabilities and equity	27,875	20,285	13,386	2,753	64,300	1,555
Liabilities to nonbanks	2,139	6,765	9,539	765	19,208	485
Deposits of U.S. residents	873	2,929	8,667	189	12,657	347
Deposits of foreigners	1,266	3,837	873	576	6,551	138
Interbank liabilities	9,384	3,153	748	787	14,072	267
U.S. banks	9,282	2,449	468	138	12,336	256
Foreign banks	102	704	280	649	1,736	11
Miscellaneous liabilities	2,796	557	564	326	4,243	49
Liabilities to parent and affiliates	13,259	9,643	1,300	703	24,904	734
Clearing balances due to others	1,515	1,509	721	434	4,179	35
Due to U.S. banking affiliates	3,182	2,136	326	22	5,667	433
Due to foreign parent and affiliates	8,561	5,997	253	247	15,058	266
Capital accounts and reserves	298	167	1,235	173	1,872	21
Number of reporting institutions	82	65	33	4	184	24*

*Includes 22 branches and 2 wholly owned subsidiaries.

Note: Details may not add to totals due to rounding.

Source: Joseph G. Kvasnicka, "International Banking: Part II," Business Conditions (economic review of the Federal Reserve Bank of Chicago) March 1976, p. 9.

TABLE 3.2

Foreign Banks Represented in California
(year-end 1975)

Country of Representation	State–Chartered Subsidiary	Agency	Repre-sentative Office
Australia			
Bank of New South Wales	—	—	SF
Brazil			
Banco do Brasil, SA	—	LA/SF	SF
Banco Real, São Paulo	—	LA	—
Canada			
Bank of British Columbia	—	—	SF
Bank of Montreal	Yes	SF	—
Bank of Nova Scotia	Yes	SF	—
Canadian Imperial Bank of Commerce	Yes	SF	SF/LA
Mercantile Bank of Canada	—	—	LA
Royal Bank of Canada	—	SF	—
Royal Trust Co. (Canada)	—	—	LA
Toronto–Dominion Bank (Canada)	Yes	SF	LA
Europe			
European–American Banking Corporation (United States)	—	LA/SF	—
France			
Banque Nationale de Paris	Yes	SF	LA
Credit Lyonnais (France)	—	LA	—
Germany			
Bayerische Vereinsbank	—	LA	—
Dresdner Bank, AG (Germany)	—	LA	LA
Hong Kong			
Hong Kong and Shanghai Banking Corp.	Yes	SF	—
Shanghai Commercial Bank, Ltd.	—	SF	—
Israel			
Bank Leumi Le–Israel	—	LA	—
Italy			
Banca Commerciale Italiana	—	LA	LA
Banca Nazionale del Lavoro (Italy)	—	—	LA
Banco di Roma	—	SF	—
Japan			
Bank of Tokyo, Ltd.	Yes	LA/SF	—
Dai Ichi Kangyo Bank, Ltd. (Japan)	Yes	LA	—

Note: San Francisco and Los Angeles locations are shown by the notations SF and LA.

TABLE 3.2 (continued)

Country of Representation	State-Chartered Subsidiary	Agency	Representative Office
Daiwa Bank, Ltd. (Japan)	—	LA	—
Fuji Bank, Ltd. (Japan)	—	LA	—
Hokkaido Takushoku Bank, Ltd. (Japan)	—	LA	LA
Industrial Bank of Japan, Ltd.	—	LA	—
Kyowa Bank, Ltd. (Japan)	—	LA	LA
Mitsubishi Bank, Ltd. (Japan)	Yes	LA	—
Mitsui Bank, Ltd. (Japan)	Yes	LA	—
Saitama Bank, Ltd. (Japan)	—	LA	—
Sanwa Bank, Ltd. (Japan)	Yes	SF	—
Sumitomo Bank, Ltd. (Japan)	Yes	SF	—
Taiyo Kobe Bank, Ltd. (Japan)	—	LA	—
Tokai Bank, Ltd. (Japan)	Yes	LA	—
Korea			
Korea Exchange Bank	Yes	LA	—
Mexico			
Banco de Comercio, SA (Mexico)	—	LA	LA
Banco Nacional de Mexico, SA	—	LA	LA
The Netherlands			
Algemene Bank Nederland	—	LA	SF
Philippines			
Philippine National Bank	—	SF	—
Portugal			
Banco Pinto & Soto Major (Portugal)	—	—	SF
Scotland			
Royal Bank of Scotland	—	—	SF
Switzerland			
Swiss Bank Corp.	—	SF	LA
Swiss Credit Bank	—	LA	LA
Union Bank of Switzerland	—	—	SF
United Kingdom			
Barclay's Bank International Ltd. (United Kingdom)	Yes	SF	—
Chartered Bank (United Kingdom)	Yes	SF	—
Lloyds Bank Ltd.	Yes	—	—
National Westminster Bank, Ltd. (United Kingdom)	—	SF	—

Source: Compiled by the author.

TABLE 3.3

Foreign Banks in New York
(year-end 1975)

Country of Origin	Organizational Status
Argentina	
Banco de la Nacion Argentina	Branch
Australia	
Australia and New Zealand Banking Group	Representative office
Bank of New South Wales	Representative office
Commercial Banking Co. of Sydney	Representative office
Commercial Bank of Australia	Representative office
National Bank of Australasia	Representative office
Austria	
Creditanstalt Bankverein (see European–American Banking Corporation)	
Bahamas	
World Banking Corporation	Representative office
Bishops International Bank	Representative office
Deltec Banking Corp.	Representative office
Belgium	
Banque de Bruxelles	Representative office
Credit General	Representative office
Kredietbank, SA	Representative office
Société Générale (see European–American Banking Corporation)	
Brazil	
Banco do Brasil	Branch
Banco do Estado de São Paulo	Agency
Banco Mercantil de São Paulo	Agency
Banco Real	Branch
Bermuda	
Bank of Bermuda	Representative office
Canada	
Bank of Montreal	Agency
Bank of Nova Scotia	Agency
Canadian Imperial Bank of Commerce	Agency
Provincial Bank of Canada	Representative office

TABLE 3.3 (continued)

Country of Origin	Organizational Status
Royal Bank of Canada	Agency
Toronto Dominion	Agency
Columbia	
Banco Comercio Antioqueno	Representative office
Banco de Bogotá	Branch
Denmark	
Den Danske Landmansbank	Representative office
Privatbanken	Representative office
Ecuador	
Banco la Filantropica	Representative office
France	
Banque de l'Union Europeene	Representative office
Banque Francaise du Commerce Exterieur	Representative office
Banque Nationale de Paris (see also French–American Banking Corporation)	Representative office
Compagnie Financiere de Suez	Representative office
Banque Vernes et Commerciale de Paris	Representative office
Banque Wormes et Cie	Representative office
Banque Francaise et Italienne pour l'Amerique du Sud	Representative office
Crédit Commercial de France	Representative office
Crédit Industriel et Commercial	Branch
Crédit Lyonnais	Branch
Société Générale (see European–American Banking Corporation)	
Germany	
Bayerische Vereinsbank	Representative office
Berliner Handels–Gesellschaft–Frankfurter Bank	Representative office
Commerzbank	Branch
Deutsche Bundesbank (see European–American Banking Corporation)	
Dresdner Bank, AG	Branch

(continued)

TABLE 3.3 (continued)

Country of Origin	Organizational Status
Hessische Landesbank	Representative office
West Deutsche Landesbank	Representative office
Hong Kong	
Hong Kong and Shanghai Banking Corp.	Branch
India	
State Bank of India	Branch
Indonesia	
Bank Ekspor Impor Indonesia	Representative office
Bank Negara Indonesia	Representative office
Bank Indonesia	Representative office
Iran	
Bank Melli Iran	Agency
Bank Saderat Iran	Agency
Ireland	
Allied Irish Banks	Representative office
Bank of Ireland	Representative office
Israel	
Bank Hapoalim	Representative office
Bank Leumi Le-Israel	Agency
Israel Discount Bank	Branch
Mercantile Bank of Israel	Representative office
Italy	
Banca Commerciale Italiana	Branch
Banca d'America e d'Italia	Representative office
Banca Nazionale dell'Agricoltura	Representative office
Banca Nazionale del Lavoro	Branch
Banco di Napoli	Agency
Banco di Roma	Branch
Banco di Sicilia	Representative office
Credito Italiano	Branch
Japan	
Bank of Japan	Representative office
Bank of Tokyo	Agency
Chuo Trust & Banking Co.	Representative office
Dai-Ichi Kangyo Bank	Agency

TABLE 3.3 (continued)

Country of Origin	Organizational Status
Daiwa Bank	Agency
Fuji Bank	Agency
Hokkaido Takushoku Bank	Agency
Industrial Bank of Japan	Agency
Japan Development Bank	Representative office
Kyowa Bank	Agency
Mitsubishi Bank	Agency
Mitsubishi Trust and Banking Corp.	Agency
Nippon Fudosan Bank	Representative office
The Saitama Bank	Agency
The Sanwa Bank	Agency
Sumitomo Bank	Agency
Sumitomo Trust and Banking	Representative office
Taiyo Kobe Bank	Agency
Tokai Bank	Agency
Toyo Trust and Banking Co.	Representative office
Yasuda Trust and Banking	Representative office
Korea	
Bank of Korea	Representative office
Korea Exchange Bank	Agency
Mexico	
Banco Commercial Mexicano	Representative office
Banco de Commercio	Representative office
Banco Mexicano	Representative office
Banco Nacional de Mexico	Agency
Norway	
Christiana Bank og Kreditkasse	Representative office
Norges Bank	Representative office
The Netherlands	
Algemene Bank Nederland	Branch
Amsterdamsche–Rotterdamsche Bank (see European–American Banking Corporation)	
Bank Mees and Hope	Representative office
Nederlandische Middenstandsbank	Representative office
Pakistan	
Habib Bank	Branch
National Bank of Pakistan	Branch

(continued)

TABLE 3.3 (continued)

Country of Origin	Organizational Status
Peru	
Banco de Credito del Peru	Representative office
Philippines	
Philippine National Bank	Branch
Poland	
Bank Handlowy	Representative office
Portugal	
Banco Totta and Acores	Representative office
Puerto Rico	
Banco Credito y Ahorro Ponceno	Branch
Banco de Ponce	Branch
Banco Popular de Puerto Rico	Branch
Singapore	
Overseas Union Bank	Agency
South Africa	
Nedbank	Representative office
Spain	
Banco Catalana	Representative office
Banco de Bilbao	Representative office
Banco de Santander	Representative office
Banco de Vizcaya	Representative office
Banco Espanol de Credito	Representative office
Bank Exterior de Espana	Representative office
Banco Urquijo	Plans to open office in November
Sweden	
Svenska Handelsbanken	Representative office
Sveriges Kreditbank	Representative office
Switzerland	
Dow Banking Corp.	Representative office
International Credit Bank Geneva	Representative office
Nordfinanz–Bank	Representative office

TABLE 3.3 (continued)

Country of Origin	Organizational Status
Swiss Bank Corporation	Branch
Swiss Credit Bank	Branch
Swiss-Israel Trade Bank	Representative office
Union Bank of Switzerland	Representative office
Taiwan	
Central Trust of China	Representative office
International Commercial Bank of China	Agency
Thailand	
Bangkok Bank	Agency
United Kingdom	
Barclays Bank International	Two branches
British Bank of the Middle East	Representative office
Chartered Bank	Two branches
Thomas Cook and Sons (Bankers) Ltd.	Agency
London Multinational Bank	Representative office
Lloyds Bank Ltd.	Representative office
Lloyds Bank International Ltd.	Branch
Midland (see European-American Banking Corporation)	
National Westminster Bank Ltd.	Branch
Nordic Bank	Representative office
Rea Bros.	Representative office
Royal Bank of Scotland	Representative office
Standard Bank	Agency
Williams and Glyn's Bank	Representative office
Uruguay	
Foreign Trade Bank	Representative office
Venezuela	
Banco Nacional de Descuento	Representative office
Yugoslavia	
JugoBanka	Representative office
Yugoslav Agricultural Bank	Representative office
Yugoslav Bank for Foreign Trade	Representative office

Source: Compiled by the author.

55

TABLE 3.4

Assets of Foreign Banks in Chicago, 1974 and 1975
(thousands of dollars)

Branches	Total Assets, December 1975	Total Assets, December 1974
Algemene Bank Nederland	92,473	12,059
Banca Commerciale Italiana	221,082	153,340
Bank Leumi Le-Israel	26,793	—
Barclays Bank International Ltd.	13,121	14,248
Banque Nationale de Paris	63,715	33,082
Banque de l'Indochine et de Suez	923	135
The Chartered Bank	2,894	—
Commerzbank	52,952	6,556
Crédit Lyonnais	122,042	14,655
Dresdner Bank	22,887	11,868
European Banking Company, Ltd.	25,157	12,022
Hong Kong and Shanghai Banking Corp.	473	262
International Commercial Bank of China	3,803	—
Korea Exchange Bank	15,017	—
Lloyds Bank International Ltd.	49,614	25,578
National Bank of Greece	29,201	21,769
National Westminster Bank Ltd.	63,616	15,279
The Sanwa Bank Ltd.	177,088	74,494
State Bank of India	2,336	—
The Sumitomo Bank Ltd.	152,565	97,831
Swiss Bank Corporation	158,304	44,761
Union Bank of Bavaria	23,256	—
Subtotal	1,319,312	537,946
Subsidiaries		
Banco di Roma	133,006	82,524
First Pacific Bank	102,751	65,754
Grand total	1,555,069	686,224

Source: Joseph G. Kvasnicka, "International Banking: Part II," Business Conditions (economic review of the Federal Reserve Bank of Chicago), March 1976, p. 11.

mented at the state level. The Federal Deposit Insurance Act does
not define a foreign branch as a bank for insurance purposes and,
thus, FDIC only insures deposits of foreign bank subsidiaries, over
which FDIC then has jurisdiction. The Federal Reserve Board only
regulates foreign bank operations insofar as they fall under the Bank
Holding Company Act and Regulation Y or are subject to Sections 25
or 25(A) of the Federal Reserve Act. A foreign bank may apply for
a national charter from the comptroller of the currency. Only one
has done so because of the requirements that national banks must belong to the Federal Reserve System and that all directors be U.S.
citizens.[7] Some foreign banks or individuals have bought minority
or majority interests in existing U.S. national banks. The most recent, perhaps, is the purchase of the stock owned by Bert Lance,
former director of the Office of Management and Budget, in the National Bank of Georgia by Ghaith R. Pharaon, Saudi Arabian business-
man.[8]

In addition, foreign banks cannot establish EACs, because a
majority of the ownership of an EAC must be held by U.S. citizens.[9]
Thus, the major prohibition facing foreign banks at the federal level
in the United States stems from the domestic ownership clauses of the
National Banking Act and the Edge Act. No provision exists for foreign banks to join the Federal Reserve System or to obtain FDIC insurance.[10] Regulation and supervision of foreign banks operating in
the United States, for the most part, is within the jurisdiction of the
states.

In terms of regulating entry by foreign banks to U.S. operations,
complete authority lies with the states. Eight states have enacted
legislation permitting foreign banks to operate within their boundaries.
These states are Alaska, California, Georgia, Hawaii, Massachusetts,
Oregon, Utah, and Washington.[11] Another source also claims that
Missouri allows foreign banking operations.[12] One foreign bank subsidiary presently operates in Puerto Rico, and three foreign bank
branches are located in the U.S. Virgin Islands.[13] The state of
Georgia recently enacted legislation allowing foreign banks to open
agency offices in that state and to make loans to foreign and domestic
corporations located in Goergia.[14] This is a direct result of the growth
and foreign trade interest in the city of Atlanta.

Other states that have recently approved legislation permitting
foreign bank operations have done so because of the competition in
this area. Oregon, until 1975, had prohibited foreign bank subsidiaries and branches, although the branches of the Canadian Imperial
Bank of Commerce and the Bank of Tokyo had been grandfathered by
the previous legislation. In 1975, Oregon enacted legislation permitting branches of foreign banks to operate in the state. The primary
reason was the influence of Washington, which had passed the Alien

Bank Act in 1973 (permitting foreign branches). European and Japanese banks had located in Seattle, and the competitive effects were felt in Oregon. [15]

Sixteen states explicitly prohibit foreign banking operations regardless of the organizational structure. These include Maine, Maryland, Minnesota, New Jersey, Ohio, Rhode Island, Texas, Virginia, and West Virginia. The remaining states have no legislation concerning foreign banks, and any application from a foreign bank to do business in these states would have to be considered by the state banking commissioner. In the cases of Maryland and North Carolina, only foreign branching is disallowed. Schroder Naess and Thomas Division, investment counselors, have a Baltimore branch. This company is a division of the New York-based holding company subsidiary of Schroders Ltd. of London. Virginia prohibits all types of foreign banking activity. Texas law does not prohibit representative offices of foreign banks, although it does prohibit branches and agencies. Credit Suisse became the ninth foreign bank to open a representative office in Houston in 1977, with eight more planning to open and at least six in the discussion stage. It is estimated that 40 foreign banks may have offices in Houston by year-end 1978. [16] It has been rumored that the Texas legislature might liberalize state laws regarding foreign banking. However, correspondence from Robert E. Stewart, commissioner of banks in Texas, dated March 26, 1976, stated that his office was not familiar with any such proposals.

Most foreign banking operations are located in New York, Illinois, and California, because of the financial markets of San Francisco, Los Angeles, Chicago, and New York. Other than cities such as Houston, Atlanta, Miami, and New Orleans—very few other areas present much interest to foreign banks locating in the United States. Even Utah, which has legislation permitting foreign banking operations, has never had an application from a foreign bank to do business there. [17]

The various organizational forms in which foreign banks operating in the United States take shape were discussed briefly in Chapter 1. In order to demonstrate the extent to which state regulation of foreign banking is implemented, they will be discussed in detail in the following sections. [18]

Representative Offices

The representative office is a mere appendage of the parent foreign bank and conducts no direct banking business. Business, which is solicited for the parent bank, appears on the parent bank's books or those of its affiliates. More than 140 such offices have been opened in the United States. California requires a representative office to obtain a license from the superintendent of banking. The latter authority may also revoke the license of an existing office.[19] Since such offices do not conduct a banking business directly, they are not regulated by most states.

Foreign Bank Branches

A branch is an office of a foreign bank licensed to operate in a particular state. It has neither a corporate charter nor capital. A branch can make loans, take deposits, and perform a full line of banking business (with a few exceptions). It is subject to state reserve requirements that are generally less onerous than Federal Reserve requirements. Since it has no capital, its lending limit is determined by the parent bank's capital.

Branch licensing has created a certain patchwork design of regulation. New York and Illinois license branches to operate. Illinois will permit foreign bank branches but only in the Chicago loop area and only if Illinois banks are permitted to branch in the foreign bank parent's home country; also, only one branch is allowed to a foreign bank parent. Massachusetts also permits branches of foreign banks to conduct full-service banking. Oregon and Washington allow branches with deposit-accepting powers because of grandfather rights.

Whereas New York allows branches to take deposits without FDIC insurance, California does not permit any banks to take deposits without FDIC insurance. Since the Federal Deposit Insurance Act does not recognize foreign bank branches for deposit insurance purposes, only subsidiaries are permitted in California to take deposits. Thus, no foreign bank branches exist in California.

The New York formula for maintenance by a foreign bank branch of assets collectible in the United States has been duplicated in entry regulation practiced by other states. A foreign bank branch must maintain assets in New York equal to 108 percent of all the branch's liabilities, except those owed to other offices of the parent bank.[20] Oregon's regulation is the same, with two exceptions. Oregon's law requires only deposits to be covered, and the approved assets need only equal the covered liabilities.[21] Illinois, Massachusetts, and Washington follow the New York 108 percent rule. In other words, the additional 8 percent serves as the capital of the branch and as a cushion against possible deposit losses. The rule creates a separate entity concept—segregating branch assets from those of the parent.

In New York, the following conditions must be present for a foreign bank branch to obtain a license:[22]

1. New York bank branches or agencies must be permitted to operate in the applicant's home country.
2. The New York superintendent of banking must believe that the foreign bank branch "will be honestly and efficiently conducted and that public convenience and advantage will be promoted."

3. A guarantee fund of cash and/or securities must be deposited in a separate New York bank, such funds to equal 5 percent of liabilities but amount to not less than $100,000.

4. The parent bank must have capital of at least $1 million.

5. The superintendent must grant a license to the branch before the applicant's approval by the State Banking Board.

To aid in supervision and examination of foreign bank branches in New York, such branches must maintain branch books and records, as well as assets and liabilities, which are completely separate from those of the parent bank's books, records, assets, and liabilities, and the parent bank must submit to these requirements as a condition of entry. Thus, New York State banking authorities believe they can completely segregate a foreign bank's branch from its parent bank. California banking, as well as FDIC officials, have held contrary views and uphold the subsidiary as the safest means of foreign bank penetration in the United States, especially when deposits are concerned.[23]

Branches are also subject to several other regulations, differing in their scope from state to state where foreign bank regulations do exist. For example, branches, as mentioned previously, may be subject to state reserve requirements. They may also be subject to interest rate ceilings, usury and lending limits, and other regulations that are imposed on other state banks, all of which are designed to ensure the safety and soundness of branch operations. Lending limits, where imposed, are usually based on the parent bank's capital.[24] As of October 1977, foreign banks had established 98 branches in five states, Puerto Rico, and the U.S. Virgin Islands.[25]

Foreign Bank Agencies

An agency is an office of the parent bank and has no separate corporate charter, as is true of the branch. However, unlike a branch, the agency cannot accept domestic deposits. It raises its funds through nondeposit sources, such as from the parent bank, or from other banks in the interbank market. Normally, an agency cannot exercise fiduciary powers. Generally speaking, there are no state reciprocity requirements for the establishment of agencies, as there are for branches. Thus, agencies are subject to much less state regulation than are branches. They can hold "credit balances," which are funds generated from their legal operations. These credit balances may resemble deposits (prohibited for agencies); state banking authorities may allow these if they are tied directly to international transactions. In New York, agency assets need only equal credit balances, whereas branch assets must be 108 percent of total liabilities.

In New York, state law prohibits a foreign bank from establishing both a branch and an agency. Since branches may not accept domestic deposits without insurance in California, foreign banks have established agencies when they do not desire to establish a separate chartered subsidiary. Canadian banks have used the agency as a means of penetrating the U.S. banking market because of the presence of state reciprocity requirements for establishing branches. Canada does not permit branches of foreign banks. Canadian bank agencies have acquired U.S. funds from several sources, among them being (1) U.S. corporations and banks, (2) Canadian residents who place with chartered banks interest-bearing U.S. dollar deposits on a swap basis free of exchange risk, (3) banks operating in the Eurodollar market, and (4) customers and correspondent banks in the Caribbean and Latin American countries. Japanese bank agencies in New York have also had an outstanding growth record, by acquiring funds in much the same way and performing a host of international financial services.[26] In the State of Washington, branches, for all intents and purposes, are agencies, because they are permitted to accept only very small domestic deposits. As of October 1977, foreign banks had 106 agencies operating in three states.[27]

During 1977, at least ten agencies were converted to branches. Also during this period, four new branches and five agency offices were established, and applications for three branches and four agencies were made. The change from agency to branch status is for the purpose of permitting these units to accept deposits. Agencies obtain funds from the parent or from the interbank market, especially the federal funds market, as mentioned previously. The change to branch status enables them to accept deposits, especially by issuing negotiable certificates of deposit (CDs). These CDs are for $100,000 or more and represent a major source of funding for American banks.[28]

Another reason for conversion of these agencies to branch status has arisen from proposed legislation that would prohibit foreign banks from operating offices in more than one state unless in operation on May 1, 1976. This proposal was part of the International Banking Act of 1977, H.R. 7325, which will be discussed in Chapter 4. The foreign banks that are establishing new branches are disregarding the proposed grandfathering date, believing Congress might change the date to protect any operations in effect at the time of passage of any federal legislation in this area.

Foreign Bank Subsidiaries

The subsidiary represents a domestic bank controlled by a foreign bank with its own board of directors and capital. It may be chartered by either state or federal authorities. Only one foreign bank subsidiary has been chartered at the federal level. Foreign banks have established 35 U.S. bank subsidiaries in three states and Puerto Rico as of October 1977.[29]

The subsidiary has access to FDIC deposit insurance and, thus, is subject to examination and supervision by both state bank authorities and FDIC. The parent bank may be subject to Federal Reserve System regulation under the Bank Holding Company Act. This will be discussed in the next section under federal regulation of foreign banking in the United States. State-chartered subsidiaries are eligible for Federal Reserve membership but usually decline to join the Fed. Although agencies, branches, and subsidiaries of foreign banks do not hold balances with Federal Reserve banks, they may sell balances in member bank correspondent accounts as federal funds. They are subject to state usury laws and lending limits. Such limits are based on the subsidiary's own capital and surplus.

The ability in California for foreign banks to tap the rich retail market because of the prohibition against branches' accepting deposits has been a factor behind the growth of British and Japanese banks. These banks have formed subsidiaries that can accept deposits and obtain FDIC insurance on such deposits.

The Japanese banks, especially in California, have, perhaps, come closest to emulating the full-service style of banking that U.S. domestic banks perform, including both retail and wholesale banking, more flexible market mechanisms, and lower loan-to-deposit ratios.[30] On the other hand, most foreign bank operations in Chicago and New York concentrate on wholesale banking operations and, thus, are not concerned with lack of deposit insurance.

Most foreign banks, however, prefer to establish branches or agencies instead of subsidiaries. The subsidiary requires a more complex organizational structure, with its own U.S. directors and capital as well as cost of incorporation. A branch is more effectively controlled by the parent bank than is the subsidiary. The loan limit of a branch, a function of the parent bank's capital, is usually much higher than for a foreign bank subsidiary, because of the subsidiary's relatively lesser capital base.[31]

New York Investment Companies

The NYIC is a foreign banking subsidiary allowed by Article 12 of the New York State Banking Law. This organization type functions in much the same way as do agencies; it cannot accept deposits but can maintain credit balances, which arise from direct transactions in international trade. NYICs can deal in securities to a certain extent. They are free from state reserve requirements, as well as the 108 percent rule in New York. Unless the parent is a bank holding company, they are not subject to federal regulation.[32]

As of October 1977, only five such subsidiaries were in operation, with total assets of less than $5 billion. These are the European-American Banking Corporation, owned by the European-American "Group"; the French-American Banking Corporation, owned by Banque Nationale de Paris; the J. Henry Schroder Banking Corporation, owned by the Schroder Group in London; the Nordic American Banking Corporation, owned by Svenska Handelsbanken; and the Baer American Banking Corporation, which is self-owned.

Federal Regulation of Foreign Banks in the United States

Bank Holding Company Act

The Bank Holding Company Act of 1956, as amended in 1966 and 1970, gives the Federal Reserve Board, under Regulation Y, jurisdiction over foreign banks operating one or more subsidiaries in the United States. The Federal Reserve Board, under the Bank Holding Company Act, may:

1. Authorize foreign banks to form or become bank holding companies under Section 3(a)(1) of the Bank Holding Company Act;
2. Approve applications for acquisition of bank affiliates in the United States made by foreign bank holding companies under Section 3(a)(3) of the Bank Holding Company Act;
3. Supervise the activities of foreign bank holding companies in the United States, including acquisition of interest in bank and nonbank entities in the United States under Section 4(c)(8) of the Bank Holding Company Act. [33]

The most important example of the foreign bank holding company under the supervision of the Federal Reserve Board concerns the large Japanese banks that have formed affiliates (chartered) in New York and California. Sumitomo Bank of California, Bank of Tokyo of California, and Bank of Tokyo Trust Company, New York, are notable examples. The California-chartered banks conduct a large retail banking business, whereas the New York-chartered foreign bank subsidiaries operate in the wholesale markets, primarily in trust and international activities. [34]

FDIC

As mentioned previously, foreign bank subsidiaries may obtain deposit insurance from FDIC. Branches of foreign banks are not banks as defined by the Federal Deposit Insurance Act[35] and are, therefore, ineligible for FDIC insurance.[36] Those subsidiaries that do have deposit insurance are supervised and examined by the banking authorities of the states where they are chartered and by FDIC. The FDIC examinations are made in the same way as are all FDIC examinations; these subsidiaries are required to submit reports of condition and income to FDIC, just as all other insured banks.

Agreement Corporations

Agreement corporations are subsidiaries permitted state-chartered banks that "agree" to operate as EACs (previously discussed). By agreeing to subject themselves to the Edge Act regulations, they become subject to regulation by the Federal Reserve System. Only two such agreement corporations are operating: European-American Banking Corporation in Chicago, owned by the European-American Banking Group, and Tokyo Bancorp International in Houston, owned by Bank of Tokyo.

The Glass-Steagall Act

The Glass-Steagall Act of 1933, for all intents and purposes, divorced commercial and investment banking operations in the United States. This is unlike almost all other industrialized nations, where a single bank can operate in both of these areas. Thus, this act sets up another parameter of regulation imposed on a foreign banking structure in this country.

Some foreign banks that desire to participate in the investment markets of the United States conduct branch, agency, or subsidiary operations that are separate from the securities affiliates that they own and control. Securities affiliates were discussed in detail in Chapter 1. It is necessary only to add that those securities affiliates which are members of regional securities exchanges, such as SoGen-Swiss, ABD Securities, and EuroPartners, are subject to the jurisdiction of the Securities Act of 1933 and the Securities and Exchange Act of 1934 and are regulated (to some extent) by the Securities and Exchange Commission.

Miscellaneous Federal Presence

Finally, foreign bank operations in the United States do voluntarily furnish data on their operations to the Federal Reserve System. This information is collected and disseminated publicly as part of the "Structure and Selected Financial Data from the FR 886 Foreign Financial File" (compiled monthly) and the "Monthly Report of Condition for U.S. Agencies, Branches and Domestic Banking Subsidiaries of Foreign Banks," published as the G.11 series (Federal Reserve statistical release). These data are collected for balance-of-payments and monetary policy considerations. Foreign banks in the United States have voluntarily complied in the past with domestically imposed balance-of-payments restraints programs. Their officials furnish congressional committees with much valuable statistical material and freely testify in Senate and House committee hearings dealing with foreign banking regulatory proposals.

CONCLUSIONS

A brief survey of state and federal regulation of foreign bank operations in the United States has been presented in this chapter. A number of important areas need to be analyzed that are pertinent to any coverage of the competitive advantages or disadvantages foreign banks operating in the United States may have vis-a-vis domestic banks as a result of the patchwork of state regulation laced with a small degree of federal presence. Such analysis is necessary to develop the optimal federal regulatory legislation proposed by Congress since 1966 but never enacted into law. These various proposals will be the subject of Chapter 4.

Interstate Operations

One area in which foreign banks are able to operate without federal regulation is interstate banking. The McFadden Act of 1927, as amended by the National Banking Act of 1933, restricts U.S. banks from branching across state lines. However, since foreign banks are not subject to the McFadden Act, they have been permitted to establish branch, subsidiary, and/or agency offices in more than one state.

As of April 1977, 94 foreign banks had offices in the United States; of these, 50 had operations in more than one state, with 22 operating in three or more states. If state law does not prohibit such interstate branching, foreign banks are allowed to operate in such a manner. A list of foreign banks having operations in more than one state is presented in Table 3.5.

The fact that foreign banks can operate in more than one state may not necessarily give them a competitive advantage over domestic banks. American banks have opened many representative offices nationwide. These offices cannot do banking business but can refer business to the home office. In addition, U.S. banks can establish EACs.

These institutions can be located in several states, and a number of U.S. banks have EACs in three or more states. BankAmerica has EACs in San Francisco, Chicago, New York, Houston, and Miami.[37] Thus, U.S. banks with both rep offices and EACs (and the possible advent of electronic funds transfer systems, as well as nationwide credit card systems) may have offset any competitive edge foreign banks have in their ability to circumvent the McFadden Act.

Investment Banking Operations

The ability of foreign banks to own securities affiliates that deal in investment banking activities, prohibited domestic banks by the Glass-Steagall Act of 1933, has been identified as a possible competitive advantage accruing to foreign banks operating in the United States. However, as pointed out in Chapter 1, the small number of such securities affiliates and their combined very small capitalization relative to the U.S. investment company industry would seem to support the argument that these operations do not constitute any competitive threat against the U.S. securities industry.

On the other hand, it can be argued that the role fulfilled by foreign bank securities affiliates in making markets for securities on regional securities exchanges, their underwriting activities, acting as specialists on some regional markets, and other market activities renders a very vital benefit to the U.S. securities markets and gives regional securities exchanges a competitive wedge vis-a-vis the major New York securities exchanges.

Federal Reserve Membership

Foreign bank branches and agencies are not eligible for Federal Reserve System membership. This is a disadvantage to them because they are unable to borrow from the Federal Reserve rediscount window and cannot take advantage of the clearing mechanism that the Federal Reserve System maintains. On the other hand, foreign offices in the United States are not required to maintain reserves with the Federal Reserve banks. This gives them a competitive advantage vis-a-vis domestic banks, although the latter do have the option of remaining nonmembers if they are state chartered. Also, foreign bank branches in most states where they operate must maintain a reserve account or set aside assets that either cover or more than cover deposits or total liabilities.

Other regulations or supervision that foreign banks operating in the United States are not subject to include the request by federal

TABLE 3.5

Foreign Bank Networks in the United States,[a] 1975

Bank	Origin	New York	Los Angeles	San Francisco	Chicago	Other Centers
Algemene Bank Nederland	The Netherlands	B	—	—	B	—
American Bank and Trust	Switzerland	S	—	—	—	—
Atlantic Bank of New York	Greece	S	—	—	B	—
Banca Commerciale Italiana	Italy	B	—	—	B	—
Banca Nazionale del Lavoro	Italy	B	—	—	—	—
Banco de la Nacion Argentina	Argentina	B	—	—	—	—
Banco de Bogotá	Colombia	B	—	—	—	—
Banco di Napoli	Italy	A	—	—	—	—
Banco di Roma	Italy	B	—	A	S	—
Banco do Brasil	Brazil	A	B	—	A	—
Banco do Estado de São Paulo	Brazil	A	—	—	—	—
Banco Mercantil de São Paulo	Brazil	A	—	—	—	—
Banco Nacional de Mexico	Mexico	A	—	—	—	—
Banco Real	Brazil	B	—	—	—	—
Bangkok Bank	Thailand	A	—	—	—	—
Bank Leumi Le-Israel	Israel	A, S	—	—	B	—
Bank Melli Iran	Iran	A	—	—	—	—
Bank of British Columbia	Canada	—	—	A	—	—
Bank of Montreal	Canada	A, S	—	A, S	—	—
Bank of Nova Scotia	Canada	A, S	—	A	—	U.S. Virgin Islands, B
Bank of Tokyo	Japan	A, S	A	A, S	—	Seattle, A
Bank Saderat Iran	Iran	A	—	—	—	Portland, B

(continued)

TABLE 3.5 (continued)

Bank	Origin	New York	Los Angeles	San Francisco	Chicago	Other Centers
Banque de l'Indochine	France	—	—	—	B	—
Banque Nationale de Paris	France	S	—	A, S	B	—
Barclays Bank International	United Kingdom	B, S	—	A, S	B	Boston, B; U.S. Virgin Islands, B
Canadian Imperial Bank of Commerce	Canada	A, S	—	A, S	—	Portland, B; Seattle, A
Commerzbank	Germany	B	—	—	B	—
Thomas Cook and Sons (Bankers) Ltd.	United Kingdom	A	—	—	—	—
Credit Industriel et Commercial	France	B	—	—	—	—
Crédit Lyonnais	France	B	—	—	B	—
Credito Italiano	Italy	B	—	—	—	—
Dai-Ichi Kangyo Bank	Japan	A	A	—	S	—
Daiwa Bank	Japan	A	A	—	—	—
Dresdner Bank	Germany	B	—	—	B	—
European American-Banking Corporation[b]		S	A	—	B	—
Fuji Bank	Japan	A	A	—	—	—
Habib Bank	Pakistan	B	—	—	—	—
Hokkaido Takushoku Bank	Japan	A	—	—	—	—
Hong Kong and Shanghai Banking Corp.	Hong Kong	B	—	A, S	B	—
Industrial Bank of Japan	Japan	A	A	—	—	—
International Commercial Bank of China	Taiwan	A	—	—	—	—
Israel Discount Bank	Israel	B, S	—	—	—	—
Korea Exchange Bank	Korea	A	A	—	—	—
Kyowa Bank	Japan	A	—	—	—	—
Lloyds Bank	United Kingdom	B	S	—	B	—
Mitsubishi Bank	Japan	A	A, S	—	—	—
Mitsubishi Trust and Banking Corp.	Japan	A	—	—	—	—

Bank	Country					Other
Mitsui	Japan	A		A		
Mitsui Trust and Bank	Japan	A				
National Bank of Pakistan	Pakistan	B				
National Westminster	United Kingdom	B		A		
Overseas Union Bank	Singapore	A				
Philippine National Bank	Philippines	B		A		
Royal Bank of Canada	Canada	A, S	A	A		Honolulu, A; Puerto Rico, B; U.S. Virgin Islands, B
Royal Trust Co.	Canada					
Saitama Bank	Japan	A				
Sanwa Bank	Japan	A			A, S	Miami, S
Schroders	United Kingdom	S			A, S	B
Shanghai Commercial Bank	Hong Kong					
Standard & Chartered	United Kingdom	A, B			A, S	B
State Bank of India	India	B				
Sumitomo Bank	Japan	A			A, S	B
Swiss Credit Bank	Switzerland	B	A		A, S	B
Swiss Bank Corp.	Switzerland	B	A		A	
Taiyo Kobe Bank	Japan	A	A		A	
Tokai Bank	Japan	A	A		A	
Toronto Dominion	Canada	A, S	A		A, S	Seattle, A
Trade Development Bank	Switzerland	S			A, S	B

[a]Foreign banks that have representation in two or more U.S. states.

[b]European-American Banking Corporation is owned by Deutsche Bank, Midland Bank, Societe Generale de Banque, Societe Generale, and Creditanstalt Bankverein.

Note: A = agency; B = branch; S = subsidiary.

Sources: Federal Reserve; New York State Banking Department; Illinois Office commissioner of banks, all received in 1976–77 as private correspondence.

regulatory agencies for some domestic banks to increase their capital for safety and soundness purposes. Again, states may not be as strict in this area as are federal bank examiners.

FDIC Insurance

Finally, foreign banks operating in the United States can only obtain FDIC deposit insurance if they establish a subsidiary. Branches in some states, such as California, cannot accept deposits without insurance. The cost of establishing a subsidiary may be a hindrance to foreign banks desiring to participate in U.S. retail banking markets.

Those foreign banks wishing to participate in the retail market have estimated that the cost of establishing subsidiaries is outweighed by the profitability of this market. Other foreign banks maintain branches in Chicago and New York that participate primarily in the wholesale markets or accept uninsured deposits from depositors unconcerned with deposit insurance.

Thus, it is difficult to find much support among foreign bankers or large U.S. bankers for a position that foreign banks have much competitive advantage vis-a-vis U.S. banks. The testimony by representatives of such groups as the Institute of Foreign Bankers, the New York Clearing House Association, the Bankers Association for Foreign Trade, or even the American Bankers Association has all seemingly demonstrated that foreign banks have little or not net competitive advantage in operations over domestic U.S. banking counterparts.

NOTES

1. George W. Mitchell, "Multinational Banking in the United States: Some Regulatory Issues" (Address to the Annual Meeting of the Bankers' Association for Foreign Trade, Coronado, California, April 8-11, 1974), p. 1.

2. "Required Reading: Foreign Units Hold 6% of Assets of All U.S. Commercial Banks," The American Banker 140 (November 19, 1975): 4, 20.

3. In "Compilation of Foreign Bank Activities in the United States," The American Banker 140 (July 31, 1975): 186-88, it was shown that foreign banks had some type of office in 14 states, the District of Columbia, and the U.S. Virgin Islands. However, operations in Colorado and Maryland were branches of an investment company and are not considered banks in the American sense of the word.

4. James C. Baker and Jacobus T. Severeins, "Federal Regulation of Foreign Banking in the United States: Implications for For-

eign Securities Affiliates" (Paper presented to the Annual Meeting of the Southern Finance Association, Atlanta, Georgia, November 1977).

5. James C. Baker, "Nationwide Branch Banking: The Edge Act Corporations and Other Methods," Issues in Bank Regulation 1 (Summer 1977): 31–36.

6. John J. Balles, "Required Reading: Federal Rule over Foreign Banks Would End State Patchwork" (Speech at School for International Banking, Boulder, Colorado, 1975), in The American Banker 140 (August 13, 1975): 4, 11.

7. "Required Reading: Foreign Units Hold 6% of Assets of All U.S. Commercial Banks," p. 20.

8. "Lance Reported Close to Selling Shares in Bank," The Wall Street Journal, December 21, 1977, p. 2.

9. J. T. Severeins, "More Controls over Foreign Branching Here?" Burroughs Clearing House 59 (December 1974): 48.

10. Charles S. Ganoe, "Foreign Banks: Reciprocity and Equality," The Bankers Magazine (United States) 157 (Spring 1974): 30.

11. Bruce J. Summers, "Foreign Banking in the United States: Movement toward Federal Regulation," Economic Review (Federal Reserve Bank of Richmond) 62 (January/February 1976): 4.

12. John H. Perkins, "The Regulation of Foreign Banking in the United States," Columbia Journal of World Business 10 (Winter 1975): 118.

13. Federal Reserve System FR886 data, as of October 1977.

14. "Ga. Enacts Law Granting Agency Offices, Lending Power to Foreign Banks," The American Banker 141 (March 22, 1976): 1.

15. Nancy Carpenter, "Oregon Opens the Door to Foreign Banks," The Banker 125 (September 1975): 1083, 1085.

16. "Why Foreign Banks Like Houston So Much," Business Week, December 5, 1977, p. 39.

17. Correspondence from C. B. Quinn, chief examiner, Utah Department of Financial Institutions, dated April 2, 1976.

18. For an excellent glossary of banking organizations (with the exception of NYICs and foreign bank securities affiliates), see Robert Johnston, "Proposals for Federal Control of Foreign Banks," Economic Review (Federal Reserve Bank of San Francisco), Spring 1976, p. 39.

19. Gary M. Welsh, "The Case for Federal Regulation of Foreign Bank Operations in the United States," Columbia Journal of World Business 10 (Winter 1975): 99.

20. Jack Zwick, "The Regulation of Foreign Banks in the United States," National Banking Review 4 (September 1966): 8.

21. Carpenter, "Oregon Opens the Door to Foreign Banks,", p. 1085.

22. Zwick, "The Regulation of Foreign Banks," p. 3.

23. Ibid., p. 16.

24. Welsh, "The Case for Federal Regulation," p. 100.

25. Federal Reserve System data.

26. See Fred H. Klopstock, "Foreign Banks in the United States: Scope and Growth of Operations," New York Federal Reserve Bank Monthly Review 55 (June 1973): 140-54.

27. Ibid.

28. Edward Foldessy, "Foreign Banks Jockey to Tap U.S. Money Market," The Wall Street Journal, August 1, 1977, p. 6.

29. Federal Reserve System data.

30. Paul Gleason, "Japanese Banks Edge Closer to U.S. Style," Banking 68 (July 1976): 86.

31. Zwick, "The Regulation of Foreign Banks, pp. 3-4.

32. Welsh, "The Case for Federal Regulation," pp. 100-1.

33. Francis A. Lees, "Foreign Investment in U.S. Banks," Mergers & Acquisitions 8 (Fall 1973): 6.

34. Ibid., p. 7.

35. See 12 U.S.C. §1812.

36. Ibid., §§ 1814 and 1815.

37. James C. Baker, "Nationwide Branch Banking: The Edge Act Corporations and Other Methods," Issues in Bank Regulation 1 (Summer 1977): 31-36.

4

PROPOSED U.S. REGULATION OF
FOREIGN BANKING

INTRODUCTION

In Chapter 1, the growth of foreign banking in the United States was discussed. The current regulatory and supervisory framework governing foreign banking in the United States was discussed in Chapter 3. Again, to place U.S. foreign bank operations in their proper perspective, the growth of such operations from 1973 to 1977 demonstrates vividly the rapid influx of foreign banks into the domestic U.S. market.

At year-end 1973, about 60 foreign banking organizations had total assets located in the United States that amounted to $38 billion, a fivefold increase from 1965 to 1973. As of June 30, 1975, a total of 79 foreign banks were represented in the United States by 32 subsidiaries or affiliates, 50 branches, 81 agency offices, and at least 141 representative offices. These operations had total assets of $57.3 billion.[1] By June 30, 1977, some 94 foreign banks had 222 subsidiaries, branches, affiliates, and agency offices in the United States and more than 100 representative offices. These operations had total assets of $77.1 billion.[2] Thus, total foreign banking assets doubled from year-end 1973 to mid-1977 after quintupling in size from 1965 through 1973.

In addition to the sizable growth of foreign banking in the United States from 1965 to 1977, the regulation and supervision of foreign banks in the United States has been primarily under the jurisdiction of the states in which these operations are located, principally New York, Illinois, and California, with some minor oversight by the Federal Reserve Board and FDIC, as discussed in depth in Chapter 3. This patchwork of state regulation[3] has caused much concern among U.S. federal bank regulators, congressional leaders, the press, and the U.S. public at large.

This public concern has resulted in various legislative proposals made since 1966, as well as others made by segments of the banking

community in the United States. These proposals will be analyzed in
this chapter.

PROPOSED LEGISLATION TO REGULATE
FOREIGN BANKING IN THE UNITED STATES

During the past decade or more, several proposals have been
advanced in the U.S. Congress for legislation to establish a federal
presence in the regulation and supervision of foreign banking operations
in the United States. Many amendments to these proposals have been
introduced as legislative proposals. The major bills will be discussed
and analyzed in this section. In the following section, several other
proposals supported by banking groups, academicians, regulators,
and other students of banking will be discussed.

Early Proposals

The earliest of the serious proposals to place supervision and
examination of foreign banking offices in the United States under federal control was a bill introduced by Senator Jacob Javits of New
York—the Foreign Banking Control Bill.[4] This bill raised questions
about the dual banking system of federal-state regulation of foreign
banking operations and more clearly defined the scope of permissible
activities by foreign banks in the United States.[5] The primary issue
underlying this legislative proposal was the influx of foreign banks into
the United States in general and into New York specifically. The
Javits proposal was never reported out of committee.

The next wave of legislative activity in the area of foreign bank
regulation arose in 1973. The late Congressman Wright Patman,
then chairman of the House Committee on Banking and Currency, introduced H.R. 11440, the Foreign Bank Control Act, and Congressman Thomas M. Rees of California, a member of that same committee, introduced H.R. 11597, the Foreign Bank Regulation Act.[6] The
latter bill was similar to the Patman bill, with three exceptions.
Neither bill was enacted into law.

The Patman bill would have required a foreign bank operating
in the United States to obtain either a state or a federal charter. The
state-chartered subsidiary could, under this bill, engage in any domestic or international banking activities permissible for a Federal
Reserve member bank organized under the laws of the chartering
state. A federally chartered foreign bank subsidiary would have been
limited in its operations in the United States and abroad to such activities as the Federal Reserve determined to be incidental to its international banking business.

Under this bill, a foreign bank could have had only one state-chartered subsidiary, no more than five federally chartered subsidiaries, and would have been precluded from establishing a branch or agency. Such subsidiaries would have been required to keep the same reserves required by Federal Reserve member banks but could not have been members of the Federal Reserve System. No mergers by such subsidiaries would have been allowed, and no domestic citizen could have owned stock in any subsidiary chartered under that bill.

The Rees bill would have allowed a minority ownership of a foreign bank subsidiary by a U.S. citizen, bank, or company under certain limited conditions. [7] That bill also implied that a state-chartered foreign bank subsidiary could have established one or more branches, which could have been located in a state outside the state in which the subsidiary was located provided it was authorized to do so by the state in which the branch or branches were located. Finally, this bill would have amended Section 25 of the Federal Reserve Act by adding an undesignated subsection authorizing the Federal Reserve Board to limit the aggregate amount of any or all classes of liabilities or assets held by any foreign bank branch established under this legislation at any one time and to prescribe any reserve ratio against all classes of liabilities held by any such foreign branches whenever necessary for the conduct of monetary policy.

Recent Proposals 1975-77

The Foreign Bank Act of 1975

In 1973, a Steering Committee on International Banking Regulation was formed by the Federal Reserve Board; it was composed of four members of the Federal Reserve Board and three presidents of Federal Reserve banks. This committee was chaired by George W. Mitchell, then vice-chairman of the Federal Reserve Board. Its primary purpose was to study the need for legislation controlling overseas activities of U.S. banks and domestic U.S. activities of foreign-based banks. [8] A primary result of this committee's work was the Foreign Bank Act of 1975, actually introduced as a proposal in December 1974 and submitted to the 94th Congress, 1st Session, as H.R. 5617 and S.958. The objectives of the steering committee in designing such legislation were as follows:

1. to achieve equality of treatment between foreign and domestic banks
2. to provide an alternative to state chartering and licensing that would be comparable to that available to domestic banks

3. to provide for reserve requirements and other aspects of monetary policy

4. to provide supervision of operations in certain areas, including FDIC insurance

5. to assure a consistent national policy toward foreign banks that would facilitate internationalization of banking, including the question of entry of foi 'ign banks, and open discussions of relevant issues among international banking authorities. [9]

The major doctrine supported by the Fed in this proposed legislation was nondiscrimination against foreign banks in the United States. This would be implemented by utilizing the national treatment or host powers doctrine. Such doctrine allows foreign bank affiliates to perform in the same manner and under the same regulatory requirements as are imposed on domestic banks. [10] The principal provisions of the Foreign Bank Act of 1975, known as "the Fed's bill," were as follows:

1. The Bank Holding Company Act would be amended to redefine "bank" to include branches and agencies of foreign banks, whether chartered under federal or state law or that of the District of Columbia, at which a full line of banking services would be performed.

2. Foreign bank operations in the United States would, therefore, be subject to the Bank Holding Company Act. *

3. All U.S. branches and agencies of foreign banks with total worldwide assets of more than $500 million would be required to become members of the Federal Reserve System and would, therefore, have to maintain reserve requirements and conform to other provisions of the Federal Reserve Act.

4. Foreign banks would be allowed to own a majority of an Edge Act subsidiary and be permitted to have a board of directors consisting of one-third foreign members. [†]

5. U.S. subsidiaries of foreign banks that merged or consolidated with or acquired assets in banks in the United States would be

---

*NYICs, organized under Article 12 of the New York banking law, and joint venture or consortium-type foreign banks were not covered by this amendment.

†Foreign banks could then form and operate EACs, allowed by Section 25(A) of the Federal Reserve Act, to perform international banking and investment activities. These organizations could be established outside the home state of the parent bank and would have to have approval of the Federal Reserve Board, the U.S. secretary of treasury, and U.S. secretary of state.

required to obtain a federal license from the U.S. secretary of the treasury for such operations.

6. The redefinition of the term bank as it relates to foreign banks operating in the United States would enable the extension of FDIC insurance to deposits of all foreign branches and agencies as a requirement. [11]

7. Nonbanking interests would be grandfathered by prohibiting de novo securities affiliates of foreign banks if such affiliates were conducting a securities business in the United States while permitting the retention of such nonbanking interests by foreign banks if acquired before December 4, 1974. *

First, however, a brief overview of the other major provisions of the act will be discussed. This bill was an attempt to end the supposed competitive inequality of U.S. banks, which are subject to the Glass-Steagall Act, by prohibiting de novo formation of securities affiliates in the United States by foreign banks. Securities affiliates owned by foreign banks as of December 4, 1974, would be grandfathered. The rationale for allowing retention of these affiliates stemmed from two bases: divestment of such affiliates in the securities market of the 1970s, even if accomplished over a ten-year period, might be quite costly; also, as with other banking legislation, such as the Bank Holding Company Act, the American tradition had been to grandfather existing institutional arrangements that had been prohibited by legislation.

It is unclear (especially from the analysis in Chapter 1) that foreign bank securities affiliates have posed a threat to domestic securities firms or placed U.S. banks at any significant advantage. In addition, U.S. banks do engage in extensive investment activities at home through trust departments, investment advisory services, and automatic investment plans, whereas the foreign bank securities affiliates concentrate on investment activities primarily for customers in their home countries. [12]

It was also felt by some in the banking community that grandfathering these operations would reduce the threat of retaliation by foreign governments. In fact, the grandfather clause, while not included in other foreign bank regulation proposals, has been labeled as a very liberal provision and one that should be practiced by other

---

*U.S. banks are prohibited from securities underwriting of certain types, as well as brokerage and other general securities investment activities, by the Glass-Steagall Act of 1933. U.S. banks cannot deal in other than so-called exempt securities for their own account.

governments.[13] The remarks of Sir John Prideaux, chairman of National Westminster Bank, welcoming the decision to permit foreign banks to continue all existing operations, seem to be typical of the foreign responses to the proposed Foreign Bank Act of 1975.[14]

The liberalization of the Edge Act (to permit foreign banks to control and operate EACs) would also equalize one area of competitive inequality of which foreign banks have complained. EACs have been established by the parent bank in more than one state in several instances. BankAmerica, it has been mentioned, has EACs in San Francisco, Chicago, New York, Miami, and Houston. EACs carry on only international banking activities, but this provision allows foreign banks similar flexibility to that allowed American banks in the organization structure they wish to develop. It remains to be seen to what extent foreign banks will use the EAC operation. Many foreign branches, agencies, and subsidiaries already have large international financing operations and have developed the expertise that goes with such experience. Only in the last few years have two foreign banks, European-American Banking Corporation and Bank of Tokyo established Agreement corporations, state-chartered subsidiaries formed in the United States, whose parents "agree" to operate as EACs, subject to Federal Reserve System regulation and supervision.

The Foreign Bank Act of 1975 was an attempt to reduce competitive inequality of operations alleged to exist by both domestic and foreign banks doing business in the United States. Furthermore, it was an attempt to bring foreign banking operations under some form of federal control (for monetary policy as well as supervisory reasons). Three major provisions of the proposal will be analyzed for their implications: subjecting foreign banks to the Bank Holding Company Act, requiring U.S. foreign branches whose parents have more than $500 million total assets worldwide to be Fed members, and mandatory extension of FDIC insurance to deposits of foreign banks in the United States

Foreign Banks and the Bank Holding Company Act

By making foreign banking operations subject to the Bank Holding Company Act, along with federal chartering, at least one advantage accrues to such banks. Foreign banks could initially enter the United States in a state that might prohibit foreign banking in its statutes. Although it has been argued that such federal regulation may be unwarranted for foreign subsidiaries, securities affiliates, and branches, such foreign operations, including agencies, would have the "rights and responsibilities" of national banks.

The argument has also been raised that a great deal of cooperation has already taken place between foreign banks operating here and

federal banking regulatory agencies. This certainly seems to be true
of those operating in New York State.[15] Although the Bank Holding
Company Act has not dictated such, the New York Banking Department
has obtained the approval of the U.S. Treasury Department and the
Federal Reserve Board before chartering or licensing a foreign banking unit. Several foreign outlets are already supervised under the
Bank Holding Company Act, as discussed previously. Foreign
branches and subsidiaries have been subject to state reserve requirements that parallel those of the Fed, and foreign banks have complied
with voluntary restrictions concerning credit expansion or U.S.
balance-of-payments problems and have furnished a great deal of information on their foreign banking activities to federal and state authorities.

However, the head of BankAmerica has also argued that foreign
banks should not be restricted to one state, as federal regulation, especially the McFadden Act, would impose. He believes that U.S.
banks should be permitted to branch on an interstate basis, that is,
foreign banks should not be restricted, as are U.S. banks, but restrictions should be lifted on U.S. banking in general.[16] Thus, by
placing foreign banks under the constraints imposed by the Bank Holding Company Act, those with large operations would be subject to the
same controls as most large American banks operating domestically.
At present, they are regulated by a hodgepodge of state authorities.
Although foreign banks would be exposed to possibly higher costs of
operations, that is, reserve requirements, prevented from further
development of their interstate branching operations, and prohibited
from establishment of de novo securities affiliates, they would inherit
a number of advantages. They could obtain federal charters to operate in states that now prohibit foreign banks' entry. They would be
permitted to establish EACs or similar subsidiaries to conduct international banking in the same way and on the same terms as do domestic banks. They would be allowed to operate nonbanking subsidiaries
throughout the United States in the same way as do domestic bank holding companies.

In most cases, the operations of foreign banks in the United
States would remain undisturbed; it seems unlikely that making them
subject to the Bank Holding Company Act would curtail their operations as much as this would permit their expansion. In addition, the
grandfather clause leaves present organizational structures undisturbed.

Federal Reserve Membership

The Foreign Bank Act of 1975 required Federal Reserve membership of all foreign banking units in the United States whose parent

banks had total worldwide assets of more than $500 million. The
Fed argued that this would equalize treatment between domestic banks
and foreign entities, because nearly all of the former with assets of
more than $500 million are members of the Fed. However, no statu-
tory requirement exists that makes Fed membership mandatory for
domestic banks. From this standpoint, the proposed provision is
discriminatory and seems to violate the announced rationale of the
bill, that is, equality of treatment for foreign banks.

Costs of operations would be increased because of the Fed's
reserve requirements, and the foreign banking unit would have to conform to other provisions of the Federal Reserve Act with respect to
its operations in the United States. Although Fed membership would
provide access to discount and lending facilities of the Federal Reserve System, such a requirement would go beyond the statutory requirements imposed on domestic banks.

The argument posed by the Fed that foreign banks in the United
States must come under reserve requirements because of monetary
policy implications needs further study. Total deposits of these banks
at year-end 1975 was $19.2 billion. Some of the $14 billion of interbank liabilities incurred by year-end 1975 by these banks may also
come within the reserve requirement area. However, the magnitude
of these combined seems quite small when compared with the deposits
of all U.S. state nonmember banks against which reserve requirements are not imposed. A further argument is that it is not the magnitude of these figures that is the important factor but the velocity.
Observations of foreign bank operations in the United States have shown
wide swings between the United States and abroad in deposit items
over a short period of time. Another disadvantage of Fed membership
is the limitation this would impose on loan limits. Foreign bank loan
limits for branches and agencies are dictated by parent bank capital
and not necessarily by domestic requirements. This "benefit" would
cease if, as Fed members, foreign branches and agencies were com-
pelled to observe the individual borrower loan-to-capital ratios cus-
tomarily imposed on domestic member banks and based upon the capital of branch or agency only.

However, a large and growing segment of U.S. banking would
be placed under a single bank regulator rather than the hodgepodge
now in existence. American banks operating overseas, it has been
argued, are subject to control by the central bank of the country in
which they operate. The dual banking system as practiced in the
United States is not found elsewhere.

Another argument concerns the separability of the assets of a
foreign branch, agency, or subsidiary in the United States from its
parent bank located overseas. While technically, the capital of a
subsidiary can be legally separated from that of its parent bank for

reserve and capital adequacy purposes, arguably, this cannot easily be accomplished in the case of a foreign branch or agency. First, it is unclear that such separation would in fact be easier in the case of a subsidiary than in the case of a branch or agency. Second, the state of New York has apparently experienced little difficulty in separating branches or agencies from parents. By law, New York requires a foreign banking corporation with an agency or branch located in the state to maintain assets in New York State totaling not less than 108 percent of its liabilities incurred and outstanding in New York and to deposit with a New York banking institution specified types of high-grade obligations in an aggregate amount of not less than $100,000.[17] Thus, this problem of maintaining a separation between the parent foreign bank and its branch or agency located in the United States does not appear to be as serious as the argument suggests.

FDIC Insurance of Foreign Banks in the United States

One argument asserts that there is no demonstrated need to require FDIC insurance for foreign bank operations in the United States. Thus, it has been argued that many foreign banks operating in the United States limit their activities to very specialized areas, such as providing multinational firms with easily accessible bank functions through a branch of the same bank as that of the parent company. These banks are interested only in those segments of the market dealing in international trade, that is, wholesale or large customer banking. For these reasons, they are not particularly interested in attracting domestic depositors.

However, as proposed, the Foreign Bank Act of 1975 would require all subsidiaries, branches, and agencies of foreign banks to carry FDIC insurance. This would assure that depositors in virtually all banking institutions in the United States would be covered by insurance with the same coverage as now allowed by the Federal Deposit Insurance Act: $40,000 maximum coverage of individual personal accounts and $100,000 maximum coverage for government accounts. Such a requirement would allow many foreign branches to accept domestic deposits that they otherwise would not be authorized to accept without FDIC insurance. This newly found authority might, it was argued, generate more interest in retail banking on the part of foreign branches and agencies, where previously very little interest may have existed, and, accordingly, increase competition in these areas.

Disadvantages of being insured by FDIC would accrue to foreign banking units. FDIC insurance premiums would be assessed, and this would increase their cost of operations. Foreign branches might also be subject to closer scrutiny in areas of supervision, examination, and capital adequacy, although as Fed members, primary responsibility on the federal level for their examination would rest with the Fed. So it would remain to be seen whether FDIC would add to the process of supervision. With respect to retail banking, one authority has stated that in New York, foreign bank branches have at least $125 million of uninsured deposits of $20,000 or less. This represents less than 0.5 percent of foreign bank assets in New York, but New York banking regulators have lobbied for federal legislation that would extend FDIC insurance to these deposits.[18]

The drafters of the Foreign Bank Act of 1975 recognized that possible technical problems might arise if FDIC insurance would be extended to deposits of foreign branches and agencies. Foreign subsidiaries are already required by the Bank Holding Company Act to carry FDIC insurance. Since foreign branches and agencies are not incorporated within the United States, the bill would allow FDIC 90 days from its enactment to submit proposals concerning the implementation and extension of insurance coverage to deposits of foreign branches and agencies.

Perhaps the most serious implication, other than those inferred previously, to the extension of FDIC insurance coverage to domestic deposits of foreign branches and agencies concerns the risk to the FDIC Fund. Little, if any, study of this question has been made. Foreign banks own more than $77 billion of assets in this country. The separability of branch and agency operations and assets from those of the parent may present a problem. Assurance is unclear that the parent bank will not immediately pull these funds back to the parent in crisis situations. Foreign banks in the United States hold about $19 billion in deposits, of which about two-thirds is owned by U.S. residents. The amount of these deposits that would be subject to the $40,000 insurance limit needs to be known. Although the FDIC Fund amounts to about $7 billion (with $3 billion standby drawing authority from the U.S. Treasury Department), this has to cover the insured deposits of the entire U.S. banking system. With failures such as Franklin National Bank, U.S. National Bank of San Diego, and Hamilton National Bank in the last few years, further risk to the FDIC Fund must be well thought out. These and related questions should be the subject of careful study before deciding whether or not the extension of FDIC insurance to deposits of all foreign banking operations in the United States is in the public interest.

In reality, the Fed's bill was the first major effort to place foreign banks in the United States under federal regulation. Thus, its significance lies in the fact that subsequent proposals were patterned after it.

The International Banking Act

The International Banking Act of 1977—H.R. 7325—is the product of more than two years of effort by the House Committee on Banking, Currency and Housing and its Subcommittee on Financial Institutions Supervision, Regulation and Insurance. The history of this bill includes its forerunners, the International Banking acts of 1975 and 1976, as well as various pieces of similar legislative proposals. These will be discussed and analyzed in this section.

Congressman Thomas M. Rees of California introduced the Foreign Bank Regulation Act as H.R. 11597 in 1973 as a means of regulating foreign banking in the United States. He was, at that time, concerned about a possible Arab takeover or investment in U.S. banks because of the surplus of so-called petrodollars. The bill was not enacted into law, as previously mentioned.

In 1975, Rees proposed a bill, entitled the International Banking Act of 1975 (hereafter referred to as "the Rees bill") to provide for federal regulation of participation by foreign banks in domestic financial markets and <u>to strengthen supervision of domestic institutions engaged in international banking</u>.* The primary emphasis of the Rees bill, however, was the development of a regulatory framework at the federal level for branches, agencies, and subsidiaries of foreign banks doing business in the United States.

The Rees bill seemed to be in accord with the Fed's objective of nondiscrimination in application of domestic laws on foreign banking in the United States. However, the proposal differed in several respects. First, with regard to Federal Reserve System membership, state-chartered subsidiaries of foreign banks would be required to join the Fed, regardless of the size of the parent. The Fed's bill limits membership to all subsidiaries, branches, and agencies of foreign banks when the parent bank has worldwide assets totaling $500 million or more. However, branches, agencies, and NYICs owned by foreign banks would not be required by the Rees bill to join the Fed; they would be made subject to reserve requirements to be imposed by the Fed and to examination by the Fed to the same extent as are state member banks.

---

*The underlining is to emphasize the major departure from Congressman Ree's first bill, which was to be more inclusive of bank regulation in general, that is, it extended more explicit and/or express supervision and regulation to at least a portion of U.S. banking operations located overseas.

With regard to reserve requirements, the Rees bill treated all liabilities as deposits for reserve purposes. In addition, the minimum reserve requirements imposed on Fed member banks by Section 19(a) of the Federal Reserve Act would be inapplicable, and the Fed would set such reserve requirements on these entities that would be appropriate to implement monetary policy objectives. Furthermore, the Federal Reserve Board was directed by the Rees bill to establish such reserve requirements not only for agencies, branches, and subsidiaries of foreign banks but also for foreign branches of U.S. member banks and EACs. Although the Fed has imposed reserve requirements on certain types of U.S. overseas branch operations, for example, Eurocurrency operations, the Federal Reserve Act has no express language at the present authorizing the Fed to impose reserve requirements against either foreign branches of U.S. banks or EACs. However, the Fed has been granted rule-making authority to administer the Federal Reserve Act and can impose reserve requirements against U.S. branches overseas by Regulation M and against EACs by Regulation K, as previously mentioned.

The Rees proposal differed from H.R. 5617, the Fed's bill, in that it made no provision for FDIC insurance for foreign branches or agencies. However, the Fed would have cease and desist powers over state foreign branches and agencies, and the U.S. comptroller of the currency would have such powers over federal foreign branches and agencies.

Furthermore, the grandfathering clauses in the Rees bill differed drastically from those in the Fed's bill. Foreign securities affiliates and other nonbanking companies in the United States that were owned by foreign banks had to be divested by end-1985. A branch or agency established outside the foreign bank's home state (the state wherein is located a foreign branch or agency having the greatest amount of assets of any of the parent's U.S. branches or agencies) could be retained if established outside the home state before December 3, 1974, and if all state branches of the parent foreign bank in all states had been converted to federal branches. The latter were permitted and were similar to those permitted by the Fed's bill, except that such a branch could not be established where prohibited by state law, the comptroller would be granted plenary power to establish rules for branches, and such branches would not need to become members of the Fed or obtain FDIC insurance on deposits.

The Rees bill restricted branches and agencies in certain areas. Foreign branches would be prohibited from accepting domestic deposits. They had to conform to existing office practices to this restriction by January 1, 1977. Credit balances from any source would be allowed foreign branches and agencies.

The Rees bill went much further in geographic scope when defining a foreign bank. A foreign bank would be one organized not only in a foreign country but also in a U.S. territory (for example, Guam, American Samoa, the U.S. Virgin Islands), as well as in Puerto Rico.

Other miscellaneous provisions of the Rees bill included the prohibition on foreign directors of EACs (although this could be waived for a national bank owned by a foreign bank). The Rees bill considered the takeover of a domestic bank by a foreign individual. Control of a domestic bank by a foreign individual could not be obtained without Federal Reserve Board approval in the case of a state bank or the comptroller's approval in the case of a national bank. In addition, the U.S. Treasury Department had to establish guidelines for the entry of foreign banks and individuals into U.S. banking, and these guidelines had to have precedence over the opinions of all other relevant regulatory agencies. Finally, foreign banks had to register representative offices with the U.S. Treasury Department.

Further amendments were made to the Rees bill, which culminated in H.R. 13876, the International Banking Act of 1976. Hearings were held in December 1975, as well as in January and March 1976 on a bill (H.R. 13211) referred by Rees to the House Committee on Banking, Currency and Housing. He had also earlier introduced H.R. 12103 on the same subject and under the same title.

H.R. 13211 was an offspring of the Financial Reform Act, proposed by the House Banking, Currency and Housing Committee in three sections, none of which was ever enacted into law. They were the culmination of the Financial Institutions and the Nation's Economy (FINE) study carried out by that committee. This bill would permit foreign banks operating in the United States to branch across state lines, subject to approval by the home and entry states; would not require Federal Reserve membership for foreign banks in the United States, but would impose member bank reserve requirements, interest rate controls, and reporting requirements on them; would not permanently grandfather multistate bank operations and securities affiliates' activities; and would impose on foreign banks the requirement of a surety bond or pledge of assets with FDIC to protect depositors. This would be in lieu of regular deposit insurance.[19]

The views of these various bills were synthesized into one final product, the International Banking Act of 1976, H.R. 13876. This bill is exactly the same as H.R. 7325, the International Banking Act of 1977; thus, both bills will be discussed as one.

During 1976, H.R. 13876 was passed by voice vote in the House. However, it was never passed by the Senate, although hearings were held on it by the Senate Subcommittee on Financial Institutions. In 1977, it was introduced to the 95th Congress as H.R. 7325 without change from its 1976 format. Hearings on this bill were held in 1977, but no committee vote on it was taken. It will probably be reconsidered in 1978.

Major Provisions of H.R. 7325

The International Banking Act of 1977 (and 1976) distinguished between foreign branches and agencies and defined a federal agency or federal branch of a foreign bank as one established with the approval of the comptroller of the currency. The bill authorized the latter to waive the requirement that all directors of a national bank be U.S. citizens and permitted only a majority of directors to be U.S. citizens if the bank was controlled by a foreign bank. The Edge Act was to be amended to allow foreign bank involvement in EACs. Interstate branching by foreign banks was prohibited by H.R. 7325 unless national banks were permitted to do so. However, multistate operations of foreign banks in operation or approved by May 1, 1976, were permanently grandfathered.

FDIC and Federal Reserve presence was mandated by H.R. 7325. Any foreign bank branch that accepted U.S. deposits must maintain with FDIC a surety bond or pledge of assets in amounts to be determined by FDIC for the purpose of protecting such deposits to the same degree as would be true of an insured bank. Second, the bill authorized the Federal Reserve Board to impose reserve requirements and interest rate controls of the system on foreign bank branches and agencies and on so-called New York Investment Companies. Reserve requirements would not be imposed on those operations whose parent bank had worldwide banking assets of less than $1 billion. Foreign bank operations in the United States would be subject to other regulations, branch approvals, reporting requirements, examinations, and use of the discount and clearing facilities of the Federal Reserve System.

Finally, nonbanking operations—primarily, securities and investment activities of foreign bank-controlled affiliates, must have been commenced on or before December 3, 1974 (and such operations thus permitted would have to be divested not later than December 31, 1985, unless permissible under Section 4 of the Bank Holding Company Act of 1956; they would then be allowed only to sell securities outside the United States).

Analysis of H.R. 7325

This bill is clearly discriminatory. West German Banking Association officials have already stated that it is so discriminatory that retaliation against our banks in Germany will be necessary.[20] The McFadden and Glass-Steagall acts notwithstanding, the nonbanking activities of foreign banks in the United States are quite small and, for the most part, for foreign customers (total capital of securities affiliates owned by foreign banks operating in the United States is about $60 million versus more than $600 million for Merrill Lynch alone).

U.S. banks can also get around the McFadden Act with the Edge Act subsidiary, which can engage in multistate operations (admittedly for only international operations but which can refer domestic business back to the parent). The rep office has certainly been prolific as a means of obtaining business nationwide.

Branches of U.S. banks are not subject to capital requirements, surety bonds on deposits, or reserve requirements. Their parents are subject to some of these. However, such states as New York and California do require certain amounts of funds to be set aside by foreign branches in other banks for safety and soundness purposes, and state-chartered foreign subsidiaries must maintain capital accounts and hold state reserve requirements.

The matter of the surety bond or pledge of assets with FDIC in order to accept domestic deposits is perhaps the principal difference in the bill: a requirement is imposed against foreign banks in the United States that is not imposed against domestic banks. FDIC was to be responsible for the design of this requirement. The Federal Deposit Insurance Act specifies an assessment formula for U.S. banks desiring deposit insurance, to be based on the level of certain items in the report of condition for a given date of insurance application. H.R. 7325 requires an annual examination of federal foreign branches and agencies and that these banks furnish certain data to federal regulatory agencies. Thus, in addition to the "capital" account set aside and required by the comptroller and Federal Reserve requirements, federal foreign branches and agencies should be assessed also for deposit insurance in the same way as are domestic banks.

Furthermore, the problems inherent in applying a surety bond or pledge of assets seem more troublesome than such a method is worth, especially when compared with the present domestic assessment method. For example, domestic deposits of these foreign banks fluctuate. Will the bond or pledge also fluctuate? If so, what institution will pay the added administrative burden? If a deposit has only $10,000 in it, will it be covered up to a possible FDIC limit of $40,000? The bond or pledge discussed herein seems to be different from that imposed on domestic banks concerning public funds on deposit. Such funds are usually more stable than ordinary deposits.

Finally, with the administrative cost of the surety bond or pledge of assets method coupled with federal foreign branches and agencies being required to maintain so-called capital accounts and reserve requirements, as well as the surety bond or pledge of assets themselves, it is doubtful whether such banks could be profitable. Little incentive would exist for changing to federal status or for accepting retail deposits. In addition, the definite risk of retaliation against our banks overseas makes H.R. 7325 a potentially dangerous bill.

To fit the letter of the law, if federal foreign branches pledge assets to FDIC, the pledge should be dollar for dollar—$1 pledge per $1 of domestic deposits up to the maximum per account, both private and public, which FDIC now insures in domestic banks. If a surety bond is written, in essence guaranteeing the deposits, the bonding firm would need to analyze the financial statement of the foreign branch or agency (not now required by law) in order to determine the amount of the bond to be written. The amount covered by the bond, thus, might not fully cover the total domestic deposits. In addition, the foreign branch or agency would have to pay a premium for the bond and maintain an escrow account with the bonding company. This, by the way, would be an entirely new area of surety bonding.[21]

After the July 1977 hearings on H.R. 7325 in the House, the bill was amended by the House Subcommittee on Banking as a result of such criticisms as discussed above. The section on multistate banking was deleted entirely, and the prohibition was lifted on non-banking affiliates if 50 percent or more of their business was performed outside the United States. The subcommittee amendments also included an exemption from Federal Reserve membership for state-chartered subsidiaries and weakened the FDIC insurance section by requiring it for state-chartered foreign bank subsidiaries in those states where domestic banks are required to insure deposits.[22] These amendments clearly alleviated many of the discriminatory sections contained in the original H.R. 7325 and may make it more palatable to foreign bankers operating in the United States.

NONLEGISLATIVE PROPOSALS TO REGULATE FOREIGN BANKING

In this section, four proposals advanced during the past few years to regulate foreign bank operations in the United States will be discussed. They are representative of many proposals in this area. These include: (1) a position reported to be held by Henry Harfield, a leading banking law expert; (2) the position of the New York Clearing House Association; (3) a proposal advanced by the Bankers Association of Foreign Trade; and (3) a proposal advanced by Franklin R. Edwards of the Columbia University Graduate School of Business.

The Harfield Proposal

In this section,[23] a viewpoint proposed by Harfield, an expert in banking law who is also a partner in a New York law firm and legal counsel to a major multinational bank, will be discussed and analyzed.

It is believed that this view, along with those of the Federal Reserve System, Congressman Rees, the New York Clearing House Association, the Bankers Association for Foreign Trade, and that of Edwards (of Columbia University), discussed in the following section, are the most representative and comprehensive proposals for regulation of foreign banking in the United States at the federal level.

The Harfield approach is based on formulation of national policies in two areas: (1) corporate powers with which a nation grants its banks that operate in foreign nations, and (2) establishment of the framework within which foreigners can enter and operate in the domestic market. Furthermore, Harfield, in his analysis of the problem, examines three objectives of any federal regulation of foreign banking that might be enacted into law. These include: (1) maintenance of competitive equality between foreign and domestic banks, (2) furtherance of the interstate and foreign commerce of the United States, and (3) responsiveness to monetary and other economic policies of the United States.

Harfield believes that any federal regulation of foreign banking in the United States should recognize international reciprocity, even though this concept may have different connotations to banking authorities from different countries. He also believes the American dual banking system should be preserved. If reciprocity is not a major consideration of such legislation, our banking operations overseas may be damaged by retaliation to a greater extent than will be the case of foreign banking operations in the United States, in light of the fact that U.S. banks have more than $225 billion in overseas assets, whereas foreign banks' assets are only $77 billion in this country.

Harfield argues that state regulation of foreign banking in the United States has been implemented satisfactorily and that Federal Reserve mandatory membership would be discriminatory against foreign banking operations, thus resulting in possible retaliation against our banks' operations overseas. Furthermore, federal control results in a diminution of states' rights in our dual banking system. He believes foreign banking should be integrated into our system rather than segregated or excluded from it. In other words, he implies that U.S. banking laws should be relaxed against U.S. banks rather than strengthened vis-a-vis foreign branches, agencies, or subsidiaries.

One area he would liberalize is multistate branching. Domestic banks have argued that foreign banks can branch across state lines if state law permits this, whereas they are prohibited by the McFadden Act of 1927 from doing so. However, the Fed's proposed bill would make all foreign branches and agencies subject to federal laws prohibiting such branching. Foreign subsidiaries are already subject to the Bank Holding Company Act and are restricted in their multistate branching. Harfield argues that multistate branching would provide the public with a wider choice of banking and, thus, would be economically beneficial.

One objective of the Fed's Foreign Bank Act of 1975 would be to extend U.S. monetary policy to foreign bank operations in this country. Harfield states that within the dual banking system, the assets of foreign-owned banks chartered in the United States, for example, subsidiaries, should be aggregated with those of national or state banks. On the other hand, the assets of foreign branches and agencies would be separately considered and left to the control of the states. Thus, he observes that "the quantum of money that escapes Federal control because it is lodged with the branches or agencies of foreign banks is of considerably less significance than has been asserted."[24] Harfield implies that a relatively small amount of funds held by foreign banks in the United States escapes U.S. monetary policy. This is true when total banking assets in this country are considered. However, one can make a case that a large amount of relatively volatile funds may not be controlled by our monetary policy.

Harfield's position, therefore, is to encourage Federal Reserve System membership but not make it mandatory; to liberalize provisions for national bank and EAC ownership to encourage foreign banks' entry into these areas; to consider unnecessary and undesirable the extension of FDIC insurance by legislation to deposits of branches, agencies, and securities affiliates; to keep the status quo on Bank Holding Company Act jurisdiction over subsidiaries and state supervision of other foreign banking entities; and to amend the Federal Reserve Act in order to permit classification of foreign banking units' deposits for the purposes of maintenance of reserves and regulation of interest rates. The latter argument is supported by the point that domestic banks that escape U.S. reserve requirements are quite small, and their assets in the aggregate are relatively small. Thus, they are afforded a special dispensation from maintaining reserves that the U.S. banking authorities are unobliged to extend to American foreign bank operations.

New York Clearing House Association Position[25]

The New York Clearing House Association (NYCH) represents 11 of the largest banks in New York City, and these are among the world's largest banks. Of the 11, 8 have numerous branches and/or subsidiaries in foreign countries and, thus, have a real stake in the matter of reciprocity. NYCH has published a position paper on regulation of foreign bank operations in the United States. The principal position of NYCH is that the dual banking system has functioned well and that no federal legislation in this area is necessary at the present time. Furthermore, this group believes the major point of contention is the so-called interstate banking issue and that the states should be able to decide this problem.

Currently, foreign banks may establish branches, agencies, or subsidiaries in more than one state if such states permit them. NYCH officials believe that foreign banking organizations and regulatory authorities have accepted the position that it is traditional for banks to be geographically circumscribed and supervised by the states. Thus, if federal legislation were to change such a structural framework, foreign retaliation might be practiced by foreign regulatory agencies against the branches of NYCH and other large U.S. banks.

The NYCH position is that reciprocity, especially with regard to traditional geographical circumscriptions, such as nationwide branch banking, may be regarded as granting permission to foreign banks to operate in the United States in the same way as U.S. banks are allowed to operate. Foreign banks in countries having nationwide banking may advance the position that reciprocity, on the other hand, means that such banks should be able to operate in the United States just as U.S. banks are allowed to operate in foreign countries. At any rate, the NYCH position is that foreign banks will not desire to branch outside of a handful of major U.S. financial centers and that state banking systems can cope adequately with this problem.

The NYCH position is that no new restrictions be imposed on multistate operations by foreign banking units. NYCH supports the permission given by Section 3(d) of the Bank Holding Company Act to state legislatures to all entry of out-of-state bank holding companies, as well as the freedom of states to authorize branches of banks incorporated in other states, except for those banks that are Fed members.

NYCH would make membership in the Fed optional for both subsidiaries and branches of foreign banks but is not concerned with foreign agencies or securities affiliates. If the foreign subsidiary or branch joins the Fed, it should be required to maintain reserves identical to those required of U.S. banks in their respective geographical regions. Otherwise, foreign branches and subsidiaries choosing not to join the Fed would be subject to host state reserve requirements.

The NYCH position with regard to FDIC insurance of deposits is that such insurance be required of foreign subsidiaries' deposits but be optional for branches. No position is taken with regard to agencies. NYCH believes that foreign branches will not desire another level of examination, that is, FDIC, and that practical problems may present themselves to the FDIC examiner in assessing the liquidity of a foreign bank whose home country banking laws are different from ours.

Finally, with regard to foreign bank securities affiliates operating in the United States in activities prohibited domestic commercial banks by the Glass-Steagall Act, the original H.R. 7325 would
have forced divestment of such activities by year-end 1985. An
NYCH official, at hearings on H.R. 7325 in July 1977, testified that
such operations were not a competitive threat to U.S. banks and
should be permanently grandfathered. NYCH members may fear retaliation against their overseas operations from countries whose
banks might have to divest their U.S. securities affiliates.

Bankers Association for Foreign Trade Position

The Bankers Association for Foreign Trade (BAFT) is an association of 141 banks, most of which are headquartered inland, founded
for the purpose of expanding bankers' knowledge of international trade,
as well as for promoting and developing international banking and foreign trade. The position discussed in this section was developed by
BAFT at its 1974 annual meeting.

The BAFT position maintains that new legislation to regulate
foreign banking will probably have an adverse effect on the internationalization of banking. BAFT believes that foreign banks should be
given as much freedom to operate in this country as is possible without jeopardizing the safety of U.S. depositors. Instead, BAFT advocates that any changes in banking regulations supposedly designed to
reduce discrimination or equalize competition between U.S. domestic
banks and foreign banks should attempt to reduce restrictions on domestic banks rather than further restrict foreign banking operations
in the United States. One such area, for example, is interstate
branch banking. Essentially, BAFT would rather U.S. banks be allowed to branch across state lines than have the U.S. federal government restrict foreign branches, agencies, and subsidiaries from increasing interstate operations.[26]

On the other hand, BAFT believes that other areas of international banking regulations are in need of change. Regulation M, BAFT
asserts, should be changed wherein it imposes a reserve requirement
on loans by U.S. banks' foreign branches to U.S. citizens (foreign
units in the United States do not have such reserve requirements imposed on them). The Fed bill, H.R. 5617, would make most of these
foreign banks Fed members, and the Rees proposal would require
all such operations to become Fed members, thus eliminating this
difference.

In another area, BAFT proposes several changes in Regulation
K, governing EACs. Among the several changes advocated are making
the reserve requirement imposed on EACs, now 10 percent, equal to

the level required of a Fed member bank in the same region and that EACs be permitted to operate at debt/equity ratios consistent with those permitted their competitors, including commercial banks, foreign branches, and foreign agencies.

Finally, in House hearings in July 1977 on H.R. 7325, BAFT officials also advocated grandfathering all securities and investment banking activities being carried on by foreign bank affiliates.

The Edwards Position

Franklin R. Edwards of the Columbia University School of Business, a student of international bank regulation, has developed a proposal for regulating foreign banking in the United States that merits attention. He developed this proposal around a concept of international reciprocity, which, in essence, treats foreign banks operating in the United States in the same manner as U.S. banks are treated in terms of banking powers and regulatory restraints. In addition, foreign banks should not be allowed to operate in a manner permitted by their home governments but disallowed by the U.S. banking laws.[27] This seems to be equivalent to the "nondiscrimination" regulatory principle designed to result in "competitive equality" between foreign and U.S. banks operating domestically. The latter principle supposedly underlies the Fed's proposed Foreign Bank Act of 1975. This principle is also referred to as the "host powers doctrine."

In keeping with this principle, Edwards makes the following recommendations for legislation:[28]

1. impose reserve requirements on foreign branches similar to those of Regulation D required of U.S. member banks
2. eliminate Regulation M reserve requirements imposed on loans by U.S. banks' foreign branches to U.S. resident borrowers because of their discriminatory implications
3. extend FDIC insurance coverage to the deposits of foreign banks' U.S. branches, at their option (although Edwards argued earlier for mandatory FDIC insurance for such deposits)
4. make federal licensing of foreign branches and subsidiaries more accessible to foreign banks
5. extend special privileges to LDCs by permitting their banks to enter U.S. financial markets without the need for reciprocity.

Edwards earlier had also proposed, in addition to mandatory FDIC insurance of foreign branch deposits in the United States, that foreign banks be prohibited from doing an investment business, as well as some type of federal, state, or dual system of interstate bank-

ing for both U.S. and foreign banks operating in the United States.
His strategy for making foreign banks conform to the Glass-Steagall
Act and for ending the McFadden Act restrictions would require foreign banks to divest themselves of securities affiliates before FDIC
insurance coverage would be granted. Such coverage would not be
made contingent upon creation of an interstate banking system. FDIC
insurance, Edwards believes, might stimulate development of interstate banking.

In some way, earlier proposals on foreign bank regulation grandfather existing securities affiliates held by foreign banks. Edwards
believes that total conformance to the Glass-Steagall Act is necessary
if adherence to his concept of international reciprocity is made. Some
authorities have suggested that such divestment might be quite costly
to foreign banks. A system of fair compensation could be implemented
at the federal level. On the other hand, one can make a case that the
very few foreign bank securities affiliates, all in New York, do not
pose a serious competitive threat to the U.S. investment community
and, furthermore, should be grandfathered under the fairness doctrine. Edwards and Zwick advocate a "thorough review" of the Glass-
Steagall Act, implying that it may not be appropriate in a multinational
banking context.[29]

ANALYSIS OF THE PROPOSALS

The proposals just discussed will be analyzed in this section in
terms of requirements imposed and/or restrictions strengthened or
relaxed and in consideration of three major parameters: international
reciprocity, diminution of discrimination, and internationalization of
banking. The analysis will concentrate on seven areas of legislative
change of supervisory-regulatory activity.

Federal Reserve System Membership

The Fed's Foreign Bank Act of 1975 requires Federal Reserve
System membership for all foreign subsidiaries, branches, agencies,
or affiliates of foreign banks whose worldwide assets are more than
$500 million. The early Rees proposal requires foreign subsidiaries
to join the Fed, makes membership optional for branches and agencies,
and would allow a different reserve requirement for foreign banking
operations than is required of domestic Fed members by Regulation
D, at least as far as minimum requirements are concerned. The International Banking Act of 1976 and 1977 would not require Federal
Reserve membership but would impose all Federal Reserve controls

on foreign bank operations in the United States whose parents have worldwide assets of more than $1 billion and which are not state-chartered institutions; in return, these foreign bank operations would have all the benefits of Federal Reserve membership, for example, discount and clearing facilities. The NYCH would preserve our dual banking system, would make Fed membership optional for foreign subsidiaries with current reserve requirements imposed, and would not consider foreign branches, agencies, or securities affiliates in its policy position. BAFT would merely reduce restrictions on domestic banks rather than impose new restrictions on foreign banks operating here. BAFT does not have a published position on Federal Reserve System membership but does believe the reserve requirements imposed by Regulation M on loans by U.S. banks' branches overseas to domestic residents to be discriminatory; thus, BAFT would abolish such Regulation M requirements. Harfield would encourage Federal Reserve membership to foreign operations but would make it optional, would preserve the dual banking system, and would amend the Federal Reserve Act to allow reclassification of foreign deposits for purposes of regulation of reserve requirements and interest rates. Edwards would eliminate Regulation M requirements but would impose Regulation D reserve requirements on foreign bank operations. He does not specifically advocate Federal Reserve System membership.

The purpose of requiring Fed membership is designed to bring foreign banking operations under U.S. monetary policy, as well as to fulfill the objective of ensuring a safe and sound banking system by requiring examination and supervision of these banks at the federal level. The Fed argues that the reason for requiring membership of subsidiaries, branches, and agencies of foreign banks with $500 million or more in assets is because nearly all U.S. members of the Fed are in this size category or larger. In fact, the House version recognizes that the foreign parent banks of U.S. operations generally have $1 billion or more in total worldwide assets.

It has also been argued that a relationship exists between the central bank in other countries and foreign banks in those countries. However, other countries do not have the dual system found in the United States. Furthermore, foreign banks in the United States do have an informal relationship with the Fed (by furnishing information on their activities to state banking authorities, which then confer with the Federal Reserve Board).[30] This requirement seems to be discriminatory against foreign banks because no similar requirement is imposed on U.S. banks in terms of their size. The Rees proposal seems to be quite discriminatory in that it requires all foreign bank subsidiaries to become Fed members, while state nonmember banks are not required to do so.

In terms of reserve requirements, Harfield would include subsidiaries' deposits within reserve requirements but would seem to ex-

clude those of foreign branches and agencies, although the assets of
the latter units amount to 75 percent of all foreign banking assets in
this country. The problem becomes one of determining whether U.S.
monetary policy is being thwarted because foreign banking deposits in
the United States are not under reserve requirement regulations and
whether these banks pose a sufficient threat to the safety and soundness of the U.S. banking system to warrant supervision and examination at the federal level. New York, Illinois, and California State
banking authorities believe they have satisfied both objectives in implementing their supervisory authority over foreign banking operations
located in their respective states.

FDIC Insurance of Foreign Banking Deposits
in the United States

The Fed's bill requires FDIC insurance for foreign branches,
agencies, and subsidiaries. The Rees bill makes no provision for
deposit insurance but does provide for cease and desist powers to be
exercised by the Fed and the U.S. comptroller of the currency. NYCH
requires insurance for foreign subsidiaries but makes coverage optional for branches. BAFT has no position on insurance of deposits.
Harfield argues against FDIC coverage. Edwards proposed mandatory insurance in 1974 but toned down this stand in 1975 to optional
FDIC coverage. The original House version of H.R. 7325 deviates
farthest from these proposals by requiring foreign banks' offices that
accept deposits in the United States to pledge assets or deposit a
surety bond with FDIC as protection for these deposits. This format
differs completely from the present method of assessing banks a flat
premium for deposit insurance. The amended version of H.R. 7325
exempts all deposits from this requirement except those in state-
chartered institutions in states requiring deposit insurance for all domestic banks.
  The major problem seems to be how to insulate the assets and
deposits of foreign branches and agencies from those of the foreign
parent bank. A subsidiary is a separate corporate entity, and in
case of bank failure, its assets, supposedly, can be easily attached,
although arguments have been presented that this has not yet been
proved. On the other hand, assets of branches and agencies could be
quickly shifted back to the parent bank, especially since they rely on
their parent banks' capital, or may be attached by other foreign
creditors of the parent bank. This problem seems to have been alleviated in most states that allow foreign banking, especially New York,
by requiring that a certain level of reserves be kept in the branch office and a specific amount of assets be deposited in a domestic bank

in such states. However, this requirement does not guarantee that these reserves will be on hand if the parent foreign bank with domestic branches fails. In fact, it has been statistically argued that provision not be made of mandatory FDIC insurance of deposits of foreign branches and agencies because of the high risk of these units as a result of the volatility of their funds and heavy dependence on foreign sources for funds.[31]

Thus, more study of the insulation of the assets of a foreign branch or agency will have to be made in order to determine the risk to the FDIC insurance fund. A second question that should be answered concerns the value in terms of the safety and soundness of the U.S. banking system, that is, will FDIC insurance of foreign branch deposits elicit growth in retail deposits which will reduce the volatility of these funds? A further question related to this is whether foreign banking in the United States will experience growth in the future (as occurred in the 1965-77 period). A recent study prepared by the U.S. Department of Commerce on foreign banking in the United States mandated by the Foreign Investment Study Act of 1974 predicts growth in the next few years but at a "much slower pace" than the recent decade or so.[32] Thus, the potential added risk to the FDIC insurance fund may not be warranted if foreign banking in the United States remains a relatively small amount of total U.S. banking. At present, foreign bank assets in the United States are only about 6.4 percent of all U.S. banking assets, a figure that could decline in future years.

A further level of federal regulation in addition to that which might be imposed by Fed membership may also present problems for foreign banks, whose management might consider this to be discriminatory. Thus, the matter of reciprocity and how the concept is interpreted by foreign bankers might result in retaliation against U.S. bank branches overseas if U.S. legislation requires FDIC insurance and concomitant examination.

Interstate Bank Branching

The McFadden Act prohibits national banks from branching across state lines. The Bank Holding Company Act permits some such branching by state-chartered units of bank holding companies, and the Edge Act amendment to the Federal Reserve Act permits U.S. banks to form EACs, which may locate anywhere in the United States, to carry on international business. Foreign banks' branches and agencies are not subject to the Bank Holding Company Act and may locate in any state that will permit their entrance.

The Fed's proposed bill will subject federally chartered foreign bank operations to the Bank Holding Company Act. Thus, foreign banks could initially enter the United States in a state that might prohibit foreign banking in its statutes. A number of bankers and state banking regulators have advocated that federal law should allow U.S. banks to branch on an interstate basis instead of further restricting foreign banks. These bankers usually represent large international banks with established overseas branch networks. On the other hand, bankers in small and medium-sized banks, especially in California and New York, have argued that they are discriminated against by not being allowed to do what multibank holding companies, multinational banks with EACs, and foreign banks can do, that is, resort to interstate branching.

The Fed bill would permit interstate branching if the Bank Holding Company and Edge acts and state law permit. The NYCH proposal discusses the traditional geographical circumscription of banking in the United States and would let the states decide this issue. The Rees bill proposes that foreign branches conform to taking only foreign deposits by 1977 and does not go further in regard to the McFadden Act restrictions on branching. Harfield implies that interstate banking, if not branching, should be permitted. And Edwards advocates interstate branching, whether by domestic or foreign banks. H.R. 7325 deleted a section on multistate banking that prohibited such operations unless allowed national banks.

A Senate Subcommittee on Financial Institutions, chaired by Senator Thomas J. McIntyre of New Hampshire, has proposed a study of branch banking and the McFadden Act. This is an issue that needs further study before restrictions are placed on foreign banks. Retaliation might result from further restriction, and the internationalization of banks might be hindered. Interstate branching, whether by domestic or foreign banks, can bring innovation and competition to communities whose economies could be enhanced by such branching.

Securities Investment Activities

The Glass-Steagall Act prohibits U.S. banks from performing certain securities investment and underwriting activities. Foreign banks are permitted to own securities affiliates, which are allowed activities not permitted U.S. banks. Thus, some of the latter believe this to be discriminatory.

Only four of the analyzed proposals discuss this issue. The Fed's bill would grandfather these under the fairness doctrine. No new securities affiliates could be formed by foreign banks in this country after December 4, 1974. The Rees bill grandfathers existing securities affiliates until 1985 and permits no new ones to be formed. Edwards advocates divestment without grandfathering in order to eliminate discrimination toward foreign banks. Apparently, his proposal might require some kind of federal compensation for those foreign banks that might suffer loss because of divestment. H.R. 7325 exempts nonbanking affiliates from the law if more than 50 percent of their business is transacted outside the United States. Otherwise, divestment by 1985 is required.

Many activities closely related to securities business are permitted U.S. banks, including large trust operations. Investment or underwriting by banks in some corporate securities, including mutual funds, might pose no more risk than the foreign exchange operations, real estate investment trusts (REITSs), and other real estate loans from which many banks have incurred losses in recent years. It seems that the Glass-Steagall Act is obsolete or at least inappropriate and might be replaced by closer supervision by federal and state authorities, higher reserve requirements on such investments by banks, more disclosure of such operations, and closer scrutiny of the prudent man concept with regard to fiduciary operations by banks. This later concept posits that a trust operation will be carried out in a manner which any prudent man would undertake.

The permission of banks in this nation to operate in the securities industry might lead to greater harmonization and internationalization of banking, since most industrialized countries permit their banks to engage in such activities. In addition, less discrimination might be claimed by U.S. banks, the reciprocity issue would be alleviated, and more competition from banks might improve our securities industry. To reiterate a point made earlier, it is unclear whether the very few U.S. securities affiliates of foreign banks actually pose a competitive threat to the U.S. securities industry or, even though they can do business that domestic banks are not permitted to do, if their operations are insufficiently important to warrant restructuring or legislation leading to costly divestment of such activities by foreign banks. At any rate, the debate may result in a comprehensive study of the appropriateness of the Glass-Steagall Act and its implications.

Miscellaneous Aspects of the Proposals

Three other areas covered in one or more of the proposals should be analyzed. These are the jurisdiction of the Bank Holding Company Act over foreign bank operations in the United States, the federal licensing of foreign branches and agencies, and liberalization of the Edge Act, Section 25(a) of the Federal Reserve Act, to permit foreign ownership of EACs.

The Fed bill would amend the Bank Holding Company Act to redefine the term "bank" so that it includes branches and agencies of foreign banks, whether established under federal or state law, thus making them subject to the Bank Holding Company Act. Only the NYCH proposal among the others discusses the Bank Holding Company Act jurisdiction, and the implication is that NYCH supports the Bank Holding Company Act but in a way that would permit states to allow out-of-state bank holding companies. H.R. 7325 redefines branches and agencies to conform to the Bank Holding Company Act.

Only three of the proposals discuss the federal licensing of foreign branches and agencies. The Fed bill would allow the alternative of federal licensing to state chartering and licensing and would authorize the comptroller to license branches of a foreign bank in any state to conduct a banking business on the same basis as a national bank, as would H.R. 7325. Edwards would merely make federal licensing "more accessible" to foreign banking operations in the United States.

EACs must be owned and controlled by U.S. citizens under Section 25(a) of the Federal Reserve Act, and all directors of an EAC must be U.S. citizens. The Fed's bill, as well as H.R. 7325, would amend 25(a) to give the Fed's board of governors the authority to waive these restrictions to permit ownership and control of EACs by foreign banks. The Rees bill would maintain the status quo on the Section 25(a) restrictions, and BAFT advocates liberalization of Regulation K, not necessarily to allow foreign ownership of EACs but to permit a wider scope in their permissible operations.

The suggestions in these three areas seem inconsistent when reciprocity, discrimination or fairness, and banking internationalization issues are considered. If foreign banking operations in the United States were to be placed under the Bank Holding Company Act constraints, those with large operations would be subject to the same controls imposed on most large U.S. banks operating domestically. Foreign banks would possibly be subjected to higher costs of operation, that is, reserve requirements, and they would be prevented from further development of interstate branching operations and establishment of de novo securities affiliates.

However, they could obtain federal charters to operate in states that now prohibit foreign banks from entry. They could establish EACs in any location to operate in the international sector, just as domestic banks can now operate. They could operate nonbanking subsidiaries in the same way as do domestic bank holding companies. Thus, subjection to the Bank Holding Company Act might permit more foreign bank expansion in the United States than it would curtail, while at the same time grandfathering might leave current organizational structures undisturbed.

CONCLUSIONS

The positions of two other groups should be included in the discussion of these issues. They are those of the Institute of Foreign Bankers (IFB), a trade group representing foreign banks operating in the United States, and the Conference of State Bank Supervisors (CSBS), the association that represents the combined efforts of the states' banking authorities.

IFB holds that mandatory Federal Reserve membership for foreign banks operating in the United States is unnecessary because these operations do not hamper monetary policy in this country. IFB believes that the Fed has not provided evidence of adverse effects to monetary policy by nonmember domestic banks, "let alone foreign banks."[33] IFB officials also testified in July 1977 House committee hearings on H.R. 7325 that foreign banks' multistate and securities affiliates operations posed no competitive threat to U.S. domestic banks.

The CSBS, in testimony on both S. 958, the Foreign Bank Act,[34] and H.R. 7325, has made a number of statements about foreign bank regulation by federal authorities. First, CSBS supported provisions of S. 958 that would eliminate certain restrictions in the National Bank Act allowing a federal chartering option for foreign banks. However, this group opposed permission for federally licensed foreign bank branches to operate interstate, regardless of state law. CSBS would grandfather securities operations of foreign banks in the United States and, thus, rejects the contention that these operations give foreign banks a major competitive advantage over domestic banks. CSBS, on the contrary, believes that nonbank subsidiaries of bank holding companies, EACs, and loan production offices of domestic banks offset any such advantage, and CSBS desires to preserve the dual banking system in this country.

In summary, it appears that federal regulation of foreign banking in the United States can be formulated in three diverse ways:[35] (1) foreign banks in the United States could be restricted to only those activities that affect trade between the United States and the rest of the world, (2) or the status quo could be maintained, that is, jurisdiction over foreign banking would be left largely with the state banking supervisors, or (3) a federal framework of regulation could be created that would allow foreign banks operating in the United States to operate in the same manner as that permitted domestic banks. This might also be an area to attempt innovation (to preserve some flexibility in the system). For example, Frank Wille, former chairman of FDIC, has suggested a reorganization of the bank regulatory system. He advocates establishment of a federal banking board, preservation of the office of U.S. comptroller of the currency, abolition of FDIC, establishment of a federal supervisor of state banks, and practice of monetary policy, but not supervision, by the Fed. The federal supervisor of state banks would examine state nonmember banks in cooperation with state banking superintendents. Thus, the dual banking system would be preserved.[36] The regulation and supervision of foreign banks in the United States might be left to the states, mainly New York, California, and Illinois, with the cooperation of the federal supervisor of state banks.

Which strategy is adopted depends on what affect it will have on U.S. monetary policy and the safety and soundness of the U.S. banking system, as well as what affect innovations in foreign bank regulation will have on the question of fairness or elimination of discrimination, the international reciprocity issue (that is, whether retaliation will be taken against our overseas bank branches), and the affect on the internationalization of banking.

The third strategy described above seems to be the one most likely to diminish discrimination, recognize international reciprocity, and result in further harmonization of international banking. If that strategy would involve federal supervision, reserve requirements, and insurance of deposits, the monetary policy and safety and soundness of banking issues might be satisfied.

It is unclear, based on current studies, just what the answers are when the discrimination question is considered, that is, does discrimination exist against any segment of foreign or domestic banking in the United States, and if so, does this discrimination create a competitive problem for one side or the other and does the practice result in unfair treatment that might lead to retaliation?

Reports have shown that foreign banking in this country will not grow in the next decade at the rapid pace that occurred in the 1965-77 period. Banking authorities and bankers have declared some current banking statutes to be obsolete or inappropriate and, perhaps, even the source of some of the alleged discrimination.

Until legislation such as the McFadden and Glass-Steagall acts and others are studied sufficiently to warrant their abolition, the fairness doctrine would seem to dictate that foreign banks be allowed to operate in those states where permitted but be prohibited from operating securities affiliates, unless it can be determined that the latter pose no threat to the U.S. securities industry and/or that the discrimination against U.S. banks is relatively insignificant.

If the relative amount of foreign bank assets in the United States will decline in the next decade, federal supervision, FDIC insurance, and federal chartering may be unnecessary. If U.S. banks can be encouraged or required to advertise that they are members of

FDIC, those foreign branches uninsured by FDIC should be required to advertise that their deposits are not covered by FDIC insurance.

The imposition of federal reserve requirements may be difficult to argue for when the fact is that state nonmember banks are "outside" U.S. monetary policy in terms of reserve requirements and their assets, loans, deposits, and so forth are all much greater than those of combined foreign subsidiaries, branches, agencies, and affiliates in the United States. The imposition of federal examination may not be necessary if state supervision, especially in California, New York, and Illinois, where most foreign operations are located, will maintain the record of examination and supervision demonstrated in the past few years.

Thus, it is unclear at the present time that any of the issues analyzed herein, for example, monetary policy, safety and soundness of banks, fairness, reciprocity, or internationalization of banking, have been adversely affected by the state patchwork of regulation of foreign banks in the United States. Nor is it clear that a federal role will improve the foreign banking system vis-a-vis the domestic banking system, except insofar as the reciprocity question may be alleviated. It may not be clear that the dual banking system should be preserved in terms of international bank regulation. However, it does seem to be clear that several areas need further study for their policy implications before legislation as far-reaching as the Fed's bill, the Rees proposal, or H.R. 7325 are enacted into law.

NOTES

1. See Elinor H. Solomon, "International Banking Competition and Cooperation," Antitrust Bulletin 20 (Spring 1975): 145; Fred H. Klopstock, "Foreign Banks in the United States: Scope and Growth of Operations," New York Federal Reserve Bank Monthly Review 55 (June 1973): 140-54; James C. Baker, "Implications of the Federal Reserve's Foreign Bank Act of 1975" (Paper presented at the Annual Meeting of the Southern Finance Association, New Orleans, November 14, 1975), p. 3; and "Required Reading: Foreign Units Hold 6% of Assets of All U.S. Commercial Banks," The American Banker 140 (November 19, 1975): 4, 20.

2. Federal Reserve Statistical Release, December 12, 1977.

3. John J. Balles, "Required Reading: Federal Rule over Foreign Banks Would End State Patchwork" (Speech at the School for International Banking, Boulder, Colorado, 1975), in The American Banker 140 (August 13, 1975): 4, 11.

4. U.S. Senate, 89th Congress, 2nd session, Congressional Record, 1966, pp. 19665-67.

5. Jack Zwick, "The Regulation of Foreign Banks in the United States," National Banking Review 4 (September 1966): 1.

6. Information on H.R. 11440 was obtained from a letter sent to Frank Wille, chairman, FDIC, by Congressman Wright Patman, February 4, 1974.

7. Information on H.R. 11597 was obtained from a letter sent to Frank Wille, chairman, FDIC, by Congressman Thomas M. Rees, January 2, 1974.

8. George W. Mitchell, "How the Fed Sees Multinational Bank Regulation," The Banker 125 (July 1974): 757, 759-60.

9. See, for example, "The Fed's Drive to Regulate Foreign Banks," Business Week, July 13, 1974, pp. 61-62; and "Foreign Bank Regulation in the USA: I—The Federal Reserve Proposals," The Banker 125 (January 1975): 47, 49, 51, 53.

10. Federal Reserve Press Release, dated March 4, 1975, on "Summary of Principal Technical Changes Made in Proposed Foreign Bank Act of 1974," p. 2, of "Summary of Principal Features."

11. J. Palmer, "Foreign Banking in North America: 1. The United States," The Banker 124 (April 1974): 342; and Francis A. Lees, "Which Route for Foreign Bank Regulation?" The Bankers Magazine 157 (Autumn 1974): 56. Actually, the redefinition was a technicality as far as FDIC was concerned. The Federal Deposit Insurance Act does not mention foreign banking operations in terms of state nonmember banks (those which are examined and supervised by the FDIC). The redefinition, by amendment of the Bank Holding Company Act, would enable FDIC to extend insurance to foreign branches and agencies in addition to subsidiaries, as is now permitted.

12. Eliot N. Vestner, "Foreign Banking Regulation—A New York State Viewpoint," The Banking Law Journal 91 (October 1974): 850.

13. Roger Anderson, "A World Financial Survey," The Economist 253 (December 14, 1974): 51 (interview with the chairman of the board, Continental Illinois Bank and Trust Company).

14. "Foreign Bank Regulation in the USA: I—The Federal Reserve Proposals," p. 49.

15. Vestner, "Foreign Banking Regulation," pp. 846-48.

16. A. W. Clausen, "A World Financial Survey," The Economist 253 (December 14, 1974): 19 (interview with the president, Bank of America).

17. See New York Banking Law § 202(b)(2) and § 202 (b)(1-2).

18. Vestner, "Foreign Banking Regulation," p. 854.

19. "Bill Would Permit Foreign Branches to Branch Interstate Subject to State Approval," BNA-Washington Financial Reports, April 19, 1976, pp. A-5, A-6.

20. Peter Reimpel, "US Bank Law, If Excessively Restrictive, Risks Retaliation," American Banker 141 (June 28, 1976): 8A; and

Peter Reimpel, "US Plans to Restrict Foreign Banks Leave a Bad Taste in German Mouths," Euromoney, September 1976, pp. 61–62.

21. Other statements for and against this legislation, specific parts of it, or other similar proposals are found in Charles S. Ganoe, "Controlling the Foreign Banks in the US," Euromoney, June 1975, pp. 75, 78; Frank Wille, "Statement on S. 958, 94th Congress, The Foreign Bank Act of 1975," presented to the Subcommittee on Financial Institutions, U.S. Senate, January 28, 1976 (obtainable from FDIC); Bruce J. Summers, "Foreign Banking in the United States: Movement toward Federal Regulation," Federal Reserve Bank of Richmond Economic Review 62 (January/February 1976): 3–7; and Clyde H. Farnsworth, "Supervision of Foreign Banks in U.S.," New York Times, May 12, 1977, p. B50.

22. Sarah Miller, "Foreign Banking in the United States," European Community, November–December 1977, p. 14.

23. The data upon which this section is based are drawn from three articles by Henry Harfield: "U.S. Shouldn't Curb Our Banks Overseas, Foreign Banks Here," The Money Manager 3 (October 7, 1974): 13–16; "Foreign Banks Subject to Fed's Jurisdiction; No Special Laws Needed," The Money Manager 3 (October 15, 1974): 5, 50; and "Legal Considerations in International Banking," The Banking Law Journal 91 (August 1974): 624–40.

24. Harfield, "Foreign Banks Subject to Fed's Jurisdiction," p. 5.

25. Based on (1) "New York Clearing House Position Paper on Regulation of Foreign Bank Operations in the United States" (unpublished paper prepared in 1974) and (2) statement of John F. Lee, executive vice-president, New York Clearing House Association, on H.R. 7325—The International Banking Act of 1977, before the Subcommittee on Financial Institutions Supervision, Regulation and Insurance, Committee on Banking, Finance and Urban Affairs, U.S. House of Representatives, July 13, 1977, 95th Cong., 1st sess.

26. Charles S. Ganoe, "Banking across Borders: Reciprocity and Equality," Burroughs Clearing House 58 (February 1974): 19.

27. Franklin R. Edwards, "Regulation of Foreign Banking in the United States: International Reciprocity and Federal-State Conflicts," Columbia Journal of Transnational Law 13 (1974): 257.

28. Franklin R. Edwards and Jack Zwick, "Foreign Banks in the United States: Activities and Regulatory Issues" (Research Paper no. 80), mimeographed (New York: Graduate School of Business, Columbia University, January 22, 1975), p. 42.

29. Ibid., p. 43.

30. Carlos Canal, "Foreign Banks under Fire," The Banker 124 (September 1974), p. 1111.

31. Gary G. Gilbert, "The Performance of Foreign Banks in the United States: Implications for Federal Regulation" (Working

Paper no. 75-9), mimeographed (Washington, D. C.: Division of Research, Federal Deposit Insurance Corporation, 1975), p. 19.

32. "Slower Pace in Growth of Foreign Banking in U.S. Forecast by Study," Washington Financial Reports, no. 44 (November 3, 1975), pp. A-7-A-11.

33. "Foreign Banking Activities in the United States and Monetary Policy" (prepared for the Institute of Foreign Bankers by Golembe Associates, January 1976).

34. CSBS Press Release, January 29, 1976.

35. Allan Frankel, "International Banking—Structural Aspects of Regulation," Federal Reserve Bank of Chicago Business Conditions, (October 1974), pp. 10-11.

36. Frank Wille, "Centralization Which Preserves a Regulatory Choice: An Intermediate Proposal for Bank Regulatory Reform" (address by then-chairman, Federal Deposit Insurance Corporation, to the Association of Registered Bank Holding Companies, Palm Beach, Florida, November 17, 1975).

INTRODUCTION

During the last decade or so, the most phenomenal growth area
in the economic arena has been international business in general.
World trade, for example, climbed to more than $1 trillion. The MNC
has become the most studied institution during this period. The Eurocurrency market has developed into a $500 billion-plus money and
capital market and, as such, has become a most significant means of
financing multinational corporate activities. International banking
has been a key factor in the growth of the Eurocurrency market, and
it is international banking and its regulation that is the principal subject matter of this book.

Because of the growth and significance of this part of the worldwide economic sector, a great deal of thought and effort has been applied in recent years to the problems of international bank regulation,
harmonization and further internationalization of banking in general,
and to the alleviation of a myriad of troubles that have beset international banking as a result of too rapid growth, management problems,
and worldwide recession and inflation.

The first chapters of this book have concentrated on international banking operations of American banks and foreign bank operations in the United States. In this chapter, the coverage is aimed at
bank supervision and regulation in the United Kingdom, West Germany,
France, Belgium, and the Netherlands. Included also is some material on the EEC. These five nations are most representative of West
European countries, and along with Japan, have the most widespread
banking systems outside the United States.

Along with the United States, the banking systems of these nations have incurred a great deal of growth. Because of the occurrence
of a number of problems in worldwide banking (problems that have
been examined earlier), the governments of most industrialized nations have been analyzing their bank regulatory and supervisory sys-

tems with the objective of streamlining them, making them more efficient, increasing the safety and soundness of their banking systems, and facilitating harmonization and internationalization of banking systems in general, while at the same time reducing discriminatory practices of regulation against foreign banks operating within their respective borders and improving reciprocity in banking operations. Thus, severe banking problems have resulted in re-evaluation of the banking systems in industrialized nations, especially the five whose systems are the subject of this chapter; this re-evaluation has resulted in a flurry of proposed legislation, implementation of executive decrees, and imposition of tighter controls aimed at the objectives mentioned previously.

It is not the author's intention to discuss monetary policy controls in this chapter. Bank regulation and supervision relating to entry, safety and soundness measures (such as examination), capital adequacy and liquidity, mergers and acquisitions, and handling of bank failures are among the main topics of this chapter. Only indirectly will monetary policy controls be discussed. Deposit insurance will be discussed briefly where applicable, but a more in-depth treatment will follow in Chapter 7.

The principal reason for examining the regulatory systems of other countries is that American lawmakers and bank regulators should know what and how other major nations are doing in bank regulation before legislation is enacted here whose objective is to regulate our banks overseas or foreign banks in the United States. Otherwise, serious problems may result in areas of reciprocity, safety and soundness of banking in general, and the further internationalization of banking. The structure and magnitude of banking in each country will be discussed in the following sections.

THE UNITED KINGDOM

The Bank of England, founded in 1694, is the central bank of the United Kingdom. The bank is the issuer of notes in England and Wales, is banker to the government, and keeps substantial balances from the London clearing banks, to be used for settlements between the clearing banks. The types of banks operating in the United Kingdom and their deposit sizes are shown in Table 5.1.

Only deposit banks have large branch networks. London clearing banks are members of the clearing house, and checks are cleared through them.[1] Categories numbered five through ten in Table 5.1 comprise the secondary banking system (it was a number of these banks that failed during the past few years). Whereas deposits and loans of deposit banks are usually short term, those of secondary banks are longer term. The accepting houses combine domestic and foreign banking with financial advisory services, arrange new issues, and manage portfolios, among other activities. Deposit banking is highly concentrated; however, there is little concentration among secondary banks.

TABLE 5.1

U.K. Banking System: Types of Bank and Deposits,
December 12, 1973
(millions of pounds)

Category	Number of Banks[a]	Deposits	
		Sterling	Other Currencies
Deposit banks			
(1) London clearing banks	6[b]	19,613	2,019
(2) Scottish clearing banks	3	1,838	151
(3) Northern Ireland banks	4	686	117
(4) Other	5	709	4
Total deposit banks	18	22,846	2,291
(5) Accepting houses	29	2,564	2,985
(6) British overseas and Commonwealth	42	3,215	9,551
(7) American	40	3,945	21,676
(8) Foreign banks and affiliates	40	1,131	7,349
(9) Other overseas banks	47	617	6,145
(10) Other U.K. banks	79	6,876	4,380
Total categories 5-10	277	18,348	52,086
Total all banks	295	41,194	54,377

[a]These figures involve some duplication where subsidiaries are listed separately; categories 5 and 10 are most affected.
[b]Includes Coutts and Co., which is a wholly owned subsidiary of the National Westminster Bank.

Source: Bank of England Quarterly Bulletin, vol. 14 (March 1974), Annex Table 8 and explanatory notes, p. 50.

WEST GERMANY

The Deutsche Bundesbank, the German central bank, is authorized to regulate money circulation and the supply of credit and to handle the execution by banks of payments within Germany and with other countries. Although the bundesbank may support government policy, the German government, unlike the U.K. government, cannot give instructions to it.

The bundesbank has sole power to issue notes in any amount and without reserve requirements. It serves as banker to the government and to the rest of the banking system, being lender of last resort. The bundesbank charges a discount rate on such loans, handles debt management, open-market operations, and, for special purposes, may levy reserve requirements.

The Deutsche Bundesbank controls the banking system and the money supply in cooperation with the Bundesaufsichtsamt für das Kreditwesen (Federal Bank Supervisory Agency). These controls are implemented by means of capital and liquidity requirements and a system of compulsory reserve deposits.

The number and types of German banks and the size of their business are shown in Table 5.2. The so-called big banks, or Gross-banken—Deutsche Bank, Dresdner Bank, and Commerzbank (and their West Berlin affiliates)—account for more than 40 percent of all commercial banking business. Slightly more business is done by the 123 regional banks, and the remainder of commercial banking is done by small private banks and foreign banks.

The commercial banks not only take deposits, make loans, and handle trust accounts but carry on investment banking activities, including underwriting securities, trade in securities for customers and for their own accounts, act as members of securities exchanges, and manage mutual funds and finance companies on a long-term basis.

Savings deposits in the German banking system play a much larger part than do demand deposits. They account for 30 percent of all commercial banking deposits and 47 percent of all deposits in the German banking system.[2] Long-term lending is a major factor of the German system, with two-thirds of all lending being for periods longer than four years. This is a further reflection of the fact that the German banking system has a much closer relationship with German industry than is true of banking in the United States. In fact, German banks own large amounts of the shares of German industrial companies for their own accounts, in return for which German companies receive large amounts of long-term financing from German banks. Reserve requirements, a major policy tool of the Bundesbank, are formulated by means of a complex formula. The ratio implemented

TABLE 5.2

Types of Banks and Numbers and Volume of Business, Germany,
December 1977

Type	Number	Volume of Business	
		Billions of Deutsche Marks	Percent
Big banks	6	184.3	10.4
Regional banks	113	193.8	10.9
Foreign banks	51	34.7	2.0
Private banks	100	29.5	1.7
Total commercial	270	442.3	24.9
Central giro institutions	12	292.4	16.5
Savings banks	622	390.4	22.0
Central institutions for cooperatives	11	75.2	4.2
Credit cooperatives	2,343	174.0	9.8
Mortgage banks	40	231.3	13.0
Installment credit institutions	134	20.3	1.1
Banks with special functions	18	114.9	6.5
Postal giro and postal savings banks	15	35.1	2.0
Total	3,465	1,775.8	100.0

Source: Monthly Report of the Deutsche Bundesbank 30 (March 1978): 28.

will depend on these factors: location, size of bank, type of deposits, whether deposits are domestic or foreign, and the rate of increase in liabilities.

FRANCE

More than 300 registered banks are operating in France, in addition to many savings banks, local banks, agricultural credit banks, and public and quasi-public agencies. Monetary policy is formulated by the National Credit Council and implemented by the Banque de France.

The Banque de France, founded in 1800 as a private bank, was operated privately until it was nationalized in 1945. It is sole note issuer, banker to the government, and banker to banks. Although not the sole monetary policy authority and having jurisdiction over only registered banks, it does have some authority to supervise the banking system to insure that it does not become overcommitted in the area of loans. The Commission de Contrôle des Bangues (Banking Control Commission) is primary supervisor of banks, but the Banque de France controls the system when monetary policy considerations are important.

The most important sector in the French banking system is comprised of the registered banks. This can be seen in Table 5.3. Registered banks are further divided into three categories: deposit banks, banques d'affaires, and medium- and long-term banks. Deposit banks take primarily short-term deposits. Banques d'affaires take longer-term deposits and carry on a wide range of commercial and investment banking activities. Medium- and long-term banks are not permitted to take short-term deposits. Since 1966, deposit banks have been managing portfolios and mutual funds and issuing securities. The "big three" nationalized banks (see Table 5.4)—Banque Nationale de Paris, Crédit Lyonnais, and Société Générale—are among the deposit banks and account for about half the deposits of all registered banks. Deposit banks may own shares in other companies but no more than 20 percent of any one company. The bank's total holdings of such securities cannot exceed the bank's own capital and reserves. Banques d'affaires, by tradition, invest in share capital of companies. Registered with the National Credit Council are 247 deposit banks, 24 banques d'affaires, and 50 medium- and long-term credit banks.[3]

Several other types of banks operate in a number of specific areas, and these and the registered banks take a wide variety of deposits. In addition, variable cash reserve ratios are applied to all but savings banks. French banks traditionally refinance much of their lending by rediscounting such paper; before 1969, they relied to a great extent on the Banque de France for much of their funds. This source has been restricted drastically in recent years.

BELGIUM

The Banque Nationale de Belgique, a public company whose stock is 50 percent owned by the Belgian government, is the monetary authority over principal financial institutions, after consultation with the minister of finance; since December 1973, it has had the power to impose balance sheet ratios on Belgian banks, call for special deposits for monetary control purposes, and fix maximum rates of interest on various categories of bank liabilities.[4]

The banque issues bank notes for both Belgium and Luxembourg. It acts as banker to the government, holds the Treasury accounts,

TABLE 5.3

Deposits of the Main Categories of Banks, France, 1971 and 1973
(millions of francs)

Type	December 1971		August 1973	
	Sight Deposits	Other Deposits	Sight Deposits	Other Deposits
Registered banks, Banque Francaise du Commerce Extérieur and Banque Centrale des Coopératives	107,450	94,560	118,890	133,860
Banques populaires	8,830	7,700	11,620	11,910
Cooperative banks (mostly Crédit Agricole)	32,400	50,160	43,910	75,300
Post Office giro	33,310	—	35,630	—
Total	181,990	152,420	210,050	221,070
Savings banks				
National Savings Bank	44,040		36,140*	
Ordinary savings banks	81,530		105,602*	
Bank notes in circulation and coin	77,950		88,590*	

*Provisional figure.

Source: E. Victor Morgan, Richard Harrington, and George Zis, Banking Systems and Monetary Policy in the EEC (London: The Financial Times, 1974), p. 29.

controls foreign exchange through a dependent body, the Institut Belgo-Luxembourgeois des Changes, holds accounts of commercial banks and of public sector financial intermediaries, and is an important source of funds through the discounting of Treasury and approved commercial bills.

Of the other financial-related agencies in Belgium, only the Commission Bancaire needs to be mentioned in this chapter. It was spawned by the banking problems of the 1930s and has supervisory powers over all commercial banks and sociétés financières. Such supervision includes the enforcement of capital and reserves adequacy, as well as ratios for liquidity.

As shown in Table 5.5, commercial banks are the most important financial institutions in Belgium, representing nearly a third of

TABLE 5.4

Combined Balance Sheet of the Three Nationalized Banks, France, October 31, 1973
(millions of francs)

Liabilities	Amount	Assets	Amount
Capital and reserves	2,971	Cash, balances with Banque de France and Treasury	31,745
Deposits of persons	77,230	Loans and advances	127,480
Deposits of firms and others	48,834	Loans to other banks and correspondents	83,101
Borrowing from other banks, correspondents, and Banque de France	103,082	Treasury bills and bonds	21,921
Cash bonds issued	29,267	Other	38,458
Other	41,321		
Total	302,705	Total	302,705

Source: E. Victor Morgan, Richard Harrington, and George Zis, Banking Systems and Monetary Policy in the EEC (London: The Financial Times, 1974), p. 27.

114

TABLE 5.5

Total Assets and Liabilities of Certain Financial Intermediaries,
Belgium, October 31, 1972*
(billions of Belgian francs)

Type	Total Assets and Liabilities
National Bank	254.3
Commercial banks	679.4
Private savings banks	192.8
Post Office giro, Institut de Réescompte et de Garantie (IRG), Fonds des Rentes	94.0
Other public sector financial intermediaries	795.0
Total (gross)	2,015.5
Less double counting	208.6
Total (adjusted)	1,806.9

*Liabilities in foreign currencies not switched into Belgian
francs; certain "mobilization" operations and forward exchange
transactions excluded.

Source: E. Victor Morgan, Richard Harrington, and George
Zis, Banking Systems and Monetary Policy in the EEC (London:
The Financial Times, 1974), p. 5.

all such assets. Three of these—Société Générale de Banque, Banque
de Bruxelles, and Kredietbank—dominate the industry. These are
holding companies, or sociétés financières, and they carry on a wide
range of short-, medium-, and long-term commercial and investment
banking activities. See Table 5.6 for the combined balance sheet for
all types of commercial banks.

THE NETHERLANDS

The central bank of the Netherlands and the sole monetary policy
authority is the Nederlandsche Bank, founded in 1814 as a private
bank and nationalized in 1948. The bank is sole bank of issue in the
Netherlands, as well as banker to the Dutch government and other public institutions. Day-to-day control of foreign exchange has been dele-
gated by the government to the bank. The bank is banker for private

banks and facilitates interbank clearing, acts as monetary authority, and maintains a register of all credit-granting financial institutions.

The Dutch banking system is comprised of commercial banks, agricultural cooperative banks, private savings banks, the Post Office Savings Banks, the Post Office giro, and a few security-credit institutions. Commercial banks comprise the largest amount of Dutch banking business.

The commercial banking system is highly concentrated among 70 institutions. However, 60 percent of their total assets are held by the two largest—Algemene Bank Nederland and Amsterdamsche-Rotterdamsche Bank—and 90 percent of all resources are held by the four largest commercial banks.[5] The largest bank in the Netherlands, on the other hand, is not a commercial bank. It is the central organization of the agricultural cooperative bank.

The "big two" banks are jointly owned by the Dutch government and private shareholders, and all large commercial banks are members of the Amsterdam Stock Exchange and combine commercial and investment banking operations. The combined balance sheet for Dutch commercial banks is shown in Table 5.7.

REGULATION AND SUPERVISION OF BANKS

The bank supervisory and regulatory systems in each of the five countries will be discussed and analyzed in this section, with some degree of comparison and contrast involved. Supervision and regulation will be discussed in terms of major overall functions, that is, bank entry regulations, including licensing and de novo or merger considerations; reporting and examination of banking operations; foreign exchange operations; insurance or safe maintenance of deposits; and maintenance of balance sheet adequacy standards, including capital and liquidity. These are the standard functions of a bank regulatory and supervisory agency whose principal objectives are the safety and soundness of the banking system and the protection of individual depositors. The exercise of monetary policy to further economic objectives of the individual governments will not be discussed further in this chapter.

Supervisory Authority

In some cases, the central bank is sole supervisory and regulatory authority abroad, whether that regulation be formal or informal. In England, the Bank of England serves in this capacity. In the Netherlands, it is the Nederlandsche Bank, whose governing

TABLE 5.6

Balance Sheet of the Commercial Banks, Belgium, September 30, 1973
(billions of Belgian francs)

Liabilities	Amount	Assets*	Amount
Liabilities abroad		Foreign lending	
Belgian francs	115.6	Belgian francs	32.5
Other currencies	384.7	Other currencies	338.2
Resident deposits		Other short-term foreign credits	51.8
At one-month notice or less	223.2	Notes and coins	5.6
At more than one-month notice	136.6	Balance with National Bank	17.9
Savings deposits	148.8	Balance with other public bodies	5.4
Foreign currency deposits	11.6	Interbank lending	79.9
Interbank deposits	79.9	Loans to the private sector, local government, and the public and semi-public organizations (including bond holdings)	428.9
Deposits of public and semipublic organizations	3.0		
Other	177.1	Loans to central government (including bond holdings)	217.2
		Other	104.0
Total	1,281.4	Total	1,281.4

*Certain of the items on the assets side of the balance sheet are provisional.

Source: E. Victor Morgan, Richard Harrington, and George Zis, Banking Systems and Monetary Policy in the EEC (London: The Financial Times, 1974), p. 6.

TABLE 5.7

Balance Sheet of the Commercial Banks, the Netherlands, December 31, 1973
(millions of guldens)

Liabilities	Amount	Assets	Amount
Capital and reserves	4,850	Notes, coins, balances with Nederlandsche Bank	382
Current accounts	10,371	Balances with other banks	3,269
Time deposits and money at call	14,913	Short and medium-term loans to government	2,848
"Genuine savings" deposits	7,110	Short-term loans to local authorities	1,535
Other long-term funds	4,639	Government bonds	2,819
Interbank borrowing	3,433	Loans and advances	33,892
Central bank borrowing	694	Securities in Dutch companies	2,474
Nonresident deposits	30,584	Claims on nonresidents	33,823
Miscellaneous	6,264	Miscellaneous	1,816
Total	82,858	Total	82,858

Source: E. Victor Morgan, Richard Harrington, and George Zis, Banking Systems and Monetary Policy in the EEC (London: The Financial Times, 1974), p. 70.

board controls the banking system; in Germany, the central bank is the Deutsche Bundesbank, but cooperation with the Banking Supervisory Office is prevalent. However, in Belgium and France, two and three agencies, respectively, regulate and supervise the banking systems. In Belgium, the Banque Nationale de Belgique acts in most monetary policy matters as central bank, while supervision of commercial banks and sociétés financières is implemented by the Commission Bancaire. In France, monetary authority over banks is formulated by the National Credit Council and implemented by the Banque de France; whereas supervisory and regulatory authority is the responsibility of the five-member Commission de Contrôle des Banques, whose chairman is the governor of the Banque de France.

Bank Entry, Licensing, and Mergers

The supervisory authorities just mentioned are the principal agencies regulating entry to the banking sector. For example, in France, the National Credit Council maintains a list of all registered banks, and any change in the structure of a bank or in the nature of a bank's business requires approval by the council. The supervisory board of the Nederlandsche Bank in the Netherlands has authority over banks' opening and closing of branches and organizational matters, including mergers and foreign participation.

Holding companies, or sociétés financières, are regulated in Belgium by the Commission Bancaire. In Germany, banking regulations in the statutes include licensing requirements; these may be administered by various banking federations. The branches of the bundesbank, the Landeszentralbanken, carry out the routine supervision of such matters. In the United Kingdom, until the secondary bank failures of the past few years, very little thought was given to the inadequacy of British laws in their definition of a bank. In the secondary level of banking, almost anyone could voluntarily establish a bank. The Bank of England has maintained a list of "authorized banks," but the distinction between a bank and a moneylender has never been made clear. Proposed legislation may correct these inadequacies.[6] Thus, until now, very little control, if any, has been exercised in the United Kingdom over bank entry, licensing, mergers, branching, acquisitions, or dissolution.

Reporting and Examination

Two areas of bank regulation and supervision that have drawn perhaps the most attention from the banking losses and failures of the past few years are the direct supervision of banks by examination and the question of desirability of implementing more stringent balance sheet ratio tests, such as capital adequacy and liquidity. Balance sheet tests will be discussed in the next section.

In nearly all industrialized nations, proposals have been made seeking tighter supervision, more bank information disclosure, and, thus, more stringent examination procedures. In the EEC, an informal discussion group was formed by the bank supervision authorities. Known as the Groupe de contact, meetings have been held on a quarterly basis for the purpose of fostering greater cooperation among national bank regulatory authorities.[7] This move coincided with the formation of a Steering Committee on International Bank Regulation by the U.S. Federal Reserve Board. Under the chairmanship of former Fed Vice-Chairman George W. Mitchell, this committee's objectives were to study how foreign banking in the United States might be regulated at the federal level, as well as how the U.S. bank regulatory agencies might further control U.S. banking operations abroad.[8]

In early 1975, the central bank governors of the Group of Ten countries formed a standing committee with other bank supervisory authorities from those nations, as well as from Switzerland and Luxembourg. The committee, chaired by George Blunden, in charge of bank supervision at the Bank of England, acted in conjunction with the Bank for International Settlements in Basel; its objectives were to strengthen banking regulations and supervisory practices in the European nations. In addition to international cooperation in the supervisory field, the committee worked toward development of an early warning system to give bank regulators better knowledge of banking difficulties before they result in large losses or failures.[9]

In analyzing specific supervisory and examination practices in the five countries, one conclusion can be inferred, that is, present practices are not as stringent, formal, or comprehensive as the federal-state system of bank regulation in the United States. For example, in Belgium, the Commission Bancaire "collects regular information on banks."[10] It is unclear what information is requested or what is meant by "regular." In the Netherlands, the Supervision of the Credit System Act of 1956 legitimized the traditional process in that country of regulation by prior consultation and gentlemen's agreements, the latter with regard to credit controls and liquidity and solvency requirements. Although the act gives the Nederlandsche Bank power to obtain whatever information necessary from any bank to facilitate its supervisory function and although it requires each bank to provide an annual balance sheet and income statement, and states that the bank may require bank examinations and audits, it does not grant powers to the bank concerning auditing procedures (and few such audits have ever been implemented). The act grants no enforcement powers to the bank. Thus, the bank can issue warnings to problem banks but can only sanction such by publication of the warnings. Such a warning to the public might result in a run on that particular bank and possible liquidation.

New legislation before the Dutch Parliament is designed to remedy these problems. It empowers the Nederlandsche Bank to audit Dutch banks, as well as their foreign branches; to appoint a supervisor to restructure the management of a bank on the verge of insolvency; to license financial institutions; and to enforce minimum liquidity and solvency ratios. The latter power may solve the problem of declining solvency of Dutch banks in general. No failures of major Dutch banks have occurred, but several mergers have been carried out (it was reported that the Amro Bank acquisition of Piersons was the result of a solvency problem).

Although in Germany, the Deutsche Bundesbank and the Federal Banking Supervisory Office cooperate in supervising German banks, routine supervision, including examination and analysis of banks' credit reports, monthly statements, and balance sheets, is handled by the Bundesbank through its branches. In the case of irregularities in a particular bank, an audit may be ordered. Until the 1974 failure of the Bankhaus I. D. Herstatt, such audits were quite rare. However, if the audit is performed, the Banking Supervisory Office can take corrective action if banking laws have been violated, including the power to withdraw a bank's license. Currently, the German government has been considering new bank regulatory legislation designed to strengthen the bank regulatory system there. This proposed legislation is concerned primarily with increased protection of deposits of nonbank depositors and limitations on lending to a single borrower (results of the Herstatt failure).

In France, a Banking Control Commission, headed by the governor of the Banque de France, implements bank regulation and supervision but operates closely with the banque. The minister of finance is at the top of the decision-making hierarchy in France and sounds his policies out on the National Credit Council, discussed earlier. The latter agency, consisting of 47 members selected from a wide cross section of the public, formulates monetary policy, which, in turn, is implemented by the Banque de France.

The Banking Control Commission audits financial information furnished quarterly by most banks and monthly by the largest banks and supplements such audits with periodical on-premise examinations of these banks. The commission has the power to enforce orders and can issue reprimands, remove bank officers, and rescind charters, subject to court review. Thus, there seems to be a relatively large degree of compliance with the commission's orders, because it, like the Banque de France, has an excellent reputation, is highly efficient, guarantees public confidence in the banking system, and is known for its professional toughness.

Another reason for the high reputation and effectiveness of the Bank Control Commission emanates from the size of its staff. France has approximately 350 banks and 400 other financial institutions. The commission has a staff of 45 to 50, in addition to 15 to 20 examiners. The 750 institutions submit documentation that is analyzed by the commission's staff, but 100 annual on-premise examinations also add to the agency's effectiveness. [11]

The British banking regulatory system has generally operated on a voluntary, or gentlemen's agreement, basis. One principal problem in the United Kingdom is that no definition of a bank has any legal standing. The legal system underlying U.K. bank regulation is based on tradition, five separate laws, and the efforts of a small, overworked department in the Bank of England.

Banking law in the United Kingdom is comprised of the following laws: (1) 1947 Exchange Control Act—contained a list of banks authorized to deal in foreign exchange; (2) 1948 Companies Act—allowed banks to hold hidden reserves; (3) 1963 Protection of Depositors Act—(merely) regulated advertisements by "banks" seeking deposits; (4) 1967 Companies Act—established functional banking criteria and gave the right to certain institutions claiming banking status in advertisements for deposits; (5) 1970 Income and Corporation Taxes Act—gave rights to bankers to pay or receive interest or dividends without the deduction of taxes. [12] Thus, no legislation exists in the United Kingdom that has either defined a bank or established a statutory system of bank supervision, regulation, and examination.

Specifically, however, Section 4.-(3) of the Bank of England Act of 1946 authorizes the bank to request information from and make recommendations to bankers. These powers have never been exercised in any clearly delineated way, and the supervision of British banks remains flexible and informal. The mere raising of an eyebrow by the governor of the bank may be sufficient reason for a banker to increase his bank's capital/deposit or capital/asset ratio. The bank maintains (given this framework) close contact with the large clearing banks, but the failures in the secondary sector during the past few years, coupled with the international economic crisis, have resulted in the bank's enlarging its supervisory department and the proposal of several more stringent regulations.

No regulations yet apply to all banks in the United Kingdom on a uniform basis. The examination process is performed on a bank-by-bank basis in light of the bank's specific characteristics, type of business, composition of assets and liabilities, quality of management, stage of development, and assessment by other banks.

In 1974, the Bank of England established a separate regulatory department and introduced new regulations. These regulations required more frequent, more detailed, and more sophisticated information from banks. An improved set of criteria were drafted for evaluating banks' capital adequacy and liquidity. Capital/deposit ratios were de-emphasized, but capital was to be evaluated in relation to risk assets. All banks except clearing banks were required to submit quarterly reports, and clearers were to report on an annual basis. Previously, secondary banks had to report only annually, and such annual accounts were examined generally long after the reporting date. [13]

The viewpoint underlying the Bank of England philosophy, however, remains that "rigid ratios and other detailed legal controls do not provide sufficient flexibility for dealing with a sophisticated and varied financial system,"[14] despite the 1974-75 secondary bank problems and the increased supervision by the Bank of England.

Regulation of Capital Adequacy

A great deal of discussion has evolved during the past decade concerning the capital adequacy of banks and its regulation. Some analysts believe that bank failures occur because banks have inadequate capital. Some believe that tighter controls are needed but that the application of simple arithmetic balance sheet ratios across the board is an inadequate regulatory method. Two banks could have identical capital ratios, but if one has invested deposits in three-month Treasury bills and the other in three-year loans to second-grade property companies, equal rankings on these banks would be absurd. However, capital is a resource that a bank may use to reduce its risk exposure, especially in light of the international economic problems of recent years.

In the United Kingdom, where, in the past, capital adequacy regulation has been informally implemented, the emphasis for secondary banks has been to use a ratio of free capital and reserves to public liabilities, with a guideline of 10 percent being the objective. The Bank of England is now advocating a ratio of capital to assets with the risk of each class of assets being evaluated. Cash is risk free, and advances and securities will have some degree of risk assigned, but a universally acceptable ratio will be difficult to quantify; thus, banks will be evaluated in terms of capital adequacy on an individual basis, with informal suggestions—"nods and winks"—still being the principal criteria used. [15]

In Germany, corporate accounting practices emphasize the asset side of the balance sheet; this is especially true in banking, where regulations relate capital to total credit, as well as to individual loans, in addition to relating long-term credit to the bank's overall resources. The Federal Banking Supervisory Office determines capital adequacy standards in cooperation with the Deutsche Bundesbank; when a bank's capital falls below these standards "by a considerable margin or repeatedly,"[16] capital is considered inadequate. These standards are based on two criteria: a bank's capital has to amount to at least 5.56 percent of total credit outstanding, and a bank's investments in long-term credit and other long-term assets may not exceed its long-term financial resources, including capital.

The French method is even less formal. The National Credit Council determines various capital ratios regarding an individual bank's total liabilities and amount of credit granted to a single borrower but never implements such ratios. The Banking Control Commission applies no specific ratios in a rigid manner but controls banks on a personal and individual basis; it is empowered to make rules regarding banking liquidity and reserves. Private banks generally maintain 5 percent capital/deposits ratios and are more stringently supervised than are the three nationalized banks, which maintain 2 to 3 percent ratios, have officers appointed by the government, and seldom have their portfolios scrutinized. Minimum capital requirements range from 1 to 10 million francs, depending on type of bank, legal form, and location.

The Nederlandsche Bank prescribes the maximum amount of loans that a Dutch bank may make, based on its capital and reserves. If a bank appears to have doubtful solvency, the bank can take specific action within a certain period of time. However, no specific guidelines on capital adequacy have been issued by the bank.

Belgian regulatory authorities believe that the larger the bank, the less risk involved and the smaller amount of capital is needed. Thus, the larger the bank, the lower will be its capital/deposits ratio. Several ratios have been formulated by Belgian authorities; these tie capital adequacy to the total volume of liabilities, with the actual ratio dependent on the overall risk of the assets in a bank's portfolio. Total capital/total liabilities ratios run from 3.5 percent for a bank in the lowest risk class to 15.0 percent in the highest risk class; the calculation of the risk factor is based on an elaborate set of complicated formulas.

Thus, the United Kingdom and France practice a direct, personal approach to capital adequacy regulation, whereas the Netherlands (to some extent), Germany, and Belgium apply formal regulations. If one looks at the record, for 1973 and 1974, capital/assets ratios for those banks in these five countries that are listed among The Bankers top 300 worldwide banks reveal some interesting points when compared with U.S. standards. Banks listed in the top 300 for all countries had lower capital/assets ratios for both years that did U.S. banks, where Congressmen and some regulators seem very concerned with overall generally declining capital ratios. In fact, French banks on this list showed ratios of only 1.75 percent in 1973 and 1.87 percent in 1974; with the exception of U.K. banks, country means of the top 300 banks were generally 40 percent or more lower than U.S. ratios. This is especially true of continental European banks. Part of the explanation for such lower ratios, as previously discussed, may be the fact that continental European banks and corporations generally are allowed to maintain hidden reserves, so that higher leverage appears to be true when merely applying traditional balance sheet ratio analysis. Thus, such practices (hidden reserves) may allow these banks to operate as safe and sound financial institutions with much less stated equity capital.[17] In addition, nationalized banks, such as those in France, maintain lower capital ratios because the government is in full support of these banks.

Insurance of Deposits

Of the five nations covered in this chapter, only one has what might be considered a statutory program insuring bank deposits. In late January, the German Parliament amended the law governing banking to give that nation "the best deposit insurance scheme anywhere in the world."[18] (The German scheme will be analyzed in greater detail in Chapter 7.) None of the other four nations has a formal deposit insurance program; however, Bank of England officials have discussed the possibility of a compulsory deposit insurance program.

In the other countries, less formal arrangements are prevalent. Banks are generally well supported by the French, Belgian, and Dutch governments, to the extent that few if any failures occur, and depositors' losses are covered on a case-by-case basis by government agencies.

Miscellaneous Areas of Regulation

This concluding subsection includes a discussion of the regulation of foreign exchange dealing by banks in these five countries, as well as regulation of foreign banks operating within their borders. The European countries have all pledged to tighten up foreign exchange operations by banks in light of the serious problems caused by overtrading in such markets by European banks. Much more frequent and detailed reporting of foreign exchange operations has been requested by central banks in all five countries.

Regulatory philosophies, however, may differ in terms of bailing out any bank in trouble. The French would probably not allow a

Herstatt, although most of the foreign exchange trading in France is done by the three large nationalized banks. Under present French foreign exchange regulations, French banks are forbidden to maintain positions in foreign currencies vis-a-vis the franc, although more leeway is permitted in dealings between third currencies.[19]

Belgian bank regulators place more emphasis on discount policy, direct controls over domestic credit expansion, and foreign exchange controls than they do on liquidity and reserve ratios, whereas the Netherlands handles such regulation with emphasis on liquidity.

With regard to regulation of foreign banks operating within their borders, for the most part, these nations follow policies of nondiscrimination, or national treatment. Thus, they generally, with a few exceptions, allow foreign banks to operate in a manner similar to their domestic banks, including operating in the investment banking area. However, where domestic banks can become members of stock exchanges, as in Germany, foreign banks cannot.

In France, domestic and foreign banks are subject to uniform national banking and credit regulations. In Germany, a foreign bank may open more than one branch, and each is treated as a separate banking entity, something akin to nationwide branching. U.S. banks in France may enter nonbank activities with little difficulty. French authorities seem to administer domestic law fairly against foreign banks. German law may permit discrimination by disapproval of a foreign branch on the basis of insufficient economic need. In addition, a domestic bank there does not require separate licenses for branches. However, few foreign banks have been discriminated against in Germany on the basis of these statutory provisions.

Amsterdam has become a leading financial center, with 25 foreign banks operating there or in Rotterdam, compared with only 22 Dutch banks overall. These 25 banks have 47 total offices in operation. They are organized as 13 incorporated subsidiaries and 12 branches. It is estimated that their total assets amount to more than 10 percent of all Dutch banking assets. In addition, foreign banks have investments in 10 Dutch banks, and all large Dutch banks have ownership interests in international consortia.[20]

As mentioned above, foreign banks have established either an incorporated subsidiary—a naamloze venootschap (NV), or limited liability company—or a branch, the latter being fully dependent on its parent bank and lacking any corporate identity. Which type of organizational form the foreign bank uses upon entry depends on both general policy of the parent firm as well as legal considerations involved. Branches, for example, do not yet have to publish their annual operating data, although future legislation being considered in the Netherlands will probably end this advantage. The branch has the parent's capital to support its operations.

On the other hand, French banks (2 of the former operate 19 offices in the Netherlands, and 5 Japanese banks operate 6 offices) have established subsidiaries, with 2 of them having 19 offices in the Netherlands. The French banks operate under the philosophy that their Dutch operations are Dutch banks and should, thus, stand on their own.[21]

The Dutch banking law is based on the principle of nondiscrimination with regard to entry, since foreign banks are subject to the same regulations as domestic banks. A credit control bill became law in 1976 and gave the Nederlandsche Bank more authority over all banks operating in the Netherlands, including licensing, monetary policy, solvency and liquidity, and antitrust. The new bill does include one discriminatory section, which gives the Nederlandsche Bank retaliatory powers over non-EEC parent banks. It is a reciprocal power in that it is designed to allow retaliation against any country which might prohibit a Dutch bank from operating or which severely restricted its activities.[22]

In the United Kingdom, the Bank of England uses administrative discretion in authorizing a foreign bank to operate there. It considers the reputation, balance sheet, and assets of the foreign bank. The latter generally must be at least $1 billion. If the Bank of England decides that the foreign bank desires to locate in London merely for prestige, brings little or no international business with it, and/or is not economically feasible, "authorized bank" status will not be granted, and the foreign bank may only be allowed to establish a representative office rather than a full-line office. Thus, the representative office would be prohibited from dealing in international currencies and from certain exchange control transactions.[23]

Foreign banks cannot maintain special clearing accounts with the Bank of England; thus, they are unable to clear gilt-edged securities at the Bank of England, as can U.K. banks. Some other competitive disadvantages of foreign banks vis-a-vis U.K. domestic banks have been discussed. Most of these are of minor consequence to foreign banks operating in the United Kingdom and include the inability for U.S. and some other foreign banks to rediscount sterling paper with the Bank of England or to count it for reserve asset purposes.[24]

CONCLUSIONS

The primary intent of this chapter was to furnish a broad overview of the bank supervisory and regulatory systems in five West European nations. It was not meant to be an in-depth study, because such could fill a large book. Instead, the highlights of bank regulation in such areas as entry, examination, reporting, foreign exchange operations, liquidity and solvency, and foreign banking in the United Kingdom, West Germany, France, Belgium, and the Netherlands were discussed, and some comparisons and contrasts were offered.

As former Deputy Secretary of the U.S. Treasury Stephen S. Gardner stated during testimony before a Senate subcommittee, that banking systems differ widely throughout the industrialized world and that it would be a futile and unproductive exercise to attempt to rationalize the U.S. banking system with those of U.S. trading partners. However, a number of bills have been introduced in the U.S. Congress in recent years to regulate foreign banking in the United States (discussed in Chapter 4). In addition, some discussion has been made of legislating further controls over U.S. banking abroad.

Without a thorough knowledge of bank regulation and supervision by foreign authorities, legislation in the United States may be passed that will be inappropriate and may be discriminatory, lack reciprocity, and impede the further internationalization of banking. One example is the current dispute with regard to the 1975 Securities Act Amendment, regulation by the Securities and Exchange Commission, and Rule 309 administered by the New York Stock Exchange (NYSE). The latter allows a foreign company to become a member of the NYSE if reciprocity exists allowing U.S. firms or banks to be exchange members in the country in which the foreign firm is domiciled. A problem arises between the United States and Canada—in the latter country, no new firms, especially foreign firms, may join the Toronto Stock Exchange, the major Canadian exchange. Thus, under NYSE Rule 309, Canadian firms would be barred from NYSE membership.[25] This represents only one small area in regulatory legislation in the United States. However, proposed legislation here and abroad contains many problem areas similar to this that could result in discrimination.

In addition to the desire by nations to further control foreign banking, a second reason for much of the discussion and consideration of changes, many drastic, in bank supervision and regulation in these countries and the United States is the need to increase the safety and soundness of the banking systems in these countries. Because of the economic problems of recent years, many bank failures have occurred, other banks have suffered heavy losses, and more problems may lie ahead. Thus, such crises are resulting in healthy discussion of more stringent controls on banking. However, without adequate knowledge of bank regulation in the major nations, overreaction may result in too many restrictions on banking at a time when more flexible (although safer) banking is necessary to assist worldwide economic systems out of the recent recession and inflation.

Finally, some evaluation of the bank regulatory systems in other major industrialized nations should be made so that a further comparison with the U.S. supervisory system can be drawn. First of all, the five nations whose banking systems were surveyed in this chapter do not have a dual federal-state bank regulatory system as does the United States. Thus, only federal or centralized regulation is practiced in these nations.

Second, the number of agencies that in any way, shape, or form might be involved at such a centralized level of supervision numbers from one in the United Kingdom (Bank of England) and the Netherlands (the Nederlandsche Bank), to two in Belgium (Banque Nationale de Belgique and Commission Bancaire) and West Germany (Deutsche Bundesbank and Bundesaufsichtsamt für das Kreditwesen, or the Bank Supervisory Authority), to three in France (Banque de France, le Conseil National du Credit, or National Credit Council, and the Commission des Contrôle des Banques, or Bank Control Commission).

Third, the degree of regulatory authority in these nations' bank supervisory agencies has, so far, run the gamut from highly informal to very formal. The British system has been based on a voluntary system, whereby a nod or a wink from a bank regulator can accomplish what might necessitate a cease and desist order in the United States. A comprehensive insurance scheme is adopted voluntarily by the West German Bank Federation before it is enacted into law. In France, where the top three banks are nationalized, the regulatory agencies have a great deal of prestige, and with government backing for the big banks, the system strictly adheres to supervision implemented by relatively small agencies. In Belgium and the Netherlands, some regulation is quite vague when statutes, as well as practice, are considered.

Finally, it appears that stronger regulatory systems are evolving in these countries in much the same manner as is currently occurring in the United States. That is to say, the severe economic crises of the past few years and resulting losses and failures in the banking sector are leading to proposals for new legislation or stronger bank supervisory procedures. It would seem, from the analysis in this chapter, that the areas of deposit insurance, bank examination, and capital/liquidity adequacy need more attention from the government officials responsible for designing bank supervisory systems.

NOTES

1. E. Victor Morgan, Richard Harrington, and George Zis, Banking Systems and Monetary Policy in the EEC (London: Financial Times, 1974), p. 82.
2. Ibid., p. 38.

3. Ibid., p. 26.

4. Ibid., p. 2.

5. Ibid., p. 71.

6. George Blunden, "The Supervision of the U.K. Banking System," Bank of England Quarterly Bulletin 15 (June 1975): 188-89.

7. Albert Dondelinger, "How to Improve International Banking Supervision," Euromoney, June 1975, p. 98.

8. James C. Baker, "Implications of the Federal Reserve's Foreign Bank Act of 1975" (Paper presented at the Annual Meeting of the Southern Finance Association, New Orleans, November 14, 1975), p. 1.

9. Dondelinger, "How to Improve International Banking Supervision"; and Richard A. Debs, "Petro-Dollars, LDCs, and International Banks," Federal Reserve Bank of New York Monthly Review 58 (January 1976): 17.

10. Morgan, Harrington, and Zis, Banking Systems, p. 3.

11. "Puncturing the Eurobubble—No Accidents in France," The Economist World Finance Survey 256 (December 14, 1974): 66.

12. Nicholas Travers, "The Bank of England Finds Old Arithmetic Best," The Bankers Magazine (United Kingdom) 219 (October 1975): 17.

13. Ibid.

14. Carol Parker, "A New Look at Banking Supervision," The Banker 124 (August 1974): 1045.

15. "The Banks and the Bank," The Economist 257 (September 20, 1975): 86.

16. Federal Reserve Bank of New York data.

17. Philip J. Hahn, The Capital Adequacy of Commercial Banks (New York: The American Press, 1966), p. 84.

18. Jess Lukomski, "Bonn Banking Law Seen Providing Best Depositor Protection Anywhere," The Journal of Commerce, February 4, 1976, p. 1.

19. "Puncturing the Eurobubble—No Accidents in France."

20. Paul Catz, "Foreign Banks in the Netherlands," The Banker 125 (November 1975): 1275.

21. Ibid., p. 1278.

22. Ibid.

23. Statement on H.R. 13876, International Banking Act of 1976, Stephen S. Gardner, deputy secretary, U.S. Treasury, before the Subcommittee on Financial Institutions, Senate Committee on Banking, Housing and Urban Affairs, 94th Cong., 2d sess., January 28, 1976, Appendix, pp. 14-18.

24. Ibid., pp. 15-16.

25. Charles Koshetz, "Big Board's Foreign Membership Proposal Holds Threat of Freezing out Canadians," The Money Manager 5 (February 23, 1976): 56.

6

BANKING AND BANK REGULATION
IN THE MIDDLE EAST
AND JAPAN

INTRODUCTION

Outside the United States and Western Europe, most banking of any significance in the non-Communist world is conducted in the Arab countries, Japan, and Iran. Thus, banking and bank regulation and supervision in these areas is the subject of this chapter. The Arab world, primarily as a result of surplus oil revenues, and Iran, for much the same reason, have recently become growth factors in worldwide banking. These surplus oil revenues, along with the almost geometric increase in per capita incomes and concomitant living standards in these countries, have necessitated a large growth in their banking sectors. These banking systems have also begun to branch out into other areas of the world, including the United States.

Japan has, since World War II and reconstruction, expanded worldwide through its trading companies and their related banks. Much of this growth has already been discussed in previous chapters involving foreign banking in the United States. Japanese banks have branches in many states where permitted and have established subsidiaries in California in order to tap the retail banking market there.

AN ARAB NATION PROFILE

Banking and financial operations in the Arab nations have grown dramatically during the past few years, since the large increases of oil prices imposed by the Arab oil-producing nations and the concomitant growth of the so-called petrodollar market. The petrodollar market and oil activity has created great interest in banking and investment in the Middle East.

However, bottlenecks have resulted from environmental conditions, as well as from traditional, cultural, social, legal, and religious heritages. These bottlenecks in the financial systems of these nations have hindered the arrival of investment goods into the Arab countries. Many foreign banks have opened branches in the area.

This chapter examines the banking structure in selected Arab nations, including the Gulf states of Kuwait, Bahrain, and the United Arab Emirates (UAE), as well as Egypt and Jordan. Some discussion of other systems is included, as well as the problems in Beirut and how banks that were located there have adapted to the Civil War in Lebanon.

The magnitude of banking and services available, including foreign aspects, will be measured and analyzed. Bank supervision and regulation in these selected Arab nations will be analyzed and evaluated. The focus is on the banking needs of the Arab world in light of current environmental conditions.

Environment

The Arab nations (including those not covered in this chapter) show contrasts in several ways. Per capita income of the UAE was $13,500 in 1976, while it was only $150 in the Sudan at the same time. Population was 36.4 million in Egypt and only 190,000 in Qatar. Banking structures were very sophisticated in Lebanon before the war, are centralized in Iraq and Algeria, and are public-private in the Gulf area.[1]

Aside from the demographic and income differences in these countries, the drastic increase in the last few years in the price of oil produced by most of these countries has added tremendous investable funds to their exchange reserves. Middle East members of OPEC had a surplus in 1975 of $36 billion.[2] The surplus of these countries is estimated to have been about $28 billion in 1976.[3] These resources have had to be channeled or recycled through money markets and banks to investment areas and have come to be referred to as petrodollars when they have been recycled through the international maze of Eurocurrency markets and facilitating institutions. For the past three years, oil states have been the leading suppliers of funds to the international money markets. But their banks have remained insignificant in international lending.

The reasons for this dichotomy are many. Arabs are conservative investors who desire control over their funds; short-term, relatively liquid investments; or assets, such as real estate. They have also been overinvolved with their own development, so surplus funds have been kept at home. However, in the first half of 1976, it has been estimated that $12 to $15 billion of surplus oil revenues were collected by Saudi Arabia, Kuwait, the UAE, and Qatar. Most of these funds were recycled through foreign banks; thus, Arabs paid much of these revenues in commissions and fees to these banks. Only about 5 percent of the $28 billion raised in international bonds or syndicated credits was directly financed by Arab banks. [4]

In addition to the petrodollars created from surplus oil revenues, a growing market in the currencies of Arab countries has also increased the need for improved banking facilities in these nations. A number of reasons can be cited for this growing market in Arab currencies. They include: (1) the stronger financial position of the Arab world, (2) the removal of foreign exchange restrictions by some of these governments, (3) better international communications, (4) a nationalistic desire to internationalize their currencies, (5) improved payment/clearing systems, and (6) the emergence of strong central banking institutions. [5] Among the currencies from this area most widely traded in international foreign exchange markets are the Saudi Arabian riyal, the Kuwaiti dinar, the UAE dirham, the Lebanese pound, and the Qatar riyal. [6]

Islamic Heritage

One major problem that may have contributed to the inhibited growth of the banking sector in Arab countries stems from Islam, the major religion of the Middle East. The Islamic religion bans the receiving of interest and makes interest and usury synonomous. A banking system is necessary to essential growth in these countries, so a substitute that satisfies Islam is necessary to banking.

For some time that alternative has been the availability of local banks to serve the public's needs in which participation or joint venture is the means of organization. [7] Moslem theologians posit that Islam permits participation in the profits of a financial institution in which the sole asset is capital. Profits and losses are shared by participants according to certain agreed formulas. An acceptable accounting system and time limit in the investment transaction between partners are important ingredients of the system. Thus, interest-free Islamic banks have been established in Egypt as local savings banks. These were replaced in 1971 by the Nasser Social Bank (with several branches), and it operates as a national Islamic bank.

In August 1974, Arab state officials agreed to establish the Islamic Development Bank (IDB), with capital of $2.4 billion. The articles of agreement to establish this bank were signed by 26 Arab countries, with Saudi Arabia being the main contributor. The IDB will invest in other banks and companies in member states, as well as in economic and social development projects in these countries. Deposits of states, groups, and individuals will be accepted, and the IDB will encourage trade between member countries. [8] This concept as a means of serving as an alternative to the Islamic prohibition of interest will certainly be controversial in years to come; it remains to be seen whether it will lead to development of banking in Arab countries.

The Beirut Problem

Another situation that although labeled a problem may actually lead to wider development of banking in the Arab countries is the Lebanese Civil War. This war has nearly eliminated Beirut as the financial capital of the Middle East. The question to be answered concerns what city or cities will fill this gap.

A few years ago, Beirut was considered the Switzerland of the Middle East. During the Lebanese Civil War, downtown Beirut became a combat zone, and the bankers fled. The recent ceasefire seems to be working, and some banks have returned. Other reports persist that Cairo or Abu Dhabi will replace Beirut.[9] The Chase Manhattan branch building was still intact, and that bank's records were still extant.[10]

Other students of Middle East banking believe that (1) Dubai is a possible replacement for Beirut; (2) that Kuwait has a long history of financial operations and is considered the most sophisticated Arab banking center; and (3) that Bahrain, besides being in a favorable time zone between London and Singapore, is the most aggressive candidate because of its foreign exchange dealers' access to 300 traders around the world, the 32 banks licensed to operate there, excellent communications (which Cairo does not have), and the permission by the government for international banks to operate as offshore banking units.[11]

When the fighting began, book assets in Beirut were actually only $8 billion, and daily foreign exchange trading there never exceeded $50 million. However, because Beirut had excellent communications and a central location; was an entrepot for Syria, Jordan, Iran, and Iraq; and because of its investment banking activities vis-a-vis New York City and its bank secrecy laws, it was considered a financial center. Some of the banks may return.[12] As the following analysis will imply, if the banks do not go back to Beirut—and some probably will not—the other centers, such as Cairo, Kuwait, Bahrain, Abu Dhabi, and Dubai, will be strengthened by the growth of domestic and foreign banks.

The Problem of Boycotting

A final problem that should be discussed before analyzing the structure and regulation of banking in selected Arab nations is the

Arab blacklisting of "Zionist" banks and the quid pro quo practice by some Jewish financial institutions in other parts of the world. Some Arab banking institutions have withdrawn from management groups of Eurobond issues because of the presence of even a few Jewish banks among the 100 or more banks in the overall group. A prime example is the withdrawal of the Kuwait International Investment Company, one of the Arab world's most experienced institutions, from the under-writing of two Eurobond issues because of the presence of Jewish banks among the group's banks. [13]

Among the principal Jewish banks boycotted by Arab financial institutions are S. G. Warburg, the London and Paris Rothschild banks, and Lazard Frères in Paris. These banks have supported the Israeli cause. In addition, some countries have boycotted, or have threatened to boycott, Israeli activities because of their reliance on Arab oil. Such restrictions on internationalization of banking in the Middle East can only impede the growth of banking there.

STRUCTURE AND REGULATION OF BANKING IN SELECTED ARAB COUNTRIES

Egypt

The Egyptian banking system consists of four commercial banks and two groups of specialized institutions, one concerned with agricultural credit and cooperative banks and the other with two mortgage banks. The system is topped off by the Central Bank, created by a 1951 law that converted the National Bank of Egypt from a de facto to a de jure central bank. The Central Bank, commercial banks, non-commercial banks, and regulation of credit were placed under tight controls by the Banking and Credit Law of 1957. [14] The Central Bank was empowered to: (1) regulate the availability and cost of credit; (2) take measures to alleviate economic and financial problems in Egypt; (3) regulate financial institutions to ensure their safety and soundness; and (4) manage the gold and foreign assets of the country A commercial bank was defined by this law as an entity that accepts demand deposits or time deposits payable within one year. Only as settlement of debts to them are they allowed to invest in movables, real estate, or their own shares. They can own up to 25 percent of the shares of companies if this ownership does not exceed the bank's paid-up capital and reserves. Such banks are supervised by the Department of Bank Control of the Central Bank.

The four commercial banks are the National Bank of Egypt, the Misr Bank, the Bank of Alexandria, and the Bank of Cairo. The National Bank of Egypt has more than 90 branches and agencies in Egypt, and upon the nationalization of banks in 1960-61, it acquired branches of Banca Commerciale Italiana, Banco Italo-Egiziano, the First National City Bank of New York, the Commercial Bank of Greece, and the National Bank of Greece. The National Bank of Egypt and Misr Bank are both nationalized; the latter accounts for about 45 percent of the country's banking units. Misr's capital is £4 million, its reserves are £13 million, and it acquired four minor banks in 1963, as well as the Bank of Port Said. Misr Bank specializes in financing cotton and rice production.

The Bank of Alexandria was formed in 1957 to take over Barclays Bank branches in Egypt and provides medium- and long-term loans to the private industrial sector through a network of 50 branches. Finally, the Bank of Cairo has capital of £3 million and 64 branches, as well as offices in Saudi Arabia, Abu Dhabi, and Bahrain; it finances the services sector.

Some leading indicators for these four commercial banks on an aggregate basis show the dramatic change between 1970 and 1974 and are presented in Table 6.1. Total assets have grown from £972.1 million in 1965 to £2.09 billion in 1974. Total capital during this period grew from £64.0 million to £130.0 million. Deposits grew from £582.0 million to £1.13 billion. Loans and advances increased from £495.2 million to £1.06 billion.[15]

Some mention should be made of the Crédit Foncier Egyptien, a mortgage bank that was established in 1880 and is the oldest financial institution in Egypt, and two regional and international banking institutions located there. These latter are the Arab African Bank, a joint venture between Egypt and Kuwait, with £20 million in capital, and the Arab International Bank, a bank that carries out full banking operations in convertible currencies and whose £26 million in capital is subscribed by Egypt, Libya, Oman, the UAE, and Qatar. Banking by either bank in Egypt may be carried out only through local banks.

Foreign banks are allowed to operate in Egypt if they are established as joint ventures, with Egyptian investors owning at least 51 percent of the venture's capital. Some European and American banks have participated in joint ventures, such as the Egyptian Iranian Investment Bank and Misr International Bank.[16] During the 1974-75 period, Cairo Barclays International Bank, Chase National Bank of Egypt, and Egyptian American Bank (American Express) were founded under this arrangement. In addition, the American Express International Banking Corporation is located in Cairo, as are the representative offices of Banco Commerciale Italiana, Deutsche Bank, and Dresdner Bank.

Bank supervision increased in intensity after the 1971 embezzlement scandal that occurred in Bank Misr.[17] A dozen prominent bank

TABLE 6.1

Leading Indicators, Egyptian Commercial Banks
(millions of pounds)

Item	1961	1974	Percent Change during Period
Total assets/liabilities	520.1	2,093.3	+302.5
Capital and reserves	49.6	130.0	+162.1
Deposits	389.6	1,128.7	+189.7
Borrowings from Central Bank	25.5	414.0	+1,523.5
Due to banks	21.7	181.2	+735.0
Cash and balances with Central Bank	82.9	289.0	+248.6
Banks and correspondents	48.9	475.9	+873.2
Securities and investments	112.6	117.0	+3.9
Loans and advances	249.8	1,062.1	+325.2

Source: Philip Thorn, Banking Structures and Sources of Finance in the Middle East (London: Banker Research Unit, 1975), p. 12.

officials and a sum of $1.1 million were involved. Total independence of the Central Bank from the administration was advocated, as well as increased supervisory powers.

A 1975 law gives Egyptian banks, as well as the Central Bank, full authority to supervise their operations in accordance with national economic planning. By this law, they are not bound to salary and wage restrictions of the civil service schedule, and they may import necessary equipment without the usual import licenses. This law makes Egyptian banks more competitive vis-a-vis foreign banks operating there or in the area. [18]

Jordan

Jordan is a nation without oil and, thus, depends heavily on outside support. Because of a number of favorable environmental factors, 50 foreign companies, along with several international banks, have established a presence in Amman. Chase Manhattan located there in early 1976. [19] A liberalization of foreign investment restrictions has encouraged this immigration, along with good communications and relative political stability. Foreign banks may set up in Amman, for example, by opening nonresident bank accounts in any currency, with no restrictions on currency movements.

Until 1949, Jordan was dominated by foreign banks, particularly British banks. At present, 12 commercial banks are operating in the East Bank of Jordan, as noted in Table 6.2. They operate a total of 70 offices. Four Jordanian banks have 27 offices outside the country.[20]

Jordanian financial institutions are of three types: the Central Bank of Jordan, the commercial banks, and specialized credit institutions. The relative size of these three groups can be seen in Table 6.3.

The Central Bank of Jordan is banker and fiscal agent for the government, has control over monetary policy, and supervises licensed banks to ensure their safety and soundness. The Central Bank prescribes the method that banks will use to compute a minimum liquid assets ratio and may prescribe a minimum capital/deposits ratio for individual banks. Several crises have been handled relatively well by the Central Bank, including banking problems resulting from the Arab-Israeli wars, the Intra Bank failure of 1966, the 1967 pound sterling devaluation, and the 1970 internal strife in Jordan.

The relative sizes of the commercial banks operating as of December 31, 1973, in Jordan—four Jordanian and five foreign banks —are presented in Table 6.4. Three banks were licensed as of year-end 1973 but were not yet in operation at that time.

Banks in Jordan, especially domestic banks, have a high degree of liquidity. This is a result of the absence of a capital market for

TABLE 6.2

Commercial Banks in Jordan

Nationality of Bank	Number of Banks	Number of Bank Offices, including Head Office
Jordanian	4	43
Lebanese	1	1
Iraqi	1	2
Egyptian	1	6
British	2	15
American	2	2
Luxembourg	1	1
Total	12	70

Source: Philip Thorn, Banking Structures and Sources of Finance in the Middle East (London: Banker Research Unit, 1975), p. 29.

TABLE 6.3

Deposits and Assets of the Banking System, Jordan,
October 31, 1974
(millions of Jordanian dinars)

Agency	Total Deposits	Total Assets
Central Bank of Jordan	28.31	156.09
Commercial banks	103.52	133.94
Domestic banks only	66.47	86.19
Specialized credit institutions	2.48*	29.03
Total	134.31	319.06

*The Housing Bank only.

Source: Philip Thorn, Banking Structures and Sources of Finance in the Middle East (London: Banking Research Unit, 1975), p. 30.

banks to deal in highly liquid assets, as well as the conservative behavior of Jordanian bankers in extending credit.

Thus, it appears that Jordan's banking system is more open, especially to foreign investment, than is the case in Egypt. Privately owned banks are tolerated, but the Central Bank does not exercise the supervisory control over these banks that is (perhaps) implicit in the Banking Law of 1971. It has certain powers but does not seem to exercise them. Specific regulations emanating from the Banking Law, as well as the openness and competition, especially from foreign banks, have kept problems from occurring, as a result of informal regulation and supervision.

Kuwait

This small Persian Gulf sheikhdom is one of the economic highlights of the Arab world, all because of the discovery of oil many years ago. For example, Kuwait's oil production incurred a recession in early 1977. Because of stockpiling before 1977 oil price increases, declining industrial production in parts of the world, and storms that hindered Persian Gulf oil loadings early in 1977, the monthly oil output in January-February 1977 declined more than 50 percent from December 1976. Still, 1976 per capita income amounted to $23,500, and reserve assets totaled $20 billion at year-end.[21]

TABLE 6.4

Total Deposits and Credits of Commercial Banks, Jordan, December 31, 1973
(millions of Jordanian dinars)

Bank	Deposits[a]	Percent Share of All Banks	Credits	Percent Share of All Banks
Jordanian banks				
Arab Bank Ltd.	31.61	36.4	16.31	26.9
The Cairo-Amman Bank	9.36	10.8	13.53	22.3
Jordan National Bank	7.99	9.2	4.49	7.4
Bank of Jordan Ltd.	7.60	8.7	4.70	7.7
Foreign banks				
Grindlays Bank Ltd. (United Kingdom)	17.29	19.9	13.55	22.3
British Bank of the Middle East (United Kingdom)	7.02	8.1	3.14	5.2
Arab Land Bank (Egypt)	4.13	4.8	3.66	6.0
Rafidain Bank (Iraq)	0.80	0.9	0.76	1.2
Bank Al-Mashrek (Lebanon)	1.03	1.2	0.59	1.0
Total	86.83[b]	100.0	60.73[c]	100.0

[a]Excludes interbank deposits.

[b]More than 90 percent of these deposits were in banks operating in the East Bank of Jordan.

[c]Nearly 90 percent of the outstanding bank credit was located in the East Bank of Jordan.

Source: Philip Thorn, Banking Structures and Sources of Finance in the Middle East (London: Banking Research Unit, 1975), p. 38.

The banking system in Kuwait consists of the Central Bank and six commercial banks, all fully owned by Kuwaitis. The Central Bank, like most foreign central banks, is the note-issuing authority for the government, advises and serves the government as its bank, exercises monetary policy, and supervises the nation's banking system. However, its supervision consists primarily of data collection concerning domestic and foreign activities of Kuwaiti banks.

The six commercial banks are the National Bank of Kuwait, the Commercial Bank of Kuwait, the Gulf Bank, Al-Ahli Bank of Kuwait, Burkan Bank, and the Bank of Kuwait and the Middle East. The latter bank is equally and jointly owned by the private and government sectors. The first five listed are privately owned banks.[22] Together, they operate 84 branches in Kuwait, so that the country seems overbanked for a population of 1 million.[23] The sources of funds for Kuwaiti banks are shown in Table 6.5.

The 699.2 million dinar total deposits shown in Table 6.5 can be further analyzed. About 87.8 percent of these deposits were made by individuals, the remainder by the government. About 60.0 percent of the total deposits were held as time deposits, savings deposits were 19.5 percent of the total, and demand deposits comprised the remainder.

The Central Bank has formulated a liquidity ratio for banks that includes a definition of what assets are liquid. Banks, according to government desire, should maintain a 25 percent liquidity ratio, with 7.5 percent of this total to be kept in Kuwaiti dinars. No reserve ratios are imposed by the Central Bank.[24]

Foreign banks are not allowed to open branches in Kuwait, but they can participate in investment companies, a specialized area needing outside expertise. The branch system of domestic banks, 1 for every 12,000 of the population, or about 1 branch for every 1,600 of the working population, seems to be quite sufficient for Kuwait's needs, without the influx of foreign competition. In fact, the Kuwaiti banking system is growing at a rate in excess of the economy as a whole. The reasons for this are the spread of the banking habit in Kuwait and the increased international activity of Kuwaiti banks.[25] Thus, although foreign banks are not allowed to form branches in Kuwait, international activity of Kuwaiti banks is a prime factor for banking growth in that country. In fact, because no money market exists there, Kuwaiti banks are entirely dependent on international markets for their liquidity. See Table 6.6 for an indication of the foreign activity of Kuwaiti banks.

Bahrain

Despite Kuwait's economic growth and long experience in international investment operations, Bahrain has been suggested as a pos-

TABLE 6.5

Sources of Funds, Kuwaiti Banks, September 30, 1974
(millions of Kuwaiti dinars)

Sources of Funds	Amount	Percentage of Total
Residential deposits	699.2	71.3
Foreign liabilities	118.0	12.0
Capital funds	47.8	4.9
Other liabilities	115.5	11.8
Total	980.5	100.0

Source: Philip Thorn, Banking Structures and Sources of Finance in the Middle East (London: Banking Research Unit, 1975), p. 177.

sible alternative for Middle East operations of international banks. Bahrain was the first Gulf country to produce oil (1932), although it has only 20 years of proven reserves remaining. It has excellent communications facilities, a small population and infrastructure, and is now serviced by the British Concorde. It is in a favorable time zone in relation to London and Singapore and has a long history of political stability under the autocratic rule of Sheikh Isa Bin Sulman al Khalifa. The nation has strong ties with Saudi Arabia and Kuwait.[26] However, the autocratic rule in the country may not be quite so stable (the sheikh set up a representative national assembly in 1974 but dissolved it in 1975, just as he opened the country to foreign bankers).[27]

Bahrain's banking system includes Arab, U.S., Pakistani, Iranian, and British banks, and 32 banks overall have been licensed to operate offshore banking units (OBUs) in Bahrain. Among these are leading banks from the nations just mentioned, as well as Brazil, the Netherlands, Scandinavia, Belgium, and France.

The Bahrain Monetary Agency (BMA) was formed in 1973 and became a full central bank in 1975. Bank regulation and taxation are favorable; thus, major banks have been encouraged to establish there. No capital or reserve requirements are imposed, and the BMA goal is to have the world's top 50 banks and leading Arab banks operating in Bahrain.

The BMA will allow OBUs to accept deposits and make loans to non-Bahrain residents in foreign currencies, deal in foreign ex-

TABLE 6.6

Foreign Assets Held by Commercial Banks, Kuwait, 1970–76
(millions of Kuwaiti dinars)

Year	Deposits with Foreign Banks	Advances to Non-residents	Foreign Securities[a]	Total Foreign Assets	Total Assets	Foreign Assets to Total Assets (percent)
1970	354.1	55.5	29.9	439.5	610.6	72
1971	394.6	49.2	34.1	477.9	679.8	70
1972	369.4	61.1	83.0	513.5	736.7	70
1973	293.9	86.7	98.5	479.1	803.4	60
1974	384.1	98.5	78.8	561.4	1,037.6	54
1975	402.3	116.3	95.8	614.4	1,300.7	47
1976[b]	346.5	113.5	107.4	567.4	1,339.5	42

[a]Consist mainly of bills and intermediate and long-term securities.
[b]First quarter of 1976.

Source: A. D. Issa and H. Elsaid, "It's Got the Banks, but . . . ," Euromoney, June 1977, p. 184.

143

change with non-Bahrain residents, and deal in money and foreign exchange with authorized banks in Bahrain. The total offshore market for OBUs at present is only $1.5 billion, compared with a Eurocurrency market of $500+ billion and a $12 billion Asian currency market. But the fact that foreign exchange operations are not taxed on their profits makes Bahrain a unique center, capable of a great deal of potential growth in this area.[28] In addition, the possibility of a single Gulf currency and potential Arab monetary fund adds to Bahrain's potential as an Arab financial center.[29]

The UAE

The UAE is a federation of seven constituent emirates located on the coastal area of the Saudi peninsula. The most important of these are Abu Dhabi, Dubai, Ajman, and Sharjah. The UAE was formed five years ago, and among the federation's objectives are economic and financial integration.

Net total oil receipts of the UAE have risen to more than $5 billion annually; although imports of machinery, transport equipment, manufactures, and food items have risen dramatically in recent years, the UAE has had large balance-of-payments surpluses. Thus, the UAE has extended large amounts of aid to other nations, bilaterally and through international institutions, and has carried on diversification of local industry and development of financial intermediaries.

Commercial banks dominate the financial system and have nearly complete freedom in which to operate. In 1973, the UAE Currency Board, the country's monetary authority, was established. At that time, 20 commercial banks were operating, 14 of them foreign. In 1976, 45 banks were licensed and 30 were operating, with 200 branches working and another 97 approved. Of these 30 banks, 26 were foreign and represented some of the world's top banks. Banking is very competitive in the UAE, especially since the population is only 450,000.[30]

Total banking assets nearly quadrupled between year-end 1973 and September 1975, rising from 3.6 billion dirhams to 13.2 billion dirhams. About 7 billion dirhams, or over 50 percent, is invested in foreign assets. About 43 percent of total bank assets is outstanding bank credit, with trade accounting for more than half of bank credit.[31]

Although the UAE Currency Board is the monetary authority, it exercises little more than a data collection function. Banks are required to furnish monthly reports concerning aggregate loans, deposits, foreign currency transactions, and balance sheet items. The few Currency Board supervisory regulations actually imposed are to alleviate cutthroat competition because of the overbanked situation in the UAE.[32] The Currency Board imposes no foreign exchange controls and no statutory reserve or liquidity requirements. The Currency Board assures a smoothly functioning foreign exchange market, by regulating the exchange rate for the dirham, and prescribes deposit rates where needed.[33]

The Currency Board is considering tighter supervision, and a new banking law is presently being considered. The growth rate and bank competition will necessitate such moves on the part of the government there.

Other developments in the area of significance to Arab banking include the decision by the UAE Currency Board in early 1976 to permit the establishment of 12 OBUs to compete with those allowed by Bahrain. The efforts of the UAE Currency Board in working with other Gulf states toward a common currency should be noted. It seems that the Currency Board's rise to eminence in that area, along with the Bahrain Monetary Agency and the Central Bank of Kuwait, has resulted in major development of the money markets in that area.

Other Nations

The preceding sections have included a discussion of only a few Arab nations and their banking systems. A few words can be said about some of the others.[34] (Lebanon has not been mentioned, except for suggestions for a Beirut substitute.) Syria has a completely nationalized banking system, with a central bank and five local commercial banks. A limited number of foreign banks may be allowed to operate in free zones. Saudi Arabia has an underdeveloped system, with the Saudi Arabia Monetary Authority acting as central bank. The system has two local banks and ten foreign banks, and a plan to nationalize foreign branches may be imminent.[35] Qatar's system is overseen by the Qatar Monetary Agency and consists of 2 local and 12 foreign banks.

Elsewhere on the Arabian peninsula, Oman's system is controlled in a limited sense by the Omani Currency Board and consists of 15 local banks or branches of foreign banks. In the Yemen Arab Republic, a central bank established in 1971 oversees one local and five foreign banks. In South Yemen, the Bank of Yemen is the central bank, and one commercial bank operates there, the result of a 1969 nationalization of foreign banks.

The Maghreb region has two mixed and two nationalized systems. In Algeria, three nationalized banks have emerged, along with a central bank. In Morocco, 13 local banks and 1 foreign bank operate under a central bank. Six of the local banks have foreign participation.

In Tunisia, 11 local and 4 foreign banks operate under a central bank. In Libya, a central bank governs a system of six banks nationalized in 1970.

Finally, in the Sudan, all banks were nationalized in 1970. There is a central bank and five commercial banks. A law was recently passed permitting private ownership in banks by Sudanese.

Conclusions and Implications

The banking systems of the Arab countries remain underdeveloped overall, but since the vast surplus oil revenues of the last few years, some systems there have had to develop rapidly. Banks in these countries are fully owned by the government, completely privately owned, or mixed, depending on the nation.

Besides the recycling of petrodollars, other problems need to be solved. A possible substitute for Beirut as a financial center may be slowly evolving. A common Gulf currency and regional monetary authority might result in international harmonization of banking in that area. Furthermore, the central banks in most of these countries exercise very informal, if any, supervision over their banks.

Development of financial systems in the Arab world will facilitate the economic and social development of these nations. Banking in this area still depends to a large extent on foreign assistance for the operations of banking in a given country, or the functioning as financial intermediary for Arab investment funds. The latter activity merely transfers some of the area's oil revenues to foreign banks in the form of fees and commissions.

As the most developed or sophisticated systems grow stronger and integrate, particularly the UAE Currency Board, Bahrain Monetary Authority, and Kuwait Central Bank, the banking structures in these countries will develop, become more competitive, and evolve into a more significant factor in the world's leading financial centers, along with New York, London, and Singapore.

BANKING IN JAPAN AND ITS REGULATION AND SUPERVISION

Japan has a banking system that has undergone significant changes since the end of World War II. The Japanese banking system can be classified into three areas: (1) the Bank of Japan—the central bank for Japan; (2) private financial institutions, consisting of commercial banks, specialized financial institutions, and miscellaneous institutions, such as securities and insurance firms; and (3) government financial institutions, such as the Japan Development Bank and the Export-Import Bank of Japan. The relative sizes of the investment of financial institutions are shown in Table 6.7, and the combined balance sheet of all commercial banks in Japan is presented in Table 6.8.

The Bank of Japan is the central bank and, as such, controls the banking sector and the money supply by acting as note-issuing bank, the banker's bank, and banker for the central government. The Bank of Japan executes monetary policy through its discount policy, open market operations, and reserve requirements on deposits in much the same way as the U.S. Federal Reserve System operates.

Japanese banks are classified as ordinary banks, long-term credit banks, and foreign exchange banks. Ordinary banks were authorized by the Banking Law of 1927 and consist of city banks and local banks. These two types, as can be seen in Table 6.7, have 35 percent of all deposits in Japanese financial institutions. Ordinary banks control nearly 42 percent of all deposits. Foreign exchange banks were established by the Foreign Exchange Bank Law of 1954, and long-term credit banks were authorized by the Long-Term Credit Bank Law of 1952. [36]

City and local banks engage mostly in short-term financing, conduct commercial banking operations, and occasionally extend medium- and long-term loans. Most of their deposit resources are from time deposits. They must obtain permission from the Ministry of Finance to do foreign exchange trading.

As of March 1974, there were 76 ordinary banks; of these, 13 were city banks and 63 were local banks. City banks branch throughout the nation and are very large organizations, whereas most local banks are medium- and small-sized. The Bank of Tokyo, a city bank, is also a specialized foreign exchange bank.

About 60 percent of city banks' loans are to firms with more than 100 million yen capital, whereas 60 percent of local banks' lending is to companies with smaller than 100 million yen in capital. Long-term credit banks engage in long-term financing by raising funds from debenture issues. Their deposit business is limited to wholesale operations. Three such banks are operating: the Industrial Bank of Japan, the Long-Term Credit Bank of Japan, and the Nippon Fudosan Bank. In addition to these banks, Japan has trust banks, small business financial institutions, mutual loan and savings banks, credit associations, credit cooperatives, and special agricultural, forestry, and fisheries financing institutions.

Bank Regulation and Supervision

The Bank of Japan is sole monetary authority, while the Ministry of Finance is supervisory authority. The latter agency has power

TABLE 6.7

Principal Funds and Investments of Japanese Financial Institutions, December 31, 1973

	Deposits, Savings, and Bank Debentures		Loans and Discounts		Total of Securities	
	Billions of Yen	Per-cent	Billions of Yen	Per-cent	Billions of Yen	Per-cent
City banks	43,706	22.0	39,010	23.6	6,839	19.4
Local banks	25,834	13.0	21,152	12.8	3,838	10.9
Trust banks	3,322	1.7	2,854	1.7	999	2.8
Long-term credit banks	10,313	5.2	8,835	5.3	1,603	4.5
Total, all banks	83,176	41.9	71,853	43.5	13,280	37.7
Trust accounts	14,508	7.3	9,400	5.8	3,400	9.7
Mutual loan and savings banks	11,880	6.0	9,575	5.8	1,174	3.3
Credit associations	14,615	7.4	11,986	7.3	1,309	3.7
Agricultural cooperatives	11,578	5.8	5,757	3.5	425	1.2
Trust Fund Bureau	26,706	13.4	19,291	11.7	7,478	21.2
Government financial institutions	—	—	12,987	7.9	97	0.3
Total, including others	198,714	100.0	165,150	100.0	35,239	100.0
Overlapping accounts	21,913	—	12,427	—	6,471	—
Net total	176,801	—	152,723	—	28,768	—

Source: Philip Thorn, ed., Banking Structures and Sources of Finance in the Far East (London: The Financial Times, 1974), p. 2.

148

TABLE 6.8

Principal Accounts of All Japanese Banks, End of March 1974
(billions of yen)

Accounts	City Banks	Local Banks	Long–Term Credit Banks
Assets			
Cash deposits with others	5,696	2,429	820
Call loans	75	544	39
Securities	7,015	3,949	1,633
Government securities	620	401	212
Local government securities	1,025	841	211
Corporate bonds	3,237	2,235	645
Stocks and shares	1,763	306	439
Loans and discounts	39,912	21,620	9,103
Bills discounted	10,535	6,040	117
Loans	29,377	15,579	8,987
Foreign exchange	3,589	95	223
Liabilities			
Deposits	44,007	26,494	1,854
Current deposits	5,162	2,603	268
Ordinary deposits	6,787	5,438	196
Deposits at notice	4,901	2,299	842
Time deposits	23,317	14,407	446
Bank debentures issued	364	—	8,619
Borrowed money	1,825	84	46
Call money	1,171	45	29
Foreign exchange	1,075	23	231
Reserves	1,092	1,475	176
Capital	625	275	133
Total	57,202	31,697	12,841

Source: Philip Thorn, ed., Banking Structures and Sources of Finance in the Far East (London: The Financial Times, 1974), p. 10.

over licensing of banks and the approval of the establishment of branches and mergers or dissolution of banks, as well as new branches.

The Ministry of Finance, in addition, can request a bank's reports of operations and examine the bank at any time. It approves capital levels, may close banks for illegal acts of their directors or officers, and has authority to approve foreign exchange dealing under the Foreign Exchange and Foreign Trade Control Law of 1949. The Ministry of Finance also advises banks on their average ratios of loans to deposits, of liquid assets to deposits, of fixed assets for business use to owned capital, and net worth to term-end deposits, as well as dividend payments.

Japanese bank supervision seems to be primarily in two forms: the use of established rules covering uniform bank accounting procedures and guidelines for balance sheet ratios (the latter designed to avoid overloaned situations). The loan-to-deposit ratio is especially useful in this area. By establishing uniform rules for accounting procedures and enforcing a number of ratios, less emphasis is required on bank examination. The so-called overloan problem is controlled on a bank-by-bank basis. The Ministry of Finance also enforces several vague restrictions concerning nonbank financial activities, for example, leasing, credit cards, factoring, insurance, and residential financing, as well as nonfinancial investments, involving travel agencies, warehouses, and so forth. Thus, Japan has placed more emphasis on standardization of reporting practices and use of ratio analysis to ensure the safety and soundness of banking.

Japan is a nation whose firms and banks maintain very high leverage levels. Since business, banking, and government are so intertwined in Japan, little need has been felt on the part of bank regulatory officials to regulate capital adequacy levels other than for the Ministry of Finance to establish and enforce certain balance sheet ratios or to advise on such ratios (discussed earlier).

In Japan, foreign exchange trading is done by the large public banks, whose management has been told by the Ministry of Finance and the Bank of Japan not to maintain open positions against the yen, so that the rules must be violated for speculation to exist. Japanese bankers do maintain open positions frequently in other currencies, such as dollars and sterling. The bigness of these banks implies breadth of management and internal controls. In addition, foreign exchange traders are not experts in trading alone but are bank officials who spend a few years in each department to gain broad experience; thus, they do not develop the expertise leading to the self-confidence that is necessary to maintain a large market operation on their own. This has served as a further control.[37]

Opening a foreign branch in Japan entails playing a complex game, because of the multitude of restrictions placed on de novo foreign branching. A representative office, for example, must precede the new branch. The representative office can do little banking and must hire a Japanese adviser to help get the branch. Parties must be held; much socializing will be done; and unofficial and informal discussions may go on for years before the Ministry of Finance grants the approval. Although the system could be legally circumvented, few, if any, officials of foreign banks would think of resorting to a process other than the "ritual."[38]

Once a foreign bank has been licensed to operate in Japan— there are at least 45 foreign banks with 67 branches and 60 to 70 foreign banks with representative offices in Tokyo—it is, in principle, treated as any Japanese bank. However, the share of banking operations held in Japan by foreign banks is only about 1.5 percent. Besides the considerable regulation of entry mentioned above, other reasons for the relatively small amount of foreign bank operations in Japan may be a result of the Japanese Banking Law, which presents a myriad of regulations for all banks operating in Japan.[39]

For example, there are 58 foreign banks operating in Japan, 22 of them branches of U.S. banks. They are referred to as gaijin (foreign) banks. Very tight surveillance and control is exercised over them by the Bank of Japan and the Ministry of Finance. Although some liberalization is expected in minor areas, foreign banks in Japan are prohibited from taking savings deposits, are subject to quotas on loans, restricted on the amount of local funding they can obtain, limited as to the amount of foreign exchange they can bring into the country, and have their currency swaps controlled. These controls on foreign banking impede Tokyo's role as an international financial center.

Finally, the closed structure of Japanese industry makes market penetration difficult. The closed structure of Japanese society makes recruitment of qualified Japanese employees difficult. Primarily, foreign bankers' interest in Japan as an area of operations is quite a recent phenomenon. It does appear that regardless of the hodge-podge of regulations facing foreign banks operating in the United States, it is easier for a Japanese bank to establish American operations than it is for a U.S. bank to enter the Japanese market.

BANKING IN IRAN AND ITS REGULATION AND SUPERVISION

Iran also has participated in the OPEC surplus revenues, so much so that economic bottlenecks during 1975-77 have caused the government there to cut back on several output sectors in order to keep inflation from becoming too rampant. This country of 32 million had oil revenues that quintupled in two years to $18.2 billion in 1974-75.[40]

TABLE 6.9

Banks in Iran, March 20, 1974

Banks	Founded	Capital (millions of rials)		Number of Branches
		Authorized and Issued Capital	Paid-up Capital	
Agricultural Co-operative Bank of Iran	1933	21,058.8	21,058.8	197
Agricultural Development Bank of Iran	1968	4,000.0	3,870.0	9
Bank Assnaf Iran	1958	100.0	100.0	441
Bank Bazargani Iran	1949	500.0	500.0	215
Bank Bimeh Iran	1958	400.0	400.0	32
Bank Dariush	1974	2,000.0	1,000.0	1
Development and Investment Bank of Iran	1973	2,100.0	1,050.0	1
Distributors Co-operative Credit Bank	1959	600.0	300.0[a]	139
Bank Etebarat Iran	1958	700.0	700.0	59
The Foreign Trade Bank of Iran	1958	700.0	700.0	19
Industrial Credit Bank	1956	4,319.9	4,319.9	1
Industrial and Mining Development Bank of Iran	1959	6,300.0	3,150.0	1
The International Bank of Iran and Japan	1959	1,000.0	1,000.0	30
Iranians Bank	1959	1,000.0	1,000.0	6

152

The Irano British Bank	1958	400.0[b]	400.0	18
The Bank of Iran and the Middle East	1959	400.0	400.0	17
Bank Kar	1958	1,030.0	1,030.0	4
Bank Melli Iran	1928	4,000.0	4,000.0	1,330
Mercantile Bank of Iran and Holland	1959	500.0	500.0	16
Bank Omran	1946	750.0	750.0	219
Bank Pars	1952	500.0	500.0	197
Bank Rahni Iran	1938	10,000.0	5,538.0[c]	151
Bank Refah Kargaran	1960	1,000.0	1,000.0	62
Russ Iran Bank	1924	600.0	600.0	1[d]
Bank Saderat Iran	1952	3,000.0	3,000.0	2,958
Bank Sakhteman	1974	6,000.0	3,000.0	1
Bank Sanaye Iran	1973	3,000.0	1,500.0	6
Bank Sepah	1925	1,500.0	1,000.0	500
Bank Shahryar	1973	5,000.0	2,500.0	6
Bank of Teheran	1952	800.0[e]	800.0	219

[a] Authorized capital of Distributors Co-operative Credit Bank was totally paid up in October 1974.
[b] The capital of the Irano British Bank was raised from R400 million to R1 billion in July 1974.
[c] R6,722 million of the total capital of Bank Rahni Iran was paid up in November 1974.
[d] Russ Iran Bank opened its first branch office is Esfahan in November 1974.
[d] The capital of Bank Teheran was raised from R800 million to R1 billion in September 1974.

Source: Padraic Fallon, "Why Iran Needs a Financial Centre," Euromoney (Special Supplement on Teheran), May 1975, p. 10.

From 1952 to 1960, the number of banks operating in Iran increased from 5 to 25.[41] More than 30 banks are operating in Iran at present, and deposits have been increasing during the last few years at 22 percent annually.[42] See Table 6.9 for a list of Iranian banks.

Since 1961, Bank Markazi Iran has been the central bank, with powers over issuance of notes and coins, supervision of banks and credit institutions, control of foreign exchange and gold trading, the sale of government bonds and bills, formulation of payments agreements, and custodian of foreign exchange and gold reserves.

The Iranian banks are comprised of ordinary commercial banks and specialized banks. The latter provide finance to such sectors as industry and mines, agriculture, and construction.[43] Most bank lending in Iran is short term, and trade financing is the principal use of these funds, with the specialized banks being the major source of long-term debt and equity.[44]

The Monetary and Banking Act of Iran was passed in 1972. This law formalized the bank supervisory role of Bank Markazi and empowered a Currency and Credit Council to supervise the central bank.[45]

The Bank Markazi supervises and examines banks in Iran under the Monetary and Banking Act in the following ways:[46]

determines the official rediscount rate and interest rate levels
determines the ratio of a bank's liquid assets to its total assets
determines reserve ratios
determines the ratio of paid-up capital and reserves to their different type of assets
formulates regulations governing the opening of savings and other accounts
audits the accounts and documents and inspects the operations of banks
limits the activities of banks to one or more specific area on a temporary or permanent basis
determines the manner in which savings and similar deposits with banks may be utilized
determines the maximum aggregate amount of overall loans and credits granted by banks
determines the general conditions under which banks may obtain loans from individuals or issue certificates of deposit.

In addition, Bank Markazi can close a bank that fails to operate according to its articles of association, ceases operations without good reason, or faces financial problems. This occurred in the case of Bank Bimah Bazargani in 1974.[47] Deposits are not insured in Iran, and there is no assurance that the government will stand behind a failed bank's depositors.

According to Iranian banking law, foreign banks cannot operate completely as a foreign bank. They must have a minimum of 60 percent Iranian participation in ownership. However, in practice, the Monetary and Credit Council permits as little as 35 percent local capital. It has been estimated that 300 banks apply weekly for licenses to operate, although this seems to be a gross exaggeration.[48]

CONCLUSIONS

Banking structure in the Middle East and Japan is quite diverse. Some systems are completely nationalized; others are predominantly privately owned; others are mixed private-public systems. Foreign banking is permitted without significant restrictions in some of these countries and not permitted at all in others. Bank supervision and regulation is highly developed in only a few areas, such as Japan and Kuwait, but very backward in others. In most of the countries, the primary government concern is with monetary policy. Except for Japan, the other nations surveyed are considered less developed. But these are primarily oil-producing nations, with rapidly increasing per capita incomes from oil revenues. Thus, their banking systems are rapidly growing, and their internationalization is a predominant factor. Supervision for purposes of safety and soundness of banking in the Middle East, especially, is just beginning to be emphasized by these nations.

NOTES

1. Anthony McDermott, "The Middle East: Land of Oil and Money," The Bankers Magazine (United Kingdom) 220 (June 1976): 9.

2. Ibid.

3. E. R. Shaw, "Arab Funds in Euro-Markets," The Bankers Magazine (United Kingdom) 220 (June 1976): 23.

4. "Arab Banks and International Lending Markets," The Banker 126 (August 1976): 957, 959.

5. Ramzi Halabi, "The Growing Market in Arab Currencies," Euromoney, April 1976, p. 80.

6. Ibid.

7. Ahmed al Najjar, "The Islamic Alternative," The Bankers Magazine (United Kingdom) 220 (June 1976): 11.

8. Nabil Megalli, "Total of 26 Nations Pledge to Establish Islamic Bank," Burroughs Clearing House 59 (October 1974): 52.

9. Halabi, "The Growing Market in Arab Currencies, p. 81.

10. "The Banks of Beirut," The Bankers Magazine (United States) 160 (Winter 1977): 84.

11. Anthony McDermott, "Beirut: Phoenix or Dodo?" The Bankers Magazine (United Kingdom) 220 (June 1976): 26-27.

12. Francis Ghiles, "Where the Bankers Went after Beirut—and Why They Will Go Back," Euromoney, November 1976, pp. 21–22, 25–26, 29.

13. "Banks and Arabs: No Grovelling," The Economist 254 (February 15, 1975): 82.

14. Philip Thorn, Banking Structures and Sources of Finance in the Middle East (London: Banking Research Unit, 1975), pp. 3–8.

15. Ibid., p. 14. The exchange rate at year-end 1974 was Egyptian £1 = $2.56, and all pound figures in this section were converted at that rate.

16. Ibid., p. 22.

17. Sami Rizkallah, "Egypt's Big Banking Scandal Brings Cries for Reform," Burroughs Clearing House 56 (October 1971): 36–37.

18. Farouk F. Mishriki, "The Structure of the Banking System in Egypt," Euromoney, March 1976, pp. 18, 20, 23.

19. Anthony Kiely, "No Oil, No Disadvantage," The Bankers Magazine (United Kingdom) 220 (June 1976): 29–30.

20. Thorn, Banking Structures and Sources of Finance, p. 29.

21. Ray Vicker, "Globan Report," The Wall Street Journal, March 14, 1977, p. 6.

22. A. D. Issa and H. Elsaid, "Kuwait: It's Got the Banks, but . . . ," Euromoney, June 1977, p. 184.

23. Thorn, Banking Structures and Sources of Finance, p. 177.

24. Hamzah Abbas Hussein, "How Kuwait Will Develop as a Financial Centre," Euromoney, March 1976, p. 26.

25. Barry Moule, "Banking and Financial Developments in Kuwait," The Banker 122 (November 1972), p. 1399.

26. K. R. Day, "Bahrain's Development as a Financial Centre," The Banker 126 (June 1976): 585.

27. "The World at Work," Barron's 56 (June 21, 1976): 4.

28. Day, "Bahrain's Development as a Financial Centre," p. 587.

29. Ibid., p. 588.

30. N. A. Sarma, "The Financial System of the United Arab Emirates," Euromoney, March 1976 , pp. 46–47.

31. Ibid., p. 47.

32. Henry G. Coregat, Jr., "The Freewheeling World of Banking in the Desert," Euromoney, March 1976, p. 53.

33. Sarma, "The Financial System of the United Arab Emirates," p. 47.

34. McDermott, "The Middle East: Land of Oil and Money," p. 10.

35. See "SAMA's Concealed Billions," International Currency Review 9: 5–16, 19; and William B. Hummer, "Saudi Arabia—World Financial Power," Bankers Monthly Magazine 94 (April 1977): 18–19.

36. Philip Thorn, ed., Banking Structures and Sources of Finance in the Far East (London: Financial Times, 1974), p. 10.

37. "Puncturing the Eurobubble—Japan Knows How to Curb 'Em," The Economist Survey on World Finance 256 (December 14, 1974): 70.

38. Norma Pearlstine, "Opening a Branch in Japan Means Playing the Game, and 8 U.S. Banks Apparently Win," The Wall Street Journal, May 11, 1973, p. 28.

39. Alexis C. Coudert, "The Regulation of Foreign Banking in Japan, Singapore, and Hong Kong," The Banking Law Journal 91 (October 1974): 822-26; "Japan: Foreign Banks Chafe at Official Controls," Business Week, February 6, 1978, p. 54.

40. "Iran's Miracle That Was," The Economist 257 (December 20, 1975), p. 68.

41. Thorn, Banking Structures and Sources of Finance, p. 134.

42. Abolghasem Kheradjou, "Banking Developments in Teheran," Euromoney (Special Supplement on Teheran), May 1975, p. 26.

43. M. H. Pesaran, "Banking and Credit Control in Iran," Euromoney (Special Supplement on Teheran), May 1975, p. 51.

44. Monroe Haegele, "Teheran's Foreign Banking Stance Puts a Brake on Its Ambitions," Euromoney, April 1976, pp. 58, 60.

45. Padraic Fallon, "Why Iran Needs a Financial Centre," Euromoney (Special Supplement on Teheran), May 1975, p. 9.

46. Thorn, Banking Structures and Sources of Finance, pp. 137-38.

47. Ibid., p. 138.

48. Shahpour Shirazi, "Changes in Financial Regulations—A Central Banker's View," Euromoney (Special Supplement on Teheran), May 1975, pp. 45, 47.

7

BANK DEPOSIT INSURANCE PROGRAMS
WORLDWIDE

INTRODUCTION

In 1967, Intra Bank of Lebanon failed. This was one of the largest banks in the Middle East. During 1973–74, the failure of several U.S. and foreign banks resulted in the initiation of many studies of the safety and soundness of banks on a worldwide basis. Among these failures were I. D. Herstatt of Germany, United Bank of California in Basel, Banca Privata of Italy, several secondary banks in England, and Franklin National Bank and U.S. National Bank of San Diego in the United States (the largest bank failures in U.S. history). Since then, other large banks in this country have failed, including Hamilton National Bank of Chattanooga and International Bank of New Orleans. A French bank has failed, and some large German banks have been in serious trouble. Even the large state bank of the USSR has been reported to be having problems.

These worldwide banking problems have stemmed from a number of reasons—discussed in depth in Chapter 1—most notably the 1974–75 recession; foreign exchange operations in excess of banks' limits; defalcation; self-dealing by bankers; bad real estate loans; loans to a declining oil tanker industry; rampant international interbank lending, including Eurodollar loans; and loans to LDCs that have had to be extended.

Thus, with banking growing on a worldwide basis and retail banking growing concomitantly, the importance of deposit protection of some type has gained more and more emphasis. More countries are considering new or more improved deposit insurance schemes or have nationalized this sector of banking in order to protect retail depositors.

In this chapter, an analysis is presented of bank deposit insurance programs now in existence in major countries, as well as those planned for implementation or change in other countries. Among them are the new scheme in West Germany (alleged to be the most comprehensive in existence) and those in the Philippines and Japan. Proposed new programs in the United Kingdom and Canada will be discussed. Other methods of deposit protection will be analyzed and evaluated, including nationalized banking systems, such as in France and India. The chapter also includes a brief discussion of thrift institution deposit protection. A brief analysis of the U.S. system of bank deposit insurance will follow.

A proposal to insure foreign bank deposits in the United States will be discussed, and the implications of these programs will be evaluated. The importance of the study of deposit insurance programs on a worldwide basis lies in the implications for safety and soundness for banking in general, international reciprocity of bank regulation, and the harmonization of banking supervision.

PHILIPPINE DEPOSIT INSURANCE CORPORATION

The Philippine Deposit Insurance Corporation (PDIC) was established by the Deposit Insurance Act in 1963 for the purpose of insuring bank deposits after one rural bank had failed and some commercial banks had nearly failed. Initially, the program was voluntary for banks, but it was made mandatory to relevant banks by a 1969 law. Relevant banks whose deposits are covered are commercial, savings, mortgage, rural, development, and cooperative banks.

Deposits (including demand, time, and savings) are covered to a maximum of 10,000 pesos. Deposits payable at the office of a bank located outside the Philippines are not considered deposits for insurance purposes. The premium assessed banks is set by the PDIC board of directors and shall not exceed 1/12 percent per annum; it presently is 1/24 of 1 percent. The assessment base is the amount of the liability of the bank for deposits, according to the definition of the term "deposit" found in Section 3.f of the Deposit Insurance Act, without any deduction for indebtedness of depositors. However, the bank may deduct certain items or exclude them from the assessment base. [1]

It has been estimated that the 10,000 peso coverage per deposit essentially protects about 96 percent of all deposits in the Philippine banks. However, the PDIC program has been highly criticized by a study done by the IMF and the Central Bank of the Philippines (CBP) because of the functions it is permitted to perform by law and the potential inadequacy of its insurance fund, given the large growth in deposits there. [2]

The principal criticism is with the provision in PDIC's charter that allows it to make loans to, purchase assets of, or make deposits in an insured bank that may be in danger of closing in order to prevent that failure, especially if it is decided the bank is needed by the public. For example, a grant of 2.52 million pesos and a 5 million peso loan were made in 1975 to a rural bank and a savings and loan association that were in trouble. It has been advocated that the PDIC fund is insufficient to do this, that the Central Bank should bail out such banks, and, thus, that the Deposit Insurance Act should be amended to limit PDIC's function to payment of depositors in closed banks.[3]

In addition to these activities in 1975, PDIC paid off 47.7 million pesos in insured deposits for depositors of 12 banks ordered closed by the Central Bank. Furthermore, 14.5 million pesos were paid to 26,000 depositors of nine banks ordered closed before 1969, when the present PDIC began operations under the 1969 law.[4]

The PDIC is managed by a three-man board comprised of the governor of the Central Bank, who serves ex officio; a chairman appointed by the president for six years, who serves full-time; and a part-time member, appointed by the president, who serves for four years.[5] The PDIC, in addition to its fund accumulated from assessed premiums, has a standby credit line from the Central Bank, although this lack of complete independence has also been criticized in the Joint IMF-CBP survey report alluded to previously.

The PDIC has the power to examine any insured bank and to have access to reports of condition of insured banks. However, the PDIC has a staffing problem, which has kept it from examining all banks needing such scrutiny.[6]

JAPAN DEPOSIT INSURANCE CORPORATION

The Deposit Insurance Corporation (DIC) of Japan was established by the Deposit Insurance Law of 1971 to protect depositors in financial institutions. These institutions include banks licensed under the Banking Law of 1927, long-term credit banks, foreign exchange banks, mutual loan and savings banks, credit associations, and credit cooperatives. Deposits covered include demand and savings deposits, installment savings, installments prescribed in the Mutual Loans and Savings Bank Law of 1951, and money accepted under a trust contract concerning money trusts, in which the replacement of the loss of principal is contracted in accordance with the provision of Article 9 of the Trust Business Law of 1922. Deposits to be excluded from coverage and from computations for insurance premium assessment purposes are as follows: foreign currency deposits, deposits accepted from the state, local public entities, and special juridical persons, deposits accepted from the Bank of Japan and financial institutions, deposits accepted from the DIC itself, and uninscribed deposits. Deposits are defined by the Deposit Insurance Law to mean those of all depositors and other obligees.

The DIC has a Management Committee of fewer than seven members, plus a chairman and executive director, who serve for one-year terms but who can be reappointed and who serve without remuneration, except for business and travel expenses.

The DIC is supervised by the Ministry of Finance, whose office also is primary supervisor of banks in Japan. In short, the DIC is a very simple organization. It has only three top officials and less than a dozen staff members. Its operations are limited to the receipt of insurance premiums and the payment of insurance claims, since it has no authority to inspect, supervise, or give loans to financial institutions. The reasoning for this simplicity is that duplication of supervisory and examination functions, already vested in the Ministry of Finance, should be avoided and financial institutions should not be further burdened.

The current insurance premium assessed banks is 0.006 percent of the total deposits assessed according to the above format. Although the Deposit Insurance Law states that the amount of insurance claims to be paid to a depositor when a banking risk occurs is the total amount of deposits he owns, a Cabinet order set a maximum limitation on this authority, which is currently 3 million yen per depositor, or about $12,400 at the exchange rate prevailing in January 1978. When the depositor is liable for a debt to a failed financial institution, that debt is offset from the amount of deposits eligible for the insurance claim.

Finally, the DIC has capital of 450 million yen (about $1.87 million) subscribed by the government, the Bank of Japan, and private financial institutions. When the DIC has insufficient funds to pay insurance claims, it can borrow up to 50,000 million yen (about $208 million) from the Bank of Japan, with the approval of the Ministry of Finance.[7]

WEST GERMAN DEPOSIT INSURANCE PLAN

Early in 1976, the Federal Association of German Banks developed a voluntary deposit insurance scheme that provided the "best depositor protection anywhere."[8] Although it is voluntary, both houses of the German Parliament have approved the scheme as an amendment to the Law on the Credit Industry in order to legalize the closing of banks that are found to be failing.

The new scheme for all German private banks, as well as foreign banks operating in Germany (and which desire to join the program), covers all private and public nonbanking deposits to an amount equal to 30 percent of a bank's own capital (equity and accumulated reserves). The Federal Bank Supervisory Authority is authorized to suspend the activity of any credit institution, including savings banks, cooperative banks, and private banks—foreign or domestic—which it considers to be in trouble. The funds supported by these member bank institutions are used to take over the suspended bank's operations and secure depositors' money. The fund is supplied by an annual assessment of each member credit institution of 0.3 percent per 1 million deutsche marks of nonbanking deposits. The executive board of the Federal Association of German Banks apparently has the power to double the annual assessment or to collect a special tax up to the amount of one annual assessment per business year. In 1976, a double assessment was made to meet losses incurred by the liquidation of Pfalz-Kredit Bank GmbH, Kaiserlautern. In addition, member credit institutions must open their books to accountants from the insurance fund for special audits. [9]

At present, all German banks belong to this system, as well as some 15 of the 40 or so foreign banks operating in West Germany. The foreign banks that are not yet members of the scheme are mostly U.S. banks, which are balking at the assessment cost and the extra audit required. [10] The German Federal Bank Supervisory Authority is attempting to make the system universal by moral suasion, but may require it in the future if the "voluntary" system does not become universal. [11] An insurance fund of at least 500 million deutsche marks is the objective of the planners of this scheme. The salient point about the German system is that besides presently being voluntary, it treats both domestic and foreign banks alike. Thus, it does not discriminate between German-domiciled banks and foreign banks operating in West Germany. [12]

Some question still exists whether the German scheme insures deposits of a German branch located in the United States, for example, Commerzbank in New York. However, it seems unlikely that West Germany or any other leading nation would allow a branch or agency to fail in another major country that would result in depositor losses.

The high limit on liability effects nearly full coverage. More than two-thirds of all German banking offices have sufficient capital to offer full insurance for deposits of up to 30 million deutsche marks each under this scheme. On the other hand, the plan may discriminate against small banks, because the insured amount per deposit is a function of in-house capital. The following powers of bank regulation have been added to the West German Federal Bank Supervisory Authority under this scheme: [13]

1. The maximum that a bank could lend to any one customer is 75 percent of the bank's liable capital. Apparently, this limit applies to actual loans advanced, as well as to total lines of credit, regardless of whether the entire line has been taken down.

2. The five largest single loans cannot be more than 300 percent of the bank's liable capital.

3. All large single loans combined cannot exceed 800 percent of the bank's liable capital. Large loans are defined as those loans that exceed 15 percent of the bank's liable capital.

4. Any single loan application in excess of 50,000 deutsche marks requires careful examination of the credit standing of the prospective borrower.

5. Federal Bank Supervisory Authority officials can walk into a bank at any time, for any reason, and demand an examination of the bank's books.

6. All banking institutions must have at least two managing directors. This suggests that no important decisions can be made by a single individual.

7. Bankruptcies of banking institutions must be approved by the Federal Bank Supervisory Authority, and such proceedings must be carried out in an orderly manner, taking into account the interest of bank borrowers in the location of the bankrupt institution.

Finally, the new West German scheme apparently does not insure interbank deposits and other correspondent-type operations. It was this area in which most of the serious international repercussions occurred when the Herstatt Bank closed in 1974. Several U.S. banks incurred losses that were not covered by any insurance scheme. This could become a serious problem with the new West German program.

FRENCH PROGRAM

In this section and the next, deposit protection in France and India are discussed. Although India has a formal program of deposit insurance, its banking system, like that of France, is highly nationalized. Thus, government protection substitutes primarily for a formal deposit insurance law, and because of this, discussion of these programs has followed the formal programs of the Philippines, Japan, and West Germany.

France has no official bank deposit insurance program. However, two factors indicate that French banks, at least small ones, will have their deposits (at least small- or medium-sized) protected by the French government. First, the big three banks in France— Banque Nationale de Paris, Crédit Lyonnais, and Société Générale, are nationalized banks. Their deposits represent about 50 percent of all deposits of registered banks in France, and registered banks are the most significant banking sector as far as the public in France is concerned. Thus, the French government will certainly stand behind these banks.

Second, on November 1, 1976, the Association of French Banking Establishments announced that all banks operating in France, including foreign bank branches, would aid small- and medium-sized depositors in the Banque Baud, which had failed earlier.[14] Full reimbursement was made for deposits of less than 100,000 francs, and partial reimbursement was declared for deposits of 100,000 to 200,000 francs.[15] This coverage was extended to all 1,500 depositors of Banque Baud. The bank was closed on October 18, 1976, when the Banking Control Commission, France's primary bank supervisory agency, found large losses in the bank from imprudent investment operations. This represented the first time since 1950 that the French banking industry had assisted a failed bank; one implication of the action is that depositors will be protected in the future by such unofficial actions of the French banking industry.

DEPOSIT INSURANCE CORPORATION OF INDIA

The Deposit Insurance Corporation of India (DICI) was formed in 1961 and represented the first such program established by a country other than the United States. The action was precipitated by the failure of two large Indian banks.[16] The premium assessed is 0.0004 percent, and deposits are covered up to an amount of 10,000 rupees held in an insured bank. Deposits and depositors are defined fairly much as they are in other plans that have been discussed, but only about 81 commercial banks and 395 cooperative banks are registered as insured banks. The premium is collected quarterly from banks and can be raised to 0.0015 percent if necessary. The DICI insurance fund increased from 92.84 lakhs rupees in 1962 to 2,541.35 lakhs rupees in 1972.* It was estimated that by year-end 1972, more than 96 percent of the deposits in insured banks were fully covered by this plan.

However, in 1969, 14 of the largest commercial banks in India were nationalized. About 85 percent of total deposits of all commercial banks are handled by these 14 banks, the State Bank of India, and its 7 subsidiaries. Foreign banks control 8 percent of total deposits, and the remaining deposits are nearly 100 percent covered by the DICI program. Thus, for all intents and purposes, assuming the foreign banks' parents would stand behind any such bank if failure occurred, all deposits in India are protected.

---

*One lakh equals $100,000; one rupee is worth about $0.1225 at the official rate of exchange (as of January 1978).

The DICI cannot grant loans or arrange a purchase and assumption (P and A), as can the U.S. FDIC, and is not required to examine banks, because the Reserve Bank of India has this authority. However, the DICI can ask the Reserve Bank to examine any bank on its behalf and can request bank operations data from any bank.[17] The operations of the DICI would have to be considered very minimal in light of the degree of nationalization of large banks in India.

CANADA AND THE UNITED KINGDOM

Finally, with regard to bank deposit insurance, two countries with recent proposals to initiate a program or to change an existing scheme are covered in this section. Canada has a bank deposit insurance program, whereas the United Kingdom is proposing one for the first time. Both countries have published white papers in this area; in the United Kingdom, new banking laws were proposed, and in Canada, major revisions were recommended.[18] Under the proposed Canadian Payments Association Act, proposed in conjunction with a new Bank Act in 1977, a Canadian Payments Association was proposed. All deposit-accepting institutions in Canada would be required to join, and belong to, the Canada Deposit Insurance Corporation, to be insured by the Quebec Deposit Insurance Board, or in the case of credit union centrals and caisses populaires fédérations, to be members of the Canadian Co-operative Credit Society.

Licensing and supervision of banks in the United Kingdom would be formalized by the proposals in its white paper. A deposit protection fund would be implemented. It would be made mandatory for licensed deposit takers and recognized banks, would be administered by the Bank of England, and would cover up to £10,000 of a deposit account. Details are yet to be formulated.

One can only speculate about the outcome of the proposals found in either of these white papers. In both countries, although a white paper is a significant document, several steps are involved in the legislative process, including several readings in both houses of each country's parliaments. Some unofficial concern has already been rumored among British officials that the amount of deposit insurance coverage proposed in the U.K. white paper is too high.

In fact, since the U.K. white paper on financial institutions was published and in light of the fact that banking in the United Kingdom has been on a more profitable level during the past few years, debate on the white paper has subsided. A committee of inquiry on financial institutions has been appointed, with former Prime Minister Harold Wilson as its chairman. Thus, the recommendations of the white paper, as well as other matters, are being studied by this Wilson committee.

FOREIGN THRIFT OR NONBANK INSTITUTIONS

Deposit insurance of thrift institutions is mentioned briefly, because these represent a large, significant sector of public individual saving (especially outside the United States, where, for example, a Sparkasse, or savings bank, is found on nearly every street corner in West Germany).

With a drastic decline of capital ratios on a worldwide basis among thrift institutions, the safety and soundness of these institutions and their individual deposits is in jeopardy. Government protection of some type exists in only West Germany, Norway, the United Kingdom (for some deposits, only at British savings banks), and the United States. None has as elaborate a system as does the United States, represented by the Federal Savings and Loan Insurance Corporation, FDIC insurance of most mutual savings bank deposits (to the statutory limit), and state insurance schemes, for example, in Maryland. Any further study of deposit insurance programs should include thrift institutions.

BANK DEPOSIT INSURANCE IN THE
UNITED STATES

A brief discussion and analysis of the U.S. system of bank deposit insurance should be included, but since several sources treat the FDIC and its history, only salient aspects will be discussed; coverage of operations of FDIC relevant to international banking is stressed.

The Federal Deposit Insurance Act of 1933 established the FDIC as an agency that (primarily) would insure individual bank deposits up to a specified limit—originally $5,000, but raised by statute to $40,000 per individual account and $100,000 per government account, provided the bank has joined the FDIC system. All national banks must have FDIC insurance, and state-chartered banks have the option of taking out FDIC insurance. Of some 14,500 banks operating in the United States, only about 200 relatively small banks do not have insured deposits.

The Federal Deposit Insurance Act rose from the debris of the more than 11,000 banks that failed between 1921 and 1933.[19] Deposit insurance has strengthened the banking system through its mandate from Congress: FDIC was to "purchase, hold, and liquidate . . . the assets of banks which have been closed; and to insure the deposits of all banks."[20]

FDIC assesses insured banks a premium against total deposits set by statute for the insurance. The statutory rate is 1/12 percent of total deposits, but since the total FDIC Fund is more than $7 billion, the agency has returned more than half the premium in recent years, so that the actual assessment has been about 1/28 percent of total deposits per bank. The same premium is assessed each bank, regardless of its size or riskiness.[21] FDIC also has a $3 billion drawing right from the U.S. Treasury.

FDIC is responsible for the examination of state-chartered nonmember banks and compiles lists of banks that have incurred financial problems. FDIC also has four procedures for dealing with a failed or failing bank: direct payment of insured deposits, deposit assumption, direct loans, and deposit insurance national bank.[22] The first two alternatives are the most commonly used. Under deposit assumption, FDIC assumes the deposits and arranges for another bank to take over the good assets of the failed bank, while liquidating the weak assets. The last alternative is used in cases where no other bank is available for a P and A and FDIC officials believe a bank is necessary for that area. It is not a permanent remedy.

Since FDIC was established, fewer than 550 banks have failed, and the agency has incurred losses of only $247 million.[23] The Federal Deposit Insurance Act has been labeled by historians as one of the two greatest social measures passed into law by Congress, the other being Social Security. It has certainly stabilized the banking system and increased its safety and soundness.

FDIC does not insure deposits in foreign branches of U.S. banks. Except in the case of state-chartered subsidiaries of foreign banks operating in the United States, FDIC insures no foreign bank deposits here. Proposals have been made to cover both these areas (discussed in detail in previous sections of this book).

CONCLUSIONS

The preceding discussion demonstrates concern in a number of countries over the bank failures and losses of the past few years; these failures and losses have resulted in the adoption of new deposit insurance schemes, proposals for new programs, and amendments to already-existing plans. The objectives of these movements have been to increase or maintain public confidence in the various banking systems involved, as well as to ensure the safety and soundness of banking in general, especially in light of the broad internationalization of banking.

The concern has spread to the United States, where proposals have been advanced to broaden coverage of U.S. bank deposit insurance. For example, insurance of deposits in overseas branches of U.S. banks has been discussed. Legislation now being considered in the U.S., House of Representatives, H.R. 7325, the International Banking Act of 1977, would require insurance of deposits held by foreign state-chartered subsidiaries in the United States by means of the maintenance of a surety bond or pledge of assets with the FDIC. (This proposal was discussed in detail in Chapter 4.)

In an international economic society, which relies to an increasing extent on the banking system for capital acquisition, programs designed to ensure the safety and soundness of the system and maintain public confidence are certainly necessary. It is believed that an international conference could be convened to discuss deposit insurance for financial institutions. The United States should take a leading role in such a conference because of its successful deposit insurance programs. The attendees might include representatives of the nations whose plans have been discussed in this chapter, as well as officials from countries without formal deposit insurance. Thrift institutions and other nonbank depository institutions also should be represented. The principal objectives of this conference would be the safety and soundness of the worldwide financial system, the internationalization of said system, and the fostering of public confidence in its institutions and their maintenance.

NOTES

1. Deposit Insurance Act of the Philippines (1963), Section 6(a)(1) and (2).

2. See "The Recommendations of the Joint International Monetary Fund-Central Bank of the Philippines (IMF-CBP) Banking Survey Commission on the Philippine Financial System" (September 1972), obtainable from the Central Bank of the Philippines, Manila.

3. Ibid.

4. See Annual Report of the Philippine Deposit Insurance Corporation, for the year ended December 31, 1975.

5. See Philippine Deposit Insurance Act, Republic Act no. 3591, as amended in Banking laws of the Philippines (Manila: National Book Store), pp. 127 ff.

6. For further information, see Robert F. Emery, The Financial Institutions of Southeast Asia: A Country-by-Country Study (New York: Praeger Publishers, 1970), p. 372.

7. See The Deposit Insurance Law and the Related Cabinet Order and Regulation, obtainable from the Deposit Insurance Corporation, Tokyo, Japan.

8. Jess Lukomski, "Bonn Banking Law Seen Providing Best Depositor Protection Anywhere," The Journal of Commerce, February 4, 1976, p. 2.

9. See "Kaiserlautern Bank to Be Liquidated," American Banker 141 (January 15, 1976): 3; and "German Banks: No Ripples," The Economist 258 (January 24, 1976): 90, 93.

10. "W. German Bank Group Seeks Members for Deposit Insurance Plan," American Banker 141 (April 21, 1976): 3, 14.

11. Jess Lukomski, "Foreign Banks in Germany Urged: Join Deposit Scheme," The Journal of Commerce, April 28, 1976, p. 2.

12. "Bank Deposit Insurance: Customer Accounts Comprehensively Protected!" Information from the Federal Association of German Banks (Cologne, May 1976); and the Law on the Credit Industry, as of May 3, 1976, the law governing banking in West Germany.

13. From unpublished report by George Troendle, research associate, FDIC, on deposit insurance programs, 1976.

14. See The Wall Street Journal, November 1, 1976, p. 4.

15. See Money Manager 5 (November 29, 1976): 23.

16. See 1972 Annual Report of DICI. Some information in this section is based on correspondence from Satish Chandra of the Embassy of India, Washington, D.C., dated December 29, 1976.

17. For further data on DICI operations, see V. N. Hukku, "Reflections on Deposit Insurance Corporation," The Journal of the Indian Institute of Bankers, January–March 1975, pp. 49–54.

18. See "White Paper on the Revision of Canadian Bank Legislation" (August 1976), p. 18, obtainable from the Canadian Department of Finance or the Canadian Minister of Finance; and "The Licensing and Supervision of Deposit-Taking Institutions" (London: Her Majesty's Stationery Office, August 1976).

19. Carter Golembe, "The Deposit Insurance Legislation of 1933," Political Science Quarterly 85 (June 1960): 194.

20. Walter A. Varvel, "FDIC Policy toward Bank Failures," Federal Reserve Bank of Richmond Economic Review, September/October 1976, p. 3.

21. See any recent FDIC Annual Report.

22. Varvel, "FDIC Policy toward Bank Failures," p. 4.

23. Ibid., p. 10.

8

SOME CONCLUDING REMARKS AND
A LOOK AT THE FUTURE

INTRODUCTION

The preceding chapters of this book have presented a quick survey of bank supervision and regulation in the United States (of foreign and international operations), selected Western European and Middle Eastern countries, and Japan. With the exception of selected countries in the Middle East, no other developing nations' banking systems have been discussed. This area remains open for future research, especially banking in Brazil, South Korea, the Philippines, Mexico, and other growth areas among LDCs. [1]

Two industrialized nations of significance have also been omitted from the previous analysis. They are Switzerland and Canada.

Switzerland

Switzerland is famous for its conservative banking system, but its regulatory agency, the Federal Banking Commission, furnishes very little information. Some information is available from the New York Federal Reserve Bank and the Bank for International Settlements. [2] In a previous chapter, several Swiss banking problems that have occurred in recent years were discussed. Drastic changes aimed at strengthening bank supervision should result from these problems, especially after the 1977 Chiasso affair involving a branch of Swiss Credit Bank.

Canada

Canada's system deserves a few comments. Canada has only ten chartered banks, but they are permitted to branch nationwide and currently operate 7,200 branches.[3] The number of foreign banks and financial institutions operating in Canada has increased from 60 in 1967, to 150 in 1974, to 200 in 1976. These include 43 representative offices of foreign banks, 7 trust companies, 78 financing companies, 38 leasing and factoring firms, and 34 firms engaged in several other activities.[4] See Table 8.1 for a list of the ten chartered banks in Canada. Foreign banks are not permitted to operate branches in Canada. The Bank Act of 1967 enacted this restriction and imposed an international reciprocity issue on, especially, U.S.-Canadian banking relations. However, many of the foreign financial institutions operate in Canada in a manner similar to Canadian banks. They simply do not refer to these activities as banking operations.[5] Canadian banks, because of the lack of reciprocity in their banking law, are often precluded from establishing operations in foreign countries.

Primarily because of this problem, that is, the ability of foreign banks to operate without regulation in Canada and the inability for Canadian banks to operate in some foreign countries, the Canadian government is proposing amendments to the Bank Act, a practice required every ten years by statute. The proposals would place foreign financial institutions on much the same level of regulation as the Canadian chartered banks.[6]

Among the specific recommendations made in 1977 by the Canadian Bankers' Association for amendment to the Bank Act of 1967 are the following: (1) provincially chartered financial institutions doing a banking business must maintain reserves with Bank of Canada; (2) Canadian federally chartered banks be allowed to operate leasing and factoring business; (3) Canadian federally chartered banks be allowed to deal in securities; and (4) foreign banks and their affiliates be supervised by the Canadian government.[7] Thus, Canadian bankers hope to place foreign banks operating in Canada under national supervision, but the proposed legislation does not treat fully the reciprocity problem mentioned earlier. The proposals also are concerned with bank deposit insurance, discussed in Chapter 7.

SUMMARY OF THE ISSUES

Certain sections of earlier chapters were designed to demonstrate both the relatively large growth and the internationalization of banking, especially by the banking systems discussed in this book. As presented earlier, the framework within which bank regulatory and supervisory systems or proposals should be evaluated include consideration of the safety and soundness of banking (not merely nationwide but also worldwide), international reciprocity, and the harmonization and further internationalization of banking in general.

TABLE 8.1

Canadian Chartered Banks, August 31, 1975

Bank	Branches		Total Assets (billions of Canadian dollars)
	In Canada	Outside Canada	
Royal Bank of Canada	1,412	93	23.90
Canadian Imperial Bank of Commerce	1,645	82	21.60
Bank of Montreal	1,242	13	18.10
Bank of Nova Scotia	919	65	15.80
Toronto-Dominion Bank	883	7	13.60
Banque Canadienne National	483	1	4.70
Banque Provinciale de Canada	423	—	2.90
Mercantile Bank of Canada	11	—	1.10
Bank of British Columbia	29	1	0.60
Unity Bank of Canada	22	—	0.16
Total	6,969	262	102.40

Sources: Canadian Bankers' Association; B. V. Gestrin, "Understanding Banking in Canada," Bankers Magazine (United States) 159 (Winter 1976): 51.

Safety and Soundness

In terms of the first of these considerations, several major bank failures or losses have occurred during the past decade. The analysis of this period has revealed several weaknesses in the regulation and supervision of financial institutions, and especially banks, by the major banking countries during this period. Every industrialized nation and the EEC have initiated discussions of proposals to strengthen bank supervision. Some of these proposals have been enacted into law; others have been shelved because of the worldwide upturn in the economy since 1975. Others are still being debated. The adverse publicity in some countries and moral suasion by some central banks or supervisory agencies have resulted in the banking systems resorting to tightening up their own banking operations.

Among the areas of banking strengthened by these activities have been capital acquisition and foreign exchange operations. The increased bank profits of 1976-77 and further retention of earnings have resulted in higher capital ratios by the leading banks worldwide. The Herstatt and Franklin Bank failures and several other major banking losses from excessive foreign exchange operations have caused sufficient government concern so that bank examiners in these countries are now placing greater emphasis on this aspect of banking operations.

In relation to this, the initiation in 1978 by the U.S. federal bank regulators of international operations examination of foreign exchange trading and international lending should furnish information, unavailable in the past, which will offer a much better picture of these areas of concern for analysts.

Examination of member banks by the Federal Reserve Board before and after its 1974 survey of 32 banks has not revealed a general lack of prudent standards concerning their foreign exchange operations. However, certain steps should be implemented or, at least, studied for their appropriateness. Extension of customer limits should be made. However, the danger in this proposal is that so few U.S. banks make a market in foreign exchange; therefore, the overall volume of foreign exchange transactions might be jeopardized. Perhaps, very strict standards could be applied to all but the largest banks dealing in these markets. Furthermore, additional information on these markets is necessary. The magnitude of the markets, the identification of their customers, what part is trade related, what part of trade-related exchange is further associated with only U.S. trade, and how much is third-country connected all represent data essential to proper economic analysis, supervision, and regulation of foreign exchange trading by U.S. banks.

Reciprocity

The question of international reciprocity has nearly become an emotional issue, especially among bank regulatory officials in the industrialized nations. First, there is reciprocity with regard to bank entry. Some states in the United States will not permit a foreign bank to establish operations unless assured that their banks are permitted to operate in that bank's home country. Some nations, Switzerland among them, do not permit foreign bank examiners to examine banks operating as foreign branches or affiliates. The foreign country, in these cases, must rely on the home bank supervisory officials. Still other nations do not permit foreign banks to establish operations in their countries, as in some Arab nations. In some of these cases, foreign participation up to some minority percentage amount may be permitted. Some of these nations permit foreign bank entry only if reciprocity exists. Canada permits foreign institutions to perform some financial activities, but not in the form of branches or full-bank subsidiaries.

The second aspect of reciprocity that has been of concern to regulators has to do with the powers permitted banks, especially foreign banks. Should foreign banks be permitted only those activities allowed domestic banks, or should they be permitted whatever is allowed banks in their own countries? This seems to be a question whose answer depends on the nationality of the interrogator.

For example, the issue of foreign bank regulation seems most significant in the United States, where a foreign bank regulation bill has been debated in Congress since 1974. The United States is one of the few countries that prohibits commercial banks from pursuing certain types of business, for example, such investment banking activities as brokerage, underwriting, and related business. In most other nations, commercial banks, or whatever they are called, can perform both commercial and investment banking activities.

The so-called national treatment policy has been espoused in several of the proposals to regulate foreign banks at the federal level in the United States. This principle, it was stated by former Federal Reserve Vice-Chairman Mitchell, means that foreign banks operating in the United States will have to abide by the same rules as do domestic banks.[8] A survey of the U.S. embassies of France, West Germany, Italy, Switzerland, and the United Kingdom by the Federal Reserve Board showed that these countries pursued policies of nondiscrimination or national treatment in their regulation of U.S. and other foreign banks operating within their borders.[9]

A few countries, such as Italy and Switzerland, practice mirror reciprocity. Since banking systems differ widely among the industrialized nations, rationalizing the U.S. system of bank regulation with those of other countries, as well as the practice of mirror reciprocity, would seem to be futile.[10] However, there is still the problem of the absence of any formal federal framework of regulation of foreign banking in the United States.[11]

The other side of this coin is the concern with U.S. banks' activities in foreign countries. For example, suppose a law is enacted restricting foreign banks to activities permitted U.S. domestic banks, even though their parent banks are allowed both commercial and investment banking operations. Should U.S. banks operating in countries whose banks are permitted greater leeway than banks in the United States be allowed wide open powers? Or should they be as restricted as their parents?

Two alternatives have been suggested.[12] One of these is to limit U.S. banks overseas to a list of permissible activities. The other is to allow U.S. banks to perform any activity permitted banks in the foreign country, except where adverse effects on the U.S. economy may occur. Thus, any legislation in the United States must recognize the implications of these principles and problems with respect to the safety and soundness of worldwide banking, as well as the internationalization of banking.

Internationalization

The preceding section contains a discussion of some of the implications of the reciprocity issue for the internationalization and harmonization of banking. Reciprocity, which has no simple definition, is frequently found in discussions of international bank regulation. The example of Canada, discussed earlier in this chapter, presents a strong example of the difficulty that the reciprocity issue brings to harmonizing international banking systems. Canada does not permit foreign operations that call themselves "banks," but more than 200 foreign financial institutions are operating in Canada at present, performing many of the same functions permitted domestic banks but with little supervision by the Canadian government.[13] The present Canadian law has fostered internationalization of banking but at the expense of reciprocity. The lack of regulation over foreign financial institutions may also have long-term adverse effects on the safety and soundness of banking.

The first step, thus, toward a sound and optimal system of worldwide bank regulation must consider these aspects: safety and soundness, reciprocity, internationalization of banking, and their interrelationships. It is with this framework in mind that the concluding section of this chapter presents recommendations aimed at an optimal system of world bank regulation.

A NEW SYSTEM OF WORLD BANK REGULATION

An American Banker editorial summarized two principles upon which the cornerstone of effective world bank regulation would be based.[14] These are the treatment of foreign banks in host countries and the resolution of the question of the financial responsibility for the operations of a foreign bank.

Foreign Banks in Host Countries

Before the host country concept of foreign bank regulation can become a part of the framework of international bank regulation, bank regulation and supervision in every nation must be improved. Without effective bank regulation in each country, it is unlikely that any concept of reciprocity will succeed. National bank regulation and supervision cannot be taken for granted, as it has in the United States, where a Franklin National Bank or a U.S. National Bank of San Diego can fail; or in Switzerland, where the Chiasso affair with the Swiss Credit Bank branch occurred after the scandals involving a Lugano branch of Lloyds Bank and a Basel branch of United Bank of California; or in the United Kingdom, where secondary banks can fail in a system whose principal means of bank supervision may be a wink or a nod from the governor of the Bank of England.

The primary fundamentals of each nation's bank regulatory and supervisory system must be the consideration of safety and soundness and reciprocity. The structure of the banking system must be considered. Bank capital adequacy, for example, must be sufficient to support the domestic banking system in times of severe economic stress. However, irrelevant academic exercises aimed at arriving at a level of capital considered by some bank regulators to be adequate may be futile, as many have been in the United States over the past three decades.[15] However, general guidelines concerning bank capital adequacy on a worldwide basis should certainly be considered and studied for implementation by major bank regulatory agencies.

Early warning systems, coupled with rigorous examination procedures by national bank supervisors, are essential ingredients of any host country's nondiscriminatory regulatory system. In this respect, the Blunden committee on banking regulations and supervisory practices, as well as the three major U.S. federal bank regulatory agencies, have been rigorously studying various early warning systems to pinpoint problem banks, so that examples such as Franklin and U.S. National of San Diego will not occur again.

These models involve very rigorous quantitative methodologies designed to incorporate many ratios and many factors from banks' reports of condition and income. The final output of these models will give leading bank regulatory officials more lead time to solve problem bank troubles before they become so severe that depositors' confidence and the safety and soundness of the banking system will decline to the danger point.

Tighter examination policies by bank regulatory agencies are needed. In the United States, FDIC has instituted a new system for examining trust departments of the banks it supervises. In 1978, new reports of condition and income submitted by American banks to federal authorities requested information about international operations. Proposals to regulate foreign financial institutions' operations in Canada have been made in the Canadian Parliament. A similar white paper suggesting drastic changes in the regulation and supervision of U.K. banks is being considered by the British Parliament.

Add these suggestions to previously analyzed plans to regulate and supervise foreign banks in the United States, new or revised bank deposit insurance programs in several countries, and Arab attempts at bank regulatory and supervisory improvement (with the Bahrain Monetary Authority and Kuwait Central Bank), and it appears that world banking regulation is in a significant era of improvement.

Financial Responsibility for Foreign Banking

The second basic foundation of world banking regulation is the financial responsibility for foreign banking. In case of failure of a foreign bank operation, who is financially responsible for any losses to depositors or to other creditors of the failed operation? This question arose in the Herstatt case, when losses were incurred by correspondent banks doing business with Herstatt. The new German deposit insurance scheme was the response by the Federation of German Bankers to eliminate the losses of another Herstatt. However, the new scheme does not address the correspondent relationship problem.

In the United States, the proposed Foreign Bank Act of 1975 and International Banking Acts of 1976 and 1977 all contained proposals to extend some type of protection to depositors of foreign banks operating in the United States. However, as mentioned previously, none of these proposals seemed devoid of discriminatory implications or considered reciprocity in the extension of deposit protection to foreign banks' depositors.

In several foreign countries, nationalized banking systems place the government in the position of final insurer of banks' depositors. In France, a French bank's depositors had their losses paid by the banking system. In India, it appears that the vast majority of the banks are backed by the central government, which owns them, or by the deposit insurance agency to which they belong. Even in the United States, it has been suggested that FDIC may, in fact, insure, by its procedures, nearly 100 percent of all deposits. At any rate, many banking scholars in the United States have recommended some form of 100 percent insurance of deposits in banks in the United States, regardless of the country of origin of the parent bank.

A lender of last resort concept has been suggested by some. [16] The Federal Reserve System has been nominated to fill this capacity in the United States. FDIC, as mentioned, has also been suggested by some to play such a role. In fact, most central banks in foreign countries, in any extreme economic collapse, may plan to act as a lender of last resort. On the international plane, the World Bank and/or IMF might perform such a role, along with the Bank for International Settlements, in acting as a lender of last resort for governments or central banks.

With regard to the origin issue, financial responsibility for foreign banks, George W. Mitchell has stated that little question seems to exist with regard to branch or agency operations of foreign banks.[17] However, subsidiary or joint venture operations pose some legal questions about severability. The subsidiary could fail with losses to depositors and creditors, with little danger to the parent.

It seems that an international convention, sponsored through the World Bank or IMF, should be drafted with regard to this question. The convention's signatories would, in fact, pledge to be responsible for foreign operations of their financial institutions. Joint responsibility between home country and host country could be optional. For example, in the United States, FDIC would insure deposits of all banks, domestic or foreign, chartered in the United States and all deposits in foreign branches of U.S. banks. Banks chartered in the United States would include foreign bank branches. However, foreign governments, on a reciprocal basis, would share, at their option, in any losses suffered by their banks operating in the United States, just as the U.S. government, through FDIC, would support U.S. banks' foreign operations.

CONCLUSIONS

Regardless of the concepts underlying any optimal world banking regulatory system, more information about all aspects of international banking is needed to refine any model optimization. The almost ridiculous inadequacy of information, discussed earlier in this book, about foreign exchange operations, Eurocurrency lending, and lending by banks to LDCs presents a problem that must be alleviated in order to develop any meaningful system of bank regulation and supervision.

Examples of this inadequacy of information can be documented in industrialized, as well as in less developed, countries and at the international, as well as national, agency levels. Most LDCs have inadequate statistical information-gathering facilities. However, even in the United States, the problem bank lists developed by the federal bank regulatory agencies are based on examinations or call reports, which in most cases are dated as much as a year or more. This was demonstrated very effectively in 1976, when several leading American newspapers used reports of examination based on 1974 data to initiate publicity calling for tighter bank supervisory procedures by federal agencies.

Furthermore, on an international level, extensive data on private lending to LDCs is available from the World Bank.[18] These data generally lag by about two years. Data on Eurocurrency lending volume compiled by the Bank for International Settlements and other institutions may vary by as much as $100 billion during a given year.

These inadequacies in data gathering by international and national agencies must be eliminated. With existing computer facilities and advanced quantitative and econometric methods, there really is very little excuse for such suboptimal information systems.

It is suggested that in addition to strengthening the data-gathering systems of international and national financial institutions and bank regulatory agencies, national governments should give them, through legislation, very tough cease and desist powers. Federal bank regulatory agencies in most countries issue cease and desist orders against problem banks, but in many, perhaps most, cases, these orders have little enforcement clout behind them. The problem banks may ignore the agencies' requests. Cease and desist orders need heavier fines and penalties to ensure that they will be observed by bankers.

Finally, in addition to previous suggestions made in this book, it is advised that the Blunden committee be encouraged to continue its study of bank regulation and supervision. Furthermore, the EEC should continue toward its goal of monetary integration and further harmonization of banking regulation and supervision in member countries. Worldwide conferences on bank deposit insurance programs, as mentioned previously, should be held. Further study of these programs, bank capital adequacy, early warning systems, worldwide electronic funds transfer systems, and other leading issues of banking, bank entry, supervision, and regulation should be implemented without further ado.

If these suggestions are not analyzed for their merit and implemented in some manner, another wave of go-go banking, followed by severe worldwide recession and/or inflation, will result in more chaotic conditions in international banking. Furthermore, if Eurocurrency lending continues to create monetary policy problems for those countries where such markets exist, governments in Western Europe may impose restrictions that, when coupled with foreign exchange restrictions to alleviate balance-of-payments disequilibriums, will lead to further tiering of the market, loss of confidence among the banking community, and loss of a significant source of funds for multinational business. Finally, if one or more of the developing nations default on loans from private banks in the industrialized world, a possible domino effect could occur. A worldwide financial panic could follow.[19] For this reason, it is important that models be developed to assess country risk incurred by private lenders.

New or revised policies that result in executive decrees or legislation by the banking nations must be well analyzed and evaluated. It has been for that purpose that this brief outline of the problems confronting international bank regulators has been compiled.

NOTES

1. However, see V. V. Bhatt, "Some Aspects of Financial Policies and Central Banking in Developing Countries," World Development 2 (October–December 1974): 59–67.
2. See, for example, "Central Bank Supervision of Banking in Major Foreign Countries" (research memorandum), October 15, 1975, pp. 10–12, obtained from the Staff of Foreign Research Division, Federal Reserve Bank of New York, and Annual Reports of the Bank for International Settlements, Basel, Switzerland.
3. B. V. Gestrin, "Understanding Banking in Canada," The Bankers Magazine (United States)159 (Winter 1976): 50.
4. "Foreign Financial Firms in Canada Multiply," Burroughs Clearing House 60 (May 1976): 31.
5. Gestrin, "Understanding Banking in Canada," p. 56.
6. "Ottawa Goes after the Foreign Banks," Business Week, April 5, 1976, p. 30.
7. James Montagnes, "Canada Looks to Changes in Banking Laws," Burroughs Clearing House 60 (May 1976): 41.
8. "World Banking Regulation," American Banker 140 (December 26, 1975): 4.
9. "Nondiscrimination in Foreign Regulation," American Banker 141 (February 4, 1976): 4.
10. Ibid.
11. "The Principle of National Treatment," American Banker 141 (April 29, 1976): 4.
12. George W. Mitchell, "Fed Mulls Possible Regulatory Changes," Bankers Monthly Magazine 90 (June 1973): 25.
13. Michael A. Harrison, "Reciprocity in International Banking," Bankers Magazine (United States) 160 (Winter 1977): 31–34.
14. "World Banking Regulation."
15. James C. Baker, "The Bank Capital Adequacy Problem—Analysis and Up-Date" (Paper presented at the Annual Meeting of the Midwest American Institute of Decision Sciences, Detroit, May 1976).
16. Allen B. Frankel, "The Leader of Last Resort Facility in the Context of Multinational Banking," Columbia Journal of World Business 10 (Winter 1975): 120–26.
17. "World Banking Regulation."
18. See Borrowing in International Capital Markets (EC–181/764) (Washington, D.C.: International Bank for Reconstruction and Development, 1976); and World Debt Tables, vols. 1 and 2 (EC–167/76) (Washington, D.C.: International Bank for Reconstruction and Development, 1976).
19. U.S., Senate, Subcommittee on Foreign Economic Policy, Foreign Relations Committee, "International Debt, the Banks, and U.S. Foreign Policy," 95th Cong., 1st sess., 1977.

Appendix A
Outline of Data on International Banking Requested by Federal Bank Regulatory Agencies in 1978

INTRODUCTION

This appendix contains the line-by-line items required in the new Report of Condition and Report of Income forms required to be submitted by American banks beginning in 1978. Notes and complete instructions concerning these items and the appropriate forms may be obtained from the Federal Reserve System. This appendix is intended to be illustrative of the move by U.S. federal bank regulatory agencies to obtain more information on international banking operations of U.S. banks and to close some of the information gaps prevalent in the field of international banking. The appropriate schedules follow both the Report of Condition and the Report of Income. The relationship of each line item to its appropriate schedule is shown in the right-hand column of each report.

EXHIBIT A.1

Consolidated Condition Statement

Line Number	Title	Relation to Schedules
	Assets	
1.	Cash and due from banks	C-IV-8
2.	Investment securities	B-IV-E
2.a.	U.S. Treasury securities	None
2.b.	Obligations of other U.S. government agencies and corporations	None
2.c.	Obligations of states and political subdivisions in the United States	None
2.d.	Other bonds, notes, and debentures	None
3.	Trading account securities	None
4.	Federal Reserve stock and corporate stock	None
5.	Federal funds sold and securities purchased under agreements to resell	D-IV
6.	Loans, net	None
6.a.	Loans, total (excluding unearned income)	A-IV

181

Line Number	Title	Relation to Schedules
6.b.	Less: reserve for possible loan losses	
7.	Direct lease financing	None
8.	Bank premises, furniture and fixtures, and other assets representing bank premises	None
9.	Real estate owned other than bank premises	None
10.	Investments in unconsolidated subsidiaries and associated companies	None
11.	Customer's liability to this bank on acceptances outstanding	None
12.	Other assets	G-6
13.	Total consolidated assets (sum of items 1-12)	None

Liabilities

Line Number	Title	Relation to Schedules
14.	Total deposits	F.IV.A.
14.a	Deposits of IPC	F(I.1.A. +II.1.A. +III.1.A.)
14.a(i)	Demand deposits of IPC (domestic offices only)	F.I.1.B.
14.a(ii)	Other deposits of IPC (all offices)	F(I.1.C.+D +II.1.A. +III.1.A)
14.b.	Deposits of U.S. government	F(I.2.A. +II.2.A. +III.2.A.)
14.c.	Deposits of states and political subdivisions in the United States	F.I.3.A.
14.d.	Deposits of foreign governments and official institutions	F(I.4.A. +II.4.A. +III.4.A.)
14.e.	Deposits of commercial banks	F(I.5+6.A. +II.5+6.A. +III.5+6.A)
14.f.	Certified and officers' checks	F(I.7.A. +II.7.A. +III.7.A.)
15.	Federal funds purchased and securities sold under agreements to repurchase	E.IV.
16.	Other liabilities for borrowed money	None

Line Number	Title	Relation to Schedules
17.	Mortgage indebtedness	None
18.	Acceptances executed by or for account of this bank and outstanding	None
19.	Subordinated notes and debentures	None
20.	Other liabilities	H.7
21.	Total consolidated liabilities (sum of items 14–20)	None

Equity Capital

Line Number	Title	Relation to Schedules
22.	Minority interest in consolidated subsidiaries	None
	Equity capital	
23.	Preferred stock	None
24.	Common stock	None
25.	Surplus	None
26.	Undivided profits	None
27.	Reserve for contingencies and other capital reserves	None
28.	Total equity capital (sum of items 23–27)	None
29.	Total liabilities and equity capital (sum of items 21, 22, and 28)	None

Note: All lines have entries, including subtotals.

EXHIBIT A.2

Consolidated Condition Statement for Domestic Offices

Line Number	Title	Relation to Schedules
	Assets	
1.	Cash and due from banks	C-I-8
2.	Investment securities	B-I-E
2.a.	U.S. Treasury securities	B-I-1-E
2.b.	Obligations of other U.S. government agencies and corporations	B-I-2-E
2.c.	Obligations of states and political subdivisions in the United States	B-I-3-E

Line Number	Title	Relation to Schedules
2.d.	Other bonds, notes, and debentures	B-I-4-E
3.	Trading account securities	LBS-C-5-A
4.	Federal Reserve stock and corporate stock	None
5.	Federal funds sold and securities purchased under agreements to resell	D-I
6.	Loans, net	None
6.a.	Loans, total (excluding unearned income) Less: reserve for possible loan losses	A-I-II
7.	Direct lease financing	None
8.	Bank premises, furniture and fixtures, and other assets representing bank premises	None
9.	Real estate owned other than bank premises	None
10.	Investments in unconsolidated subsidiaries and associated companies	None
11.	Customer's liability to this bank on acceptances outstanding	None
12.	Other assets	None
13.	Domestic office component of total consolidated assets (sum of items 1-12)	None
13.a.	Intra-assets of domestic offices	J-3
13.b.	Total assets (sum of items 13 and 13a)	None

Liabilities

Line Number	Title	Relation to Schedules
14.	Total deposits	F.I.A.
14.a.	Deposits of IPC	F.I.1.A.
14.a(i)	Demand deposits of IPC	F.I.1.B.
14.a(ii)	Other deposits of IPC	F.I.1.C.+D
14.b	Deposits of U.S. government	F.I.2.A.
14.c.	Deposits of states and political subdivisions in the United States	F.I.3.A.
14.d.	Deposits of foreign governments and official institutions	F.I.4.A.
14.e.	Deposits of commercial banks	F.I.5+6.A.
14.f.	Certified and officers' checks	F.I.7.A.
15.	Federal funds purchased and securities sold under agreements to repurchase	E.I.
16.	Other liabilities for borrowed money	None
17.	Mortgage indebtedness	None
18.	Acceptances executed by or for account of this bank and outstanding	None
19.	Subordinated notes and debentures	None

Line Number	Title	Relation to Schedules
20.	Other liabilities	None
21.	Domestic office component of total consolidated liabilities (sum of items 14–20)	None
21.a.	Intra–liabilities of domestic offices	K–1
21.b.	Total liabilities (sum of items 21 and 21a)	None

Note: All lines have entries, including subtotals.

EXHIBIT A.3

Consolidated Condition Statement for Foreign Offices

Line Number	Title	Relation to Schedules
	Assets	
1.	Cash and due from banks	C–II–8
2.	Investment securities	B–II–E
2.e.	MEMO: securities of foreign official institutions included in line 2	None
3.	Trading account securities	None
4.	Corporate stock and other equity interests	None
6.	Loans, net	None
6.a.	Loans, total (excluding unearned income)	A–II–9
6.b.	Less: reserve for possible loan losses	
7.	Direct lease financing	None
8.	Bank premises, furniture and fixtures, and other assets representing bank premises	None
10.	Investments in unconsolidated subsidiaries and associated companies	None
11.	Customer's liability to this bank on acceptances outstanding	None
12.	Other assets	None
13.	Foreign office component of total consolidated assets (sum of items 1–12)	None
13.a.	Intra–assets of foreign offices	L–3
13.b.	Total assets (sum of items 13 and 13a)	None

Line Number	Title	Relation to Schedules
	Liabilities	
14.	Total deposits	F.II.A.
14.a.	Deposits of IPC	F.II.1.A.
14.b.	Deposits of U.S. government	F.II.2.A.
14.d.	Deposits of foreign government and official institutions	F.II.4.A.
14.e.	Deposits of commercial banks	F.II.5+6.A.
14.f.	Certified and officers' checks	F.II.7.A.
16.	Other liabilities for borrowed money	None
18.	Acceptances executed by or for account of this bank and outstanding	None
19.	Subordinated notes and debentures	None
20.	Other liabilities	None
21.	Foreign office component of total consolidated liabilities (sum of items 14-20)	None
21.a.	Intra-liabilities of foreign offices	M-1
21.b.	Total liabilities (sum of items 21 and 21a)	None

Note: All lines have entries, including subtotals.

EXHIBIT A.4

Schedule A—Loans
(including rediscounts and overdrafts)

I. Loans at Domestic Offices

    1. Real estate loans (include only loans secured primarily by real estate), total

        a. Construction and land development

        b. Secured by farmland (including farm residential and other improvements)

        c. Secured by 1-4 family residential properties:
            (1) Insured by FHA and guaranteed by VA
            (2) Conventional

        d. Secured by multifamily (5 or more) residential properties:
            (1) Insured by FHA
            (2) Conventional

        e. Secured by nonfarm nonresidential properties

2. Loans to financial institutions, total

    a. To real estate investment trusts and mortgage companies

    b. To domestic commercial banks and domestic offices of their banking Edge corporations

    c. To U.S. agencies and branches of foreign banks

    d. To foreign branches of other U.S. banks

    e. To other banks in foreign countries

    f. To other depository institutions (Mutual Savings Banks, Savings and Loan Associations, Credit Unions)

    g. To other financial institutions

3. Loans for purchasing or carrying securities (secured and unsecured):

    a. To brokers and dealers in securities

    b. Other loans for purchasing or carrying securities

4. Loans to farmers (except loans secured by real estate; include loans for household and personal expenditures)

5. Commercial and industrial loans (except those secured primarily by real estate), total

6. Loans to foreign governments and official institutions

7. Loans to individuals for household, family, and other personal expenditures (include purchased paper), total

    a. To purchase private passenger automobiles on installment basis

    b. Credit cards and related plans:
      (1) Retail (charge account) credit card plans
      (2) Check credit and revolving credit plans

    c. To purchase other retail consumer goods on installment basis
      (1) Mobile homes (exclude travel trailers)
      (2) Other retail consumer goods (exclude credit cards and related plans)

    d. Installment loans to repair and modernize residential property

    e. Other installment loans for household, family, and other personal expenditures

    f. Single-payment loans for household, family, and other personal expenditures

8. All other loans

9. Total loans at domestic offices

10. Less: any unearned income on loans reflected in items above

11. Total loans at domestic offices (net of unearned income)

II. Loans at Foreign Offices

1. Real estate loans
2. Loans to financial institutions, total

   a. To U.S. commercial banks (excluding their foreign offices) and U.S. offices of their banking Edge corporations
   b. To foreign branches of U.S. banks
   c. To non-U.S. banks
   d. To other financial institutions

3. Commercial and industrial loans, total

   a. To U.S. customers (addresses)
   b. To non-U.S. customers (addresses)

4. Loans to individuals
5. Loans to foreign governments and official institutions
6. All other loans
7. Total loans at foreign offices
8. Less: any unearned income on loans reflected in items above
9. Total loans at foreign offices (net of unearned income)

III. Loans at Domestic Offices of Edge Corporations

1. To foreign branches of other U.S. banks
2. To other banks in foreign countries
3. Commercial and industrial loans

   a. To U.S. customers (U.S. addressees)
   b. To non-U.S. customers (non-U.S. addressees)

4. Loans to foreign governments and foreign official institutions
5. Other loans
6. Total loans at domestic offices of Edge corporations
7. Less: any unearned income on loans reflected in above items
8. Total loans at domestic offices of Edge corporations (net of unearned income)

IV. Total Loans at All Offices (net of unearned income) = Items I11 + II9 + III8. Equals Item 6a on Face of Consolidated Statement.

EXHIBIT A.5

Schedule B—Securities/Distribution by Remaining Maturity
(book value)

	A. One Year or Less		B. Over One through Five Years		C. Over Five through Ten Years		D. Over Ten Years		E. Total		
	Mil-lion	Thou-sand	Mil-lion	Thou-sand	Mil-lion	Thou-sand	Mil-lion	Thou-sand	Bil-lion	Mil-lion	Thou-sand
I. Investment securities in domestic offices, total											
1. U.S. Treasury securities											
2. Obligations of other U.S. government agencies and corporations											
3. Obligations of states and political subdivisions in the United States											
4. Other bonds, notes, and debentures											
II. Investment securities in foreign offices											
III. Investment securities in Edge Corporation(s)											
IV. Total investment securities (= items I + II + III). Equals item 2 on face of Consolidated Statement											

EXHIBIT A.6

Schedule C—Cash and Due from Banks

	I Domestic Offices	II Foreign Offices	III Domestic Offices of Edge Corporations	IV Total
1. Cash items in process of collection and unposted debits	___	___	___	___
2. Demand balances with banks in the United States	___	___	___	___
a. Demand balances with U.S. agencies and branches of foreign banks	___	___	___	___
b. Demand balances with other banks in the United States	___	___	___	___
3. Interest-bearing balances with banks in the United States	___	___	___	___
a. Interest-bearing balances with U.S. agencies and branches of foreign banks	___	___	___	___

b. Interest-bearing balances with other banks in the United States

4. Interest-bearing balances with banks in foreign countries

a. Interest-bearing balances with foreign branches of other U.S. banks

b. Interest-bearing balances with other banks in foreign countries

5. Other balances with banks in foreign countries

a. Other balances with foreign branches of other U.S. banks

b. Other balances with other banks in foreign countries

6. Currency and coin

a. U.S. currency and coin

b. Foreign currency and coin

7. Balances with Federal Reserve Bank

8. Total (sum of items 1 through 7)

EXHIBIT A.7

Schedule D—Assets—Federal Funds Sold and Securities Purchased under Agreements to Resell

	Bil-lion	Mil-lion	Thou-sand
I. Domestic offices, total	―	―	―
1. With domestic commercial banks	―	―	―
2. With brokers and dealers in securities and funds	―	―	―
3. With others	―	―	―
III. Total in Edge Corporation(s)	―	―	―
IV. Total (sum of I and III above; must equal item 5 on consolidated statement)	―	―	―

EXHIBIT A.8

Schedule E—Liabilities—Federal Funds Purchased and Securities Sold under Agreements to Repurchase

	Bil-lion	Mil-lion	Thou-sand
I. Domestic offices, total	―	―	―
1. With domestic commercial banks	―	―	―
2. With brokers and dealers in securities and funds	―	―	―
3. With others	―	―	―
III. Total in Edge Corporation(s)	―	―	―
IV. Total (sum of I and III above; must equal item 15 on consolidated statement)	―	―	―

EXHIBIT A.9

Schedule F—Deposit Liabilities
(XXX indicates not to be reported)
(000 indicates reported items)

Deposit Liabilities	A. Total	B. Demand	C. Savings	D. Time
I. Deposit liabilities at domestic offices, total (sum of items 1–7)	000	000	000	000
1. Deposits of individuals, partnerships and corporations, total (sum of items 1a–1c)	000	000	000	000
a. Mutual savings banks	000	000	000	000
b. Deposits accumulated for payment of personal loans	000	XXX	XXX	000
c. All other IPC deposits	000	000	000	000
i. Individuals and nonprofit or organizations	XXX	XXX	000	XXX
ii. Corporations and other profit organizations	XXX	XXX	000	XXX
2. Deposits of U.S. government	000	000	000	000
3. Deposits of state and political subdivisions in the United States	000	000	000	000
4. Deposits of foreign governments and official institutions, central banks, and international institutions	000	000	000	000
5. Deposits of commercial banks in the United States	000	000	000	000
a. Deposits of U.S. agencies and branches of foreign banks	000	000	000	000
b. Deposits of all other commercial banks in the United States	000	000	000	000
6. Deposits of banks in foreign countries	000	000	000	000
a. Deposits of foreign branches of other U.S. banks	000	000	000	000
b. Deposits of all other banks in foreign countries	000	000	000	000
7. Certified and officers' checks, travelers' checks, letters of credit	000	000	XXX	XXX

(continued)

EXHIBIT A.9 (continued)

	A. Total	E. Interest-Bearing	F. Non-Interest Bearing
II. Deposit liabilities at foreign offices, Total (sum of items 1, 2, 4–7)	000	000	000
1. Deposits of individuals, partnerships, and corporations	000	000	000
2. Deposits of U.S. government	000	000	000
4. Deposits of foreign governments and official institutions, central banks, and international institutions	000	000	000
5. Deposits of commercial banks in the United States	000	000	000
a. Deposits of U.S. agencies and branches of foreign banks	000	000	000
b. Deposits of all other commercial banks in the United States	000	000	000
6. Deposits of banks in foreign countries	000	000	000
a. Deposits of foreign branches of other U.S. banks	000	000	000
b. Deposits of all other banks in foreign countries	000	000	000
7. Certified and officers' checks, travelers' checks, letters of credit	000	000	000

	A. Total	B. Demand	C. Savings	D. Time
III. Deposit liabilities at Edge Corporations, total (sum of items 1, 2, 4–7)	000	000	000	000
1. Deposits of individuals, partnerships, and corporations	000	000	000	000
2. Deposits of U.S. government	000	000	000	000
4. Deposits of foreign governments and official institutions, central banks and international institutions	000	000	000	000
5. Deposits of commercial banks in the United States	000	000	000	000
a. Deposits of U.S. agencies and branches of foreign banks	000	000	000	000
b. Deposits of all other commercial banks in the United States	000	000	000	000
6. Deposits of banks in foreign countries	000	000	000	000
7. Certified and officers' checks, travelers' checks, letters of credit	000	000	000	000
IV. Total deposits (sum of I + II + III). (Equal to item 14 on fully consolidated statement)	000	000	000	000

EXHIBIT A.10

Schedule G—Other Assets

	Bil-lion	Mil-lion	Thou-sand
I. Domestic offices, total	——	——	——
1. Securities, borrowed	——	——	——
2. Income earned or accrued but not collected	——	——	——
3. Prepaid expenses	——	——	——
4. Cash items not in process of collection	——	——	——
5. All other (itemize)	——	——	——
a. _____	——	——	——
b. _____	——	——	——
c. _____	——	——	——
d. _____	——	——	——
II. Foreign offices, total	——	——	——
1. Income earned or accrued but not collected	——	——	——
2. All other (itemize)	——	——	——
a. _____	——	——	——
b. _____	——	——	——
c. _____	——	——	——
d. _____	——	——	——
III. Edge corporations	——	——	——
IV. Total other assets (sum of I + II + III) (Equals item 12 of fully consolidated statement)	——	——	——

EXHIBIT A.11

Schedule H—Other Liabilities

	Bil-lion	Mil-lion	Thou-sand
I. Domestic offices, total	—	—	—
1. Securities borrowed	—	—	—
2. Dividends declared but not yet payable	—	—	—
3. Expenses accrued and unpaid	—	—	—
4. Amounts in transit to banks	—	—	—
5. Deferred incomes taxes	—	—	—
a. IRS bad debt reserve	—	—	—
b. Other	—	—	—
6. All other (itemize)	—	—	—
a. _____	—	—	—
b. _____	—	—	—
II. Foreign offices, total	—	—	—
1. Income collected but not earned	—	—	—
2. Dividends declared but not yet earned	—	—	—
3. All other (itemize)	—	—	—
a. _____	—	—	—
b. _____	—	—	—
c. _____	—	—	—
d. _____	—	—	—
III. Edge corporations	—	—	—
IV. Total other liabilities (sum of I + II + III) (Equals item 20 of fully consolidated statement)	—	—	—

197

EXHIBIT A.12

Consolidated Domestic Offices
Schedule J—Intra-Assets[a]

1. Balances due from other offices in the fully Consolidated Report

    a. From foreign branches, net
    b. From foreign subsidiaries[b]
    c. From own Edge corporations[c]

2. Stock in foreign subsidiaries and in Edge corporations

3. Total intra-assets (Equal to item 13a on domestic-only consoli-
    dated statement)

[a]Claims on foreign branches, foreign subsidiaries, and Edge
Act subsidiaries that are consolidated in the Consolidated Condition
Statement. Claims on unconsolidated subsidiaries are recorded in
other items.
[b]Including due from foreign subsidiaries of Edges. Excludes
stock in unconsolidated subsidiaries.
[c]Excluding due from foreign subsidiaries of Edges.

EXHIBIT A.13

Consolidated Domestic Offices
Schedule K—Intra-Liabilities[a]

1. Balances due to other offices in the fully Consolidated Report
    (Equal to item 21a on domestic-only consolidated statement)

    a. To foreign branches, net
    b. To foreign subsidiaries[b]
    c. To own Edge corporations[c]

[a]Claims by foreign branches, foreign subsidiaries, and Edge
Act subsidiaries that are consolidated in the Consolidated Condition
Statement. Claims by unconsolidated subsidiaries are recorded in
other items.
[b]Including due to foreign subsidiaries of Edges.
[c]Excluding due to foreign subsidiaries of Edges.

EXHIBIT A.14

Consolidated Foreign Offices
Schedule L—Intra-Assets[a]

1. Balances due from other offices in the fully Consolidated Report

   a. From domestic offices, net
   b. From own Edge corporations[b]

2. Stock in domestic subsidiaries (including Edges)

3. Total intra-assets (Equal to line 13a on foreign-office consolidated statement)

---

[a]Claims on Edge Act subsidiaries (excluding claims on foreign subsidiaries of the Edge Corporations) and on head office, domestic branches and domestic subsidiaries that are consolidated in the Consolidated Condition Statement. Claims on unconsolidated subsidiaries are recorded in other items.
[b]Excludes claims on foreign subsidiaries of the Edges.

EXHIBIT A.15

Consolidated Foreign Offices
Schedule M—Intra-Liabilities[a]

1. Balances due to other offices in the fully Consolidated Report (Equal to item 21a on foreign-office consolidated statement)

   a. To domestic offices, net
   b. To own Edge corporations[b]

---

[a]Claims by Edge Act subsidiaries (excluding claims by foreign subsidiaries of the Edge corporations) and by head office, domestic branches and domestic subsidiaries that are consolidated in the Consolidated Condition Statement. Claims by unconsolidated subsidiaries are recorded in other items.
[b]Excludes claims by foreign subsidiaries of the Edges.

EXHIBIT A.16

Consolidated Income Statement

Line Number	Title	Relation to Consolidated Condition Statement (Exhibit A.1)
1.	Operating income	
1.a.	Interest and fees on loans	6
1.b.	Interest on balances with banks	C.IV. (3+4)
1.c.	Income on federal funds sold and securities purchased under agreements to resell	5
1.d.	Interest on bonds, debentures, and the like, held in investment accounts, total	2
1.d.1.	Interest on U.S. Treasury securities	2.a.
1.d.2.	Interest on obligations of other U.S. government agencies and corporations	2.b.
1.d.3.	Interest on obligations of states and political subdivisions of the United States	2.c.
1.d.4.	Interest on securities of foreign governments and official institutions	Unidentified
1.d.5.	Interest on other bonds, notes, and debentures	Parts of 2.d.
1.e.	Dividends on stock	4
1.f.	Income from direct lease financing	7
1.g.	Income from fiduciary activities	
1.h.	Service charges, total	
1.h.1.	Service charges on deposit accounts in domestic offices	
1.h.2.	Other service charges, commissions, and fees	
1.i.	Other operating income (from Section D, line 4, column IV)	
1.j.	Total consolidated operating income (sum of lines 1.a. through 1.i.)	Roughly F.I.B.

200

		F.II.E.	
2.	Operating expense		
2.a.	Salaries and employee benefits		
2.b.	Interest on deposits		
2.b.1.	Interest on time certificates of deposit of \$100,000 or more issued by domestic offices		
2.b.2.	Interest on deposits in foreign offices	15	
2.b.3.	Interest on other deposits	16	
2.c.	Expense of federal funds purchased and securities sold under agreements to repurchase	19	
2.d.	Interest on other borrowed money		
2.e.	Interest on subordinated notes and debentures		
2.f.	Occupancy expense of bank premises, net		
2.f.1.	Occupancy expense of bank premises, gross		
2.f.2.	Less: rental income		
2.g.	Furniture and equipment expense		
2.h.	Provision for possible loan losses (from Section C, line 4, column IV)		(d)
2.i.	Other expenses (from Section E, line 2, column IV)	6.b.	(w)
2.j.	Total consolidated operating expenses (sum of lines 2.a. through 2.i.)		(d)
3.	Net consolidated operating income (line 1.j.−2.j.)		(bb)
4.	Minority interest in the income of consolidated subsidiaries	22	(ff)
5.	Income before income taxes and securities gains or losses (line 3 minus line 4)		(d)
6.	Applicable income taxes		(d)
7.	Income before securities gains or losses (line 5 minus line 6)		(d)
8.	Securities gains (losses, net) (line 8.a. minus line 8.b.)		
8.a.	Securities gains (losses), gross		(v)
8.b.	Applicable income taxes		
9.	Income before extraordinary items (line 7 plus line 8)		(d)
10.	Extraordinary items, net of tax effect (from Section F, line 2.c.)		(d)
11.	Net income (line 9 + line 10)		(d)

EXHIBIT A.17

Consolidated Income Statement for Domestic Offices

Line Number	Title	Relation to Domestic Offices Condition Statement
1.	Operating income	
1.a.	Interest and fees on loans	6
1.b.	Interest on balances with banks	C.I. (3+4)
1.c.	Income on federal funds sold and securities purchased under agreements to resell	5
1.d.	Interest on bonds, debentures, and the like, held in investment accounts, total	2
1.d.1.	Interest on U.S. Treasury securities	2.a.
1.d.2.	Interest on obligations of other U.S. government agencies and corporations	2.b.
1.d.3.	Interest on obligations of states and political subdivisions of the United States	2.c.
1.d.4.	Interest on securities of foreign governments and official institutions	Unidentified
1.d.5.	Interest on other bonds, notes, and debentures	Parts of 2.d.
1.e.	Dividends on stock	4
1.f.	Income from direct lease financing	7
1.h.	Service charges	
1.i.	Other operating income (from Section D, line 4, column I)	

1.j.   Domestic office component of total consolidated operating income (sum of lines 1.a.-1.i.) — F.I. (C+D)

2.   Operating expenses

2.a.   Salaries and employee benefits

2.b.   Interest on deposits

2.b.1.   Interest on time certificates of deposit of $100,000 or more — 15

2.b.3.   Interest on other deposits — 16

2.c.   Expense of federal funds purchased and securities sold under agreements to repurchase — 19

2.d.   Interest on other borrowed money

2.e.   Interest on subordinated notes and debentures

2.f.   Occupancy expense of bank premises, net

2.f.1.   Occupancy expense of bank premises, gross

2.f.2.   Less: rental income

2.g.   Furniture and equipment expense

2.h.   Provision for possible loan losses (from Section C, line 4, column I)

2.i.   Other expenses (from Section E, line 2, column I) — 6.b.

2.j.   Domestic office component of total consolidated operating expenses (sum of lines 2.a.-2.i.)

3.   Domestic office component of net consolidated operating income (line 1.j.-line 2.j.)

3.a.   Net intra-operating-income of domestic offices (lines 3.a.1.-3.a.2.)

3.a.1.   Intra-operating income

3.a.2.   Intra-operating expenses

3.b.   Net operating income (lines 3 + 3.a.)

EXHIBIT A.18

Consolidated Income Statement for Foreign Offices

Line Number	Title	Relation to Foreign Office Condition Statement (Exhibit A.1)
1.	Operating income	
1.a.	Interest and fees on loans	6
1.b.	Interest on balances with banks	C.II. (3+4)
1.d.	Interest on bonds, debentures, and the like, held in investment accounts, total	2
1.d.1.	Interest on U.S. Treasury securities	
1.d.2.	Interest on obligations of other U.S. government agencies and corporations	
1.d.3.	Interest on obligations of states and political subdivisions of the United States	
1.d.4.	Interest on securities of foreign governments and official institutions	2.e.
1.d.5.	Interest on other bonds, notes, and debentures	
1.e.	Dividends on stock	4
1.f.	Income from direct lease financing	7
1.g.	Income from fiduciary activities	
1.h.	Service charges	
1.i.	Other operating income (from Section D, line 4, column II)	
1.j.	Foreign office component of total consolidated operating income (sum of lines 1.a.-1.i.)	
2.	Operating expenses	
2.a.	Salaries and employee benefits	
2.b.	Interest on deposits	F.II.E.
2.d.	Interest on other borrowed money	16
2.e.	Interest on subordinated notes and debentures	19
2.f.	Occupancy expense of bank premises, net	
2.f.1.	Occupancy expense of bank premises, gross	
2.f.2.	Less: rental income	
2.g.	Furniture and equipment expense	
2.h.	Provision for possible loan losses (from Section C, line 4, column II)	6.b.
2.i.	Other expenses (from Section E, line 2, column II)	
2.j.	Foreign office component of total consolidated operating expenses (sum of lines 2.a.-2.i.)	

Consolidated Report of Income

	Section B—Changes in Equity Capital Year-to-Date									
	A. Preferred Stock (par value)		B. Common Stock (par value)		C. Surplus		D. Undivided Profits and Capital Reserves		E. Total Equity Capital	
Indicate decreases and losses in ( )	Mil-lion	Thou-sand	Mil-lion	Thou-sand	Mil-lion	Thou-sand	Mil-lion	Thou-sand	Mil-lion	Thou-sand
1. Balance beginning of period	XXX	XXX	XXX	XXX	XXX	XXX	—	—	—	—
2. Net income (loss)	—		—		XXX	XXX	—	—	—	—
3. Sale, conversion, acquisition, or retirement of capital	—		—		XXX	XXX	—	—	—	—
4. Changes incident to mergers and absorptions	XXX	XXX	XXX	XXX	XXX	XXX	—	—	—	—
5. Cash dividends declared on common stock	XXX	XXX	XXX	XXX	XXX	XXX	(XXX)	(XXX)	( )	( )
6. Cash dividends declared on preferred stock	XXX	XXX	XXX	XXX	XXX	XXX	(XXX)	(XXX)	( )	( )
7. Stock dividends issued	XXX	XXX	XXX	XXX	XXX	XXX	XXX	XXX	XXX	XXX
8. Other increases (decreases) (itemize)	XXX	XXX	XXX	XXX	XXX	XXX	XXX	XXX	XXX	XXX
	—	—	—	—	—	—	—	—	—	—
	—	—	—	—	—	—	—	—	—	—
	—	—	—	—	—	—	—	—	—	—
9. Balance end of period										

EXHIBIT A.20

Consolidated Income Statement for Foreign Offices

Line Number	Title	Relation to Foreign Office Condition, Statement (Exhibit A.3)
3.	Foreign office component of net consolidated operating income (lines 1.j.–2.j.)	
3.a.	Net intra–operating income of foreign offices (lines 3.a.1–3.a.2.)	
3.a.1.	Intra-operating expenses	
3.b.	Net operating income (lines 3+3.a.)	

EXHIBIT A.21

Consolidated Report of Income
Section C—Reserve for Possible Loan Losses

	I. Domestic Offices	II. Foreign Offices	III. Edges	IV. Total
1. Balance beginning of period				
2. Recoveries credited to reserve				
3. Changes incident to mergers and absorptions				
4. Provision for possible loan losses				
5. Losses charged to reserve				
6. Intra–bank net reallocations				
7. Balance end of period				

206

Consolidated Report of Income
Section D—Other Operating Income

	I. Domestic Offices	II. Foreign Offices	III. Edges	IV. Total
1. Trading account income, net				
2. Equity in net income of unconsolidated sub-sidiaries and associated companies				
3. All other (itemize amounts over 25 percent of item 4)				
4. Total (must equal Section A, item 1.i, of appropriate statement)				

EXHIBIT A.23

Consolidated Report of Income
Section E—Other Operating Expenses

	I. Domestic Offices	II. Foreign Offices	III. Edges	IV. Total
1. Other operating expenses (itemize amounts over 25 percent of item 2)				
2. Total (must equal Section A, item 2.i, of the appropriate statement)				

Consolidated Report of Income
Section F—Memoranda

	Year-to-Date
1. Provision for income taxes for period	
a. Provision for U.S. federal income taxes	_____
b. Provision for U.S. state and local income taxes	_____
c. Provision for foreign income taxes	_____
d. Total (must equal sum of items 6 and 8b of Section A and item 2b of Section F)	_____
2. Extraordinary items (itemize and note as part of itemization whether applicable to domestic offices, foreign, or Edge corporations)	
a. Gross of tax effect: list and subtotal	_____
b. Less: total applicable income taxes	_____
c. Extraordinary items, net of tax effect (must equal item 10 of Section A)	_____
3. Interest and fees on commercial and industrial loans, total	_____
a. On C&I loans at domestic offices to U.S. customers	_____
b. On C&I loans at domestic offices to non-U.S. customers	_____
c. On C&I loans at foreign offices to U.S. customers	_____
d. On C&I loans at foreign offices to non-U.S. customers	_____
e. On C&I loans at Edge corporations to U.S. customers	_____
f. On C&I loans at Edge corporations to non-U.S. customers	_____
4. Number of employees on payroll at end of period	_____
5. Number of subsidiaries consolidated	_____
6. List all mergers, consolidations, and purchases during reporting period	_____

Name and location	Date
_____	_____
_____	_____
_____	_____

Consolidated Report of Income
Section G—Derivation of Income Attributable to Domestic
and International Operations

---

1. Net operating income (line 3 of Section A of Consolidated Report of Income)

2. Net operating income of domestic offices (line 3.b. of substatement for income of domestic offices)

3. Net operating income of foreign offices (line 3.b. of substatement for income of foreign offices)

4. Net operating income of Edges (lines 1-2-3 above)

5. Net operating income of international departments of domestic offices (estimated component of line 2 above)

6. Estimated adjustments for appropriate allocations not already made in calculation of lines 3, 4, and 5 above, total

6.a. Head office expenses not included above

6.b. Capital expense allocations not included above

6.c. Net income from foreign minority and joint venture investments not included above

6.d. Other adjustments not included above

7. Net operating income from international operations (lines 3+4+5+6 above)

8. Net operating income from domestic operations (lines 1-7 above)

Model Checklists for Country Risk Assessment for Lending to Less Developed Countries by U.S. Banks

INTRODUCTION

Banks should be concerned with both country exposure and country risk. These are two very different things. Country exposure is a term of measurement that refers to the volume of assets held and off-balance sheet items considered to be subject to the risk of a given country. In practice, one important aspect of this measurement is based on identifying the country domicile of the entity ultimately responsible for the credit risk of a particular transaction.

On the other hand, banks should be interested primarily in the concept and measurement of country risk. Country risk refers to a spectrum of risk arising from the economic, social, and political aspects of a given foreign country (including government policies framed in response to trends in these environments) having potential favorable or adverse consequences for foreigners' debt and/or equity investments in that country. Examples are shown in Exhibit B.1.

EXHIBIT B.1

Country Risk Factors

A. Events that may adversely affect profitability and/or recovery of equity investments in a given foreign country include:

1. Confiscation;
2. Nationalization;
3. Branching limitations;
4. Restrictions on earnings remittances;
5. Higher local taxes levied on earnings;
6. Market conditions (deflation);
7. Devaluation, and the like.

B. Events that affect profitability of debt investments in a given foreign country include:

1. Withholding and other special taxes that impact on existing outstandings;
2. Interest rate controls;
3. Government-imposed delays on the liquidation of private and/or public sector external obligations.

C. Events that often affect potential recovery of debt investments include:

1. Certain types of foreign exchange controls including government-imposed restrictions on the liquidation of public and/or private sector external obligations;
2. Domestic policies often imposed in a sudden, unpredictable manner which affect a client's ability to generate the necessary cash flow to repay loans; examples are:

   a. Fiscal policy (for example, increase in taxes)
   b. Restrictive monetary policy and/or
   c. Price controls, and the like

The above types of country risk are incurred as a result of activities undertaken in a foreign country and are distinct from considerations relating to a given borrower's creditworthiness. In varying degrees, the above examples of events can affect both local and foreign currency investments. In this context, the term "investments" is often used synonymously with exposure.

MODELS FOR COUNTRY RISK ASSESSMENT

EXHIBIT B.2

Outline of Typical Qualitative Country Evaluation Report

I. Economics

   A. Background

      (1) Natural resources
      (2) Demographics
      (3) Other

   B. Current indicators

      (1) Internal

         a. GNP
         b. Inflation
         c. Government budget
         d. Consumption
         e. Investment

      (2) External

         a. Trade account
         b. Current account

       c. Capital account and/or foreign debt analysis
       d. Other

         i. Export diversity
        ii. Import compressibility
       iii. Main trading partners

  C. Long-run indicators

    (1) Managerial capability
    (2) Investment in human capital
    (3) Long-run projections

       a. Internal economic indicators
       b. External economic indicators

II. Politics

  A. Stability

    (1) Type of government
    (2) Orderliness of political successions
    (3) Homogeneity of the populace

  B. External relations

    (1) Quality of relationships with major trading partners
    (2) Quality of relationships with the United States

  C. Long-run social and political trends

Sources: Stephen Goodman, "How the Big U.S. Banks Really Evaluate Sovereign Risks," Euromoney, February 1977, pp. 105, 107, 108, 110; and "1976 Survey of Lending Practices of U.S. Banks Taken by the U.S. Export-Import Bank, mimeographed, U.S. Export-Import Bank, Washington, D.C. (March 1976).

EXHIBIT B.3

Statistics Frequently Used by Banks in Evaluating Country Risk

I. Internal economy

  A. GNP per capita

    (1) Absolute
    (2) Rate of growth

  B. Inflation rate
  C. Money supply growth
  D. Net budget position

II. External economy

   A. Balance of payments

      (1) Trade balance

         a. Exports and export growth
         b. Imports and import growth

      (2) Current account balance
      (3) Long-term capital flows

   B. External ratios

      (1) Debt service ratio (debt principal and interest-to-exports)
      (2) Reserves-to-imports ratio

   C. International reserves

Source: Stephen Goodman, "How the Big U.S. Banks Really Evaluate Sovereign Risks," Euromoney, February 1977, pp. 105, 107, 108, 110.

EXHIBIT B.4

Checklist System Indicators for Country Risk Assessment

I. Variables relating to the internal economy

   A. GNP
   B. GNP per capita
   C. Growth in GNP per capita
   D. Inflation rate
   E. Money supply growth
   F. Investment-to-income ratio
   G. Net budget position
   H. Income growth-to-fixed capital formation ratio

II. Variables relating to the external economy

   A. Exports and export growth
   B. Imports and import growth
   C. International reserves
   D. Reserves-to-import ratio
   E. Trade and current account balances
   F. Debt service ratio
   G. IMF borrowings
   H. Current collection experience of U.S. suppliers
   I. Debt service payments

J. Principal payments–to–total external debt ratio
K. Share of gold in reserves
L. Share of leading non–oil export in total export revenue
M. Share of trade in GNP
N. Share of short–term credit in total credit
O. Total external debt

III. Social and political variables

A. Political stability
B. International banking division's region rating
C. Past trend in unemployment

Source: "1976 Survey of Lending Practices of U.S. Banks Taken by the U.S. Export-Import Bank," mineographed, U.S. Export-Import Bank, Washington, D.C. (March 1976).

EXHIBIT B.5

Quick Analysis of Country Risk

I. Priority: high/medium/low

Facts			Statistic
A.	Size	Population	1. Latest figure
		GNP	2. Latest figure
B.	Level of development	GNP per capita	3. Latest figure
		Percent GNP from industry	4. Latest figure
		Percent population in agriculture	5. Latest figure
		Literacy rate	6. Latest figure
C.	Economic growth	Real growth per capita	7. Lowest/average/highest of last five years
		Trend	8. Up/down/stable/erratic/stagnant
		Industrial growth	9. Lowest/average/highest of last five years
D.	Potential	Minerals/oil	10. Known mineral/oil deposits
		Investment ratio (investment/GNP)	11. Most recent/five years ago

E. U.S. involve- Percent imports from 12. Most recent/trend
    ment   United States
                    Percent exports to   13. Most recent/trend
                       United States
                    U.S. investment   14. Most recent/trend

II. Credit worthiness: acceptable/unacceptable

A. Political   Past stability?   15.
                     Social unrest?   16.
                     Ethnic/religious dif- 17.
                       ferences explosive?
                     Government popular/   18.
                       effective?
                     Stability in area?   19.
                     Trend/change likely   20.
                       that will lead to in-
                       ability/unwilling-
                       ness to pay?

B. Ability to   Export-import ratio   21. Lowest/average/
    generate for-   highest of last five
    eign exchange   years
                     Expected trend Xm/
                       Im ratio   22.
                     Oil bill; oil imports/ 23. Latest figures
                       total imports
                     Exports + imports/   24. Most recent
                       GNP
                     Percent major export   25. Average of last
                       products   three years
C. Reserves   Reserves   31. Most recent
                     Reserves, months of   32. Most recent
                       imports
                     Net foreign assets   33. Most recent
                     Trend reserves   34. Last five years;
                                                within last year
D. Debt burden   Debt servicing ratio   35. Most recent
                     Debt servicing trend   36. Last three years
                                                projected
                     Total external debt/   37. Most recent
                       exn.
                     Average maturity   38. Most recent
                     Suppliers/bank debt   39. Most recent
                     Past debt reschedul-   40. Year and terms (if
                       ings   available)

E. Financial management	Inflation	41. Last three years
	Development plan	42. Most recent
	Percent current budget surplus/deficit	43. Last three years
	Percent total budget surplus/deficit	44. Last three years

Source: Antoine W. van Agtmael, "Evaluating the Risks of Lending to Developing Countries," Euromoney April 1976, pp. 16, 18, 20, 22, 25 27, 28, 30.

EXHIBIT B.6

Country Political Checklist

I. Internal aspects

A. History

1. Time and mode of independence
2. Record of stability

B. Homogeneity

1. Sense of national duty?
2. History of conflicts between ethnic or religious groups?
3. Is there a dominant ethnic group or are groups of equal strength?

C. Form of government if democracy

1. a. Strong opposition parties with radically different ideology?
   b. Effective government or chaotic situation?
   c. Corruption?
   d. Voting along ethnic lines?
   e. Is government sensitive to needs of population?
2. If military government
   a. Widespread popular support or national liberation front?
   b. How strong is the army?
   c. Rivalries among army commanders?
   d. Underground opposition strong?
   e. Did military government follow ineffective, unpopular democracy?
   f. Does the regime have to rely heavily on repression or can it afford a certain degree of freedom?
   g. Do civil servants play a major role or are they alienated?

        h. What alternative power bases are there?

        i. Return to civil rule planned?

    3. If one-man, one-party state

        a. What if present leader dies?

        b. Are various ethnic groups represented in government?

        c. Is military large enough to be a major contender for power?

        d. Is civil service strong and independent?

        e. Is opposition effectively organized; does it have moral stature?

        f. Are there specific interest groups opposing the regime?

D. Sources of potential unrest

    1. Is there a suppressed minority group?

    2. Are the students, intellectuals, civil servants, military, businessmen, or public opinion alienated from government?

    3. Are there conflicts between the central government and traditional, regional centers of power?

    4. Is strong foreign influence resented?

    5. Is unemployment high?

    6. Has the cost of living risen sharply without offsetting wage increases?

    7. Is corruption widespread? Who are the victims?

    8. Is there a sense that the government is unusually ineffective or that there is no economic progress?

    9. Is economic progress confined to the center or purposely spread over the country as a whole?

  10. Do the farmers own the land they till or are they mostly tenants with absentee landlords?

  11. Is the economic gap between elite and the populace widening or narrowing?

E. Drastic political changes

    1. Will a change in government or a coup lead to a drastic change in political orientation or economic chaos?

    2. Is there any chance of a civil war?

    3. Would a coup lead to political paralysis and a counter-swing?

    4. Would the next political regime be more/less likely to renounce or reschedule debt for political/ideological reasons?

II. External aspects

A. Danger of war

    1. Is the area as a whole explosive or calm?

    2. Are there major sources of conflict with neighbors?

    3. Will a war seriously impair the economy?

B. Economic relations

    1. Is there a threat of an effective economic boycott?

    2. Are relations with major aid donors stable?

    3. Are relations with World Bank and IMF healthy?

    4. Are there plans for political agreements with major trade-blocs for ensured access to major markets?

    5. Does the country want to increase U.S. investment and trade?

    6. Does the U.S. government have any leverage?

Source: Antoine W. van Agtmael, "How Business Has Dealt with Political Risk," Financial Executive 44 (January 1976): 28-29.

EXHIBIT B.7

Country Risk Indicators Used by Citibank of New York

A. Changes in factors affecting internal and external liquidity/balance of payments

    1. The rate of change in the net domestic assets of the central bank, giving consideration to factors such as requirements which might offset liquidity

    2. The change in domestic assets of the banking system

    3. The extent to which a country's foreign exchange rate serves to equilibrate the domestic price level in relation to external price levels

    4. Rate of inflation

    5. The trend line of international reserves in relation to imports

    6. Budget performance, that is, expenditures relative to GNP and/or rate of growth of expenditures

    7. Rates of change in imports, exports, and current account balance

    8. Changes in total external debt service charges plus profit remittances from foreign private investment versus earnings from goods and services

    9. Changes in commercial arrears

   10. Changes in controls and regulations

B. Indicators of near-term structural vulnerability

1. Diversity and stability of exports as indicated, for example, by the percentage of manufactures in exports
2. Marginal import elasticity, where available, or proportion of imports to GNP
3. Market concentration—proportions of exports to two largest national markets
4. Imports and exports as a percentage of GNP
5. Per capita income
6. Real growth rate of real GNP, total and per capita
7. Domestic savings as a percentage of GNP
8. Degree of industrialization, that is, percentage of labor force in secondary industry
9. Quality of financial planning and management
10. Political stability

C. External debt

1. Foreign debt profile and structure, including maturities, interest rates, source (that is, by type of creditor), and purposes; IMF gold and credit tranche positions
2. Payment record and willingness, that is, character, to meet world obligations

Source: "A Panel Discussion—Assessing Country Exposure," Journal of Commercial Bank Lending 57 (December 1974): 29-31.

INDEX

ABOUT THE AUTHOR

JAMES C. BAKER is professor of finance, Kent State University. He was chairman of finance, Kent State University, 1971 to 1975, and served as a Federal Faculty Fellow at Federal Deposit Insurance Corporation, 1975-76, where he was a consultant specialist in international finance. He has remained a consultant to that agency since then. From 1968 to 1971, he was associate professor of world business, California State University, San Francisco, and served from 1965 to 1968 as assistant professor of business administration, University of Maryland.

Dr. Baker is author of The International Finance Corporation and The German Stock Market, coauthor (with M. G. Bradford) of American Banks Abroad, and coauthor (with T. H. Bates) of Financing International Business Operations. His articles have appeared in such journals as Journal of World Trade Law, Columbia Journal of World Business, Issues in Bank Regulation, Journal of Business Finance and Accounting (United Kingdom), The Bankers Magazine (United Kingdom), and Management Decision (United Kingdom).

Dr. Baker received his doctorate in international business administration from Indiana University.

RELATED TITLES
Published by
Praeger Special Studies

THE FUTURE OF COMMERCIAL BANKING
                    Edited by Wray O. Candilis

AMERICAN BANKS ABROAD: Edge Act Companies and
Multinational Banking
                    James C. Baker and
                    M. Gerald Bradford

INTERNATIONAL FINANCIAL MARKETS: Development
of the Present System and Future Prospects
                    Francis A. Lees and
                    Maximo Eng

DATE DUE

NOV 0 3 1997 DEC 1 2 1997 NOV 2 4 1997			
GAYLORD			PRINTED IN U.S.A.

WITHDRAWN FROM
OHIO NORTHERN
UNIVERSITY LIBRARY

HETERICK MEMORIAL LIBRARY
341.751 B167i
Baker, James Calvin / International bank r

onuu

3 5111 00064 3571